Four Moments of Aesthetic Experience

Four Moments of Aesthetic Experience

Reading Huysmans, Proust, McCarthy, and Cusk

Bryan Counter

ANTHEM PRESS

Anthem Press
An imprint of Wimbledon Publishing Company
www.anthempress.com

This edition first published in UK and USA 2025
by ANTHEM PRESS
75–76 Blackfriars Road, London SE1 8HA, UK
or PO Box 9779, London SW19 7ZG, UK
and
244 Madison Ave #116, New York, NY 10016, USA

© 2025 Bryan Counter

The author asserts the moral right to be identified as the author of this work.

All rights reserved. Without limiting the rights under copyright reserved above, no part of this publication may be reproduced, stored or introduced into a retrieval system, or transmitted, in any form or by any means (electronic, mechanical, photocopying, recording or otherwise), without the prior written permission of both the copyright owner and the above publisher of this book.

British Library Cataloguing-in-Publication Data
A catalogue record for this book is available from the British Library.

Library of Congress Cataloging-in-Publication Data: 2024951176
A catalog record for this book has been requested.

ISBN-13: 978-1-83999-343-5 (Hbk)
ISBN-10: 1-83999-343-X (Hbk)

This title is also available as an e-book.

CONTENTS

Acknowledgments		vii
Introduction: An Aesthetic Paradox		1
1.	Curated Moments in Joris-Karl Huysmans's *À rebours*	23
2.	Quiet Moments in Marcel Proust's *À la recherche du temps perdu*	53
3.	Violent Moments in Tom Mccarthy's *Remainder*	97
4.	Disconnected Moments in Rachel Cusk's *Outline* Trilogy	135
Conclusion: Nearly Impossible to Represent		167
References		171
Index		177

ACKNOWLEDGMENTS

This book is the result of several years of thought, research, and writing, and would have been impossible without an immense amount of assistance and encouragement. First, I want to thank Jeffrey Di Leo, whose faith in this project is a large part of why it's appearing in this form and at this time. I also want to thank the staff at Anthem Press, whose work on the manuscript was timely and meticulous. In addition, I am grateful to the anonymous reviewers who commented on the manuscript as I was preparing it for Anthem Press; their comments were instrumental in my restructuring of the earlier parts of the book.

Next, from my time at SUNY Buffalo, I must thank Rodolphe Gasché and Fernanda Negrete, who both read and provided invaluable comments on some of the earliest drafts of what became this book: Rodolphe for reminding me to take into consideration the limits of certain texts and paths of thinking, and Fernanda for posing questions that helped bring to light implicit undercurrents in my writing. Above all, warm gratitude is due to Kalliopi Nikolopoulou for her consistent support, honest conversation, perceptive feedback, and friendship. Thinking causes much pleasure and much pain, indeed!

I owe an immense debt to Nathan Wainstein, who read and discussed several drafts of this text at various stages, and whose practical advice was lifesaving. Joseph LaBine gets my sincere thanks for great conversation, motivation, disagreement, and collaboration. Endless thanks to Ben Farber for providing a steady soundtrack and much-welcome conversation, which helped keep me grounded throughout the writing and revising process. Finally, a wholehearted thanks to my family, especially Penny, mom, and Matt. You've all inspired and supported me in different ways. And thank you to Emily for surviving my stubborn obsession with this project, and for listening to me as it developed.

A small section of the introduction was published as part of "Spiralling Relations: Barthes, Kant, and Balzac" in *Barthes Studies*, vol. 9 (2023). Earlier iterations of parts of Chapter 2 were published as "'Pour cet état si particulier': Disinterest and the Impersonal Resonance of Aesthetic

Experience" in *SubStance*, vol. 49, no. 3 (2020) and "'Peut-être aurais-je dû penser': Research and Event in Proust" in *Literature and Event: Twenty-First Century Reformulations* (Routledge Press, 2022). Thanks to the editors of these publications, as well as the anonymous readers who gave feedback on my initial drafts.

Introduction

AN AESTHETIC PARADOX

This book begins with a deceptively simple question, one stemming mainly from philosophy: what is aesthetic experience? What warrants the designation of aesthetic experience, and how do we recognize it? In the philosophical tradition, the aesthetic has often been discussed in terms of judgment (i.e., I pronounce the aesthetically grounded judgment that this rose is beautiful), and in common parlance, it is often discussed in terms of style (i.e., somebody or something has this or that "aesthetic"). In each case, therefore, the realm of aesthetics and/or the aesthetic tends to be located somewhere on the binary of subject and object. If we consider the standpoint of judgment, we are thrust into a subjective expression of will and discernment, even when the subject strives for a certain objectivity; if we take up the idea of style, we think mainly of artistic characteristics and effects, "looks" that we can often identify with the eye (or with the organ relevant to the medium in question). Rather than cleave to either side of this binary—which would leave a critical middle ground untouched, namely, a lived fact of our engagement with our surroundings—this book will argue for an understanding of aesthetic experience as depending just as much on subjective attunement as it does on any object out in the world. In this way, it is possible to address the paradox inherent in aesthetic experience: the necessity of disinterestedness on the one hand, and the likelihood of interest in aesthetic experience itself on the other hand. This is especially a problem on the subjective level and can affect a subject's relationship to canonical aesthetic objects, as well as objects encountered privately or individually. Part and parcel of this issue, as we will see, is the tendency to mistake the object as the cause of aesthetic experience, which in turn obfuscates the gap between subject and object, the way that the subject *experiences* that object.

This vital encounter with the world, as I will argue here through close readings of works by four literary authors, *is* aesthetic experience. Christopher Prendergast has recently remarked that "the terms of the affirmation of 'literature' and 'art' are continuous with what from the eighteenth century onwards was to become 'aesthetics' as a branch of theoretical inquiry, but whose principal object (aesthetic experience) lies below the threshold of rational cognition and abstraction, in the immediacy of the 'lived.'"[1] The bifurcated nature of aesthetics—stemming from life, but more recognizably given shape in works of art that can be organized, studied, and written about in a manner arguably more communicable than first-hand accounts—demands that we make a distinction between aesthetics in general and aesthetic experience, and perhaps even between aesthetics, aesthetic experience, and aesthetic judgment. Without wishing to wade into the murky waters of Kantian aesthetic judgment just yet, I will note that this book will approach aesthetic experience with a focus on life, taking as its starting point the provisional, minimal definition of aesthetic experience as "the sensuous mode of apprehension that Kant distinguished from the cognitive, moral, and practical aspects of human experience."[2] What is cognitive, moral, and practical will still undoubtedly be intertwined with what is aesthetic in my readings of novels in the chapters that follow, but it will be as it were secondary, external to, or imposed upon the moment of aesthetic experience.

Though I began above by setting this book's concern apart from the philosophical tradition, this vital quality of aesthetic experience is, of course, by no means absent from the tradition. My contention is instead that the lineage of interpretation of the aesthetic, and its bastardization in common parlance, has (as Prendergast suggests) allowed its nuance to become occluded in favor of more easily identifiable characteristics of the object (either the work of art or the object of natural beauty) or the potential judgments pronounced by the subject, as well as their psychological and sociological ramifications. Even thus far, the necessity of constantly navigating between different modes of considering this question (e.g., subjective and objective, psychological and sociological) points toward the true difficulty and all-pervasiveness of the question of aesthetic experience, and the near-impossibility of doing it justice with precision. To propose an alternate, but hopefully still philosophically serviceable understanding of aesthetic experience, I will turn toward literature in the four main chapters of this book, a gesture that I will justify toward the end of this introduction. First, I will turn to an author not dealt with in the main chapters, Honoré de Balzac, whose 1831 novel *La Peau de chagrin* thematizes an indispensable consideration for my understanding of aesthetic experience: the workings of chance.

Les hasards de la destinée humaine

Though we do not yet know his reasons, Balzac's as-yet-unnamed Raphaël enters a gambling hall in the Palais-Royal with the goal of allowing the outcome of one wager to decide his fate: whether he will continue in life or kill himself. His engagement with chance is thus doubled. Not only does he stake his bet, whose consequences will be decided according to the chance of the game, but he also leaves the wager itself up to chance: he "jeta sans calcul sur le tapis une pièce d'or qu'il avait à la main, et qui roula sur Noir [blindly threw on to the cloth a gold coin he had been holding. It rolled on to black]."[3] Two instances of chance are then joined by a third: his general ignorance of the rules of the game in the first place. He does not even realize that he has lost until the coin is raked in by the croupier, at which point "il affecta l'air d'un Anglais pour qui la vie n'a plus de mystères [...]. Combien d'événements se pressent dans l'espace d'une seconde, et que de choses dans un coup de dé! [he put on the air of an Englishman who sees no further mystery in life [...]. How many events can be crowded into the space of a second! How much depends on the throw of a dice!]" (30/27–28). The croupier, however, sees the effect of this loss on Raphaël—"Voilà sans doute sa dernière cartouche [I bet that was the last shot in his locker!]"—but significantly, it is an old gambler who can read Raphaël's demeanor all too accurately: "C'est un cerveau brûlé qui va se jeter à l'eau, répondit un habitué en regardant autour de lui les joueurs qui se connaissaient tous ['A young idiot who's going to jump into the river!' said an old *habitué*, looking round him at the gamblers, who all knew one another]" (30/28).

Shortly afterward, Raphaël wanders into the shop where he will acquire the titular skin. Possessing magical powers, this skin fulfills his desires at the price of its diminishing, taking his life with it. After learning of Raphaël's plans of suicide, the shop attendant offers him the skin, by which Raphaël seemingly gains insurmountable powers. Immediately running into some friends upon exiting the shop, he marvels at the alteration of his demeanor and the deferral of his death, as if it were heralded by the very same skin: "Quoiqu'il lui fût impossible de croire à une influence magique, il admirait les hasards de la destinée humaine [Although he found it impossible to believe in the intervention of magic, he was lost in wonderment at the changes and chances of human destiny]" (72/59). This marks the moment where Raphaël, and the text itself, makes a distinction between two kinds of chance— gambling on the one hand, and destiny on the other—a distinction that bears on the rest of the novel.

If life—before and beyond any concern with categories—is where we find aesthetic experience, then chance underlies the four moments of aesthetic experience that I will propose and discuss in what follows. Chance, or unpredictability, allows us to take the long view (i.e., to avoid a purely sociological or cynical view of aesthetic judgment) while maintaining close attention to the subject's role. If the aesthetic is not merely about distinction or cultural capital, and if on the other hand it is not merely about seeking out certain objects to enjoy certain sensations, then there must be something accidental about it. Through this contingency, aesthetic experience does attune us to nature in a way that we cannot anticipate or consciously will ourselves into. Chance is the unthematized (even when it is thematized, as in Raphaël's gambling) dimension of experience that requires our listening, our close attention, and our patience.

While the remainder of the first part of *La Peau de chagrin* is largely occupied with Raphaël's initial wish to dine and drink extravagantly with his friends, the second part finds him in that same environment narrating his own life in the past tense, looking back to the life that led up to the novel's beginning and his plans for suicide. After telling this tale, which revolves around his unrequited infatuation with the beautiful Foedora, he returns to the present moment and reveals the skin, and its powers, to his friends. He first wishes for an immense income, and upon awakening is notified that his uncle has died, leaving him with six million francs. As if in disbelief at the proof of the skin's powers, and annoyed by his friends' biting requests for donations, this section ends with Raphaël attempting to forget the power he now wields as a result of possessing the skin. Citing this moment, Peter Brooks finds the novel exemplary for the way in which it "violates the usual structure of desire in the novel, which is oriented toward the end."[4] Initially full of desire, Raphaël pulls back and will continue to pull back in various ways up to the novel's end. Seeming to remember that he possesses the skin, this moment marks an instance where "the story of the past catches up with the present, intersects with it, in a formulation of the desire that subtended the story of the past."[5] But equally as interesting, I would argue—and importantly for what will follow—is precisely the inability of this supernatural wish-fulfillment (embodied by the skin) to fully eliminate the role of chance in desire and experience, especially experiences of the aesthetic kind. As is already made clear by the novel's opening passage, chance is not mere randomness, however often we might interpret it to be so; it can perhaps more accurately be described as our general inability to "read" or interpret something before truly encountering it and grappling with it. If destiny participates in chance, then chance also must include some degree of subjective choice. Destiny is nothing if not retrospective, able to be constructed as a narrative only after the fact,[6] which is mirrored by the structure of Balzac's text and which anticipates the other novels I will discuss in the following chapters.

As far as Raphaël's desires are concerned, the skin's limitations are made clear by the third part of the novel, which takes place sometime after the first two parts. At this point, having exercised the skin many times, causing it to shrink and his health to deteriorate, we find Raphaël ill. He attempts to stifle his desires in hopes of prolonging his life, cementing a certain shift in his—and the text's—attitude toward chance. As Warren Johnson writes, "*vouloir* figures the flux of energies that attempt to bring the outside within the individual's grasp, to impose his stamp on the inescapably alien."[7] In this struggle to master what comes from the outside, certain problems with will and control become painfully clear. And yet, Raphaël seems to do exactly this. But instead of imposing his will, he avoids willing altogether and instead attempts to live in a passive way, almost merging with the natural world around him, which may otherwise seem untouchable, or at the very least indifferent to human affairs. If, as Patrick Bray writes, the magic skin "as the concrete materialization of the old man's theory of will, lets Raphaël interpret his past with a teleological certainty, even as he seems incapable of acting in the present or caring about the future,"[8] the situation in this moment is arguably reversed: Raphaël, seeking to preserve his life force (rather than expend all of his desire in a mad orgy of decadence), suppresses his will in an attempt to safeguard the very possibility of the future, even if this means the next moment only. While this seems to be emblematic of a teleological impulse, it also points to Raphaël as having progressed to a more intimate understanding of chance. Being in touch with chance to the point of truly comprehending it does not amount to being immersed in gambling, nor does it equate simply and unproblematically to a complete renunciation of will. There is something at play here that is much more difficult to see at first glance.

On the run after winning a duel, Raphaël comes across a family living in a small cottage and takes up with them. As his health continues to deteriorate, he seems to grow increasingly attuned to nature:

> se familiarisant avec des phénomènes de la végétation, avec les vicissitudes du ciel, il épiait le progrès de toutes les oeuvres, sur la terre, dans les eaux ou dans l'air. Il tenta de s'associer au mouvement intime de cette nature, et de s'identifier assez complètement à sa passive obéissance, pour tomber sous la loi despotique et conservatrice qui régit les existences instinctives. (355–356)
> familiarizing himself with the phenomena of vegetation and the vicissitudes of the weather, he studied the sequence of all processes of change, on the land, in the water and in the air. He attempted to associate himself with the intimate movement of this natural order around him, to identify himself so completely with its passive obedience that he might come under the despotic law that governs and protects all creatures that live by instinct. (272)

Some pages earlier, describing the landscape surrounding him, the text reads: "C'était une nature naïve et bonne, une rusticité vraie, mais poétique, parce qu'elle florissait à mille lieues de nos poésies peignées, n'avait d'analogie avec aucune idée, ne procédait que d'elle-même, vrai triomphe du hasard [Here nature was simple and kindly, giving an impression of rusticity both genuine and poetic, blossoming a world away from our contrived idylls, with no reference to the universe of ideas, self-generated, the pure product of chance]" (350–351/268). In both instances, chance is aligned with nature insofar as Raphaël strives to become more attuned to what is natural, and therefore to exert less of his will. Balzac specifically names nature's "passive obéissance," meaning the passive obedience both *of* and *to* nature. As noted previously, chance, from this perspective, looks like something else entirely than a simple game or a wager and seems closer to an interpretive position or attunement wherein Raphaël understands nature insofar as he begins to move closer to it, rather than simply subjecting himself to it. His familiarity or alignment with nature is passive in a way that reaches beyond the superficial instance of passivity put into play by a game of roulette. His passivity is more meaningful, more thorough, even as (and maybe even because) it does not lead him where he expects.

David F. Bell stresses that the French *hasard*, in distinction from ideas of fortune, encounter, and contingency, "does not depend on order for its definition. It suggests, on the contrary, that chance is primordial, that it precedes order."[9] That is, although chance is almost excessively thematized in the opening gambling-hall scene of *La Peau de chagrin*, Stéphane Mallarmé must be kept in mind insofar as the throw of the dice not only doesn't abolish chance, but furthermore does not even come close to exhausting chance. Instead, chance is perhaps always at play naturally, even in Raphaël's decision to forestall rather than go through with his suicide, once the dice have been cast, which leads him to the shop where he finds the skin. Chance is operative in his decision to give the game of roulette the last word on his life, as well as in his decision to disregard that last word. In other words, chance is primordial both within and beyond decisions made when chance is not explicitly thematized, and the fact that this chance is tied up with narrative necessity only strengthens its potency.

This mutual imbrication of chance and necessity also points us back to the relationship between literature and philosophy. This provides part of the rationale for investigating aesthetic experience specifically through literature: literature is never quite the "object" that we may objectively deem it to be, and as such it resists our attempts to derive totally coherent and self-contained theories out of any of its singular examples. But as stated above, it is equally necessary to establish the roots of my main argument in a few thinkers who have contributed greatly to our understanding of the aesthetic today: Immanuel Kant, Friedrich Nietzsche, Arthur Schopenhauer, and Marcel Proust, in that order.

Kant's Four Moments

In the *Critique of the Power of Judgment*, Kant lays out the four moments of the judgment of taste as follows: (1) disinterest; (2) universality; (3) purposiveness without representation of an end (i.e., purposiveness without purpose); and (4) necessity. These four moments are the requirements of the judgment of the beautiful, which also means that they are the boundaries for the judgment of the beautiful. What exactly this means is difficult to pin down, as the four moments unfold across a number of complex pages, but not until Kant prefaces his discussion by first laying out the characteristics of two categories that don't quite meet the standards of the beautiful: the agreeable and the good.

The agreeable is pleasurable through sensation, which, for Kant, is always objective, as opposed to subjective feeling. This means that interest is involved, and an encounter with an agreeable object will in a straightforward way cause us to desire more of such objects and encounters. The agreeable is also what allows Kant to make the distinction between objective and subjective sensation. Kant gives the example of "the green color of the meadows," which "belongs to **objective** sensation, as perception of an object of sense; but its agreeableness belongs to **subjective** sensation, through which no object is represented."[10] What is given to us merely through perception is objective, but what we affectively do with that perception is subjective. To find something agreeable "presupposes not the mere judgment about it but the relation of its existence to my state insofar as it is affected by such an object."[11] In other words, the agreeable not only allows for but is based upon a direct and interested relation to the object.

The good swings to the opposite pole, since it is that which we like through concepts, rather than for reasons of appetite. Kant writes: "That is **good** which pleases by means of reason alone, through the mere concept."[12] The good requires us to have knowledge of what the thing is supposed to be, that is, a concept of the object. It is worth citing Kant's delineation of the agreeable and the good, which employs the metaphor of taste to great effect:

> Of a dish that stimulates the taste through spices and other flavorings one may say without hesitation that it is agreeable and yet at the same time concede that it is not good; because while it immediately **appeals to** the senses, considered mediately [...] it displeases. [...] But in order to say that it is good it must still be referred by reason to ends, as a state, namely, that makes us fit for all our tasks.[13]

The difference between the agreeable and the good depends on the employment either of the mere senses or of intellect—that is, of pure interest, or of interest and concepts. As Kant writes, "despite all this difference between the agreeable and the good, the two still agree in this: that they are always combined with an interest in their object."[14] The good is like the agreeable insofar as they each involve interest, but they are different because the good calls upon concepts external to the object being judged as good. The beautiful is something very different and introduces a new subjective dynamic into the judgment proper to it.

The beautiful excludes both interest and concepts and is therefore located somewhere between, or perhaps beyond, the agreeable and the good. But it is clearly not a question of simply finding a middle ground, or of finding objects that one can judge without interest or concept. As Kant makes clear consistently throughout the third *Critique*, the agreeable, the good, the beautiful, and even the sublime are not liked *objectively*. They are not forms of liking that depend upon a certain object or class of object. Instead, they all depend on certain subjective attunements in the face of objects. The restrictions placed upon the judgment of the beautiful are thus subjective, concerning only *how* something is liked, *how* it is experienced, which cannot definitively be situated in terms of objectivity: "Flowers, free designs, lines aimlessly intertwined in each other under the name of foliage, signify nothing, do not depend on any determinate concept, and yet please."[15] Flowers please not because of what they are, but despite what they are—that is, despite the fact that we cannot locate a concept for them. But this lack of concept becomes pleasurable in a way that is distinct from the pleasure we find in the agreeable and the good. In the absence of any particular kind of object that could categorically satisfy the requirements of this pleasure, the restrictions of the beautiful might seem to give it the status of a near-ideal, or to at least require a massive effort on the part of the subject, a subject therefore compromised, only able to experience the beautiful in a state of self-alienation. In light of this conundrum, it is worth considering what the beautiful and the sublime have in common, despite their differences.

In contrast to the beautiful, which "carries with it a purposiveness in its form, through which the object seems as it were to be predetermined for our power of judgment, and thus constitutes an object of satisfaction in itself," the sublime is "contrapurposive for our power of judgment, unsuitable for our faculty of presentation, and as it were doing violence to our imagination, but is nevertheless judged all the more sublime for that."[16] Importantly, Kant points out that "we express ourselves on the whole incorrectly if we call some **object of nature** sublime, although we can quite correctly call very many of them beautiful; for how can we designate with an expression of approval that which is apprehended in itself as contrapurposive?"[17] Though Kant allows that objects in nature may rightly be called beautiful, while the sublime is more absolutely untethered from objects, this passage points to something held in common by both the beautiful and the sublime. What is in question is the disposition, mood, or atmosphere of the subject judging the object, and the object is lent the classification of "beautiful" or "sublime" depending on the feeling that it provokes or coincides with; the object, even with the beautiful, does not define or otherwise designate the feeling ahead of time, in a way that could be anticipated. Instead, the object is deemed beautiful or sublime—even if it is incorrect to call any given *object* sublime—retroactively, in response to the disposition it prompts.

Nietzsche takes issue with what seems to be the effort required by Kant's aesthetic subject. He focuses on the first moment, disinterest, and while his reading of Kant may seem dismissive, it is useful for thinking through the implications of disinterest beyond what Kant states explicitly and as such is provocative in its insistence on the vitality of aesthetic experience. To begin with, Nietzsche critiques disinterest as if it truly does lend the beautiful the status of an ideal, something for the subject to aspire to, therefore posing an injunction to the subject whereby he must attempt, through an act of will, to become disinterested in order to properly experience the beautiful. In this way, Nietzsche broaches the question—indeed, the problem—of the will and its place in aesthetic judgments. Nietzsche seems to suggest that the Kantian aesthetic subject, in bad faith as it were, assesses the beautiful object in a sterile way. In other words, Nietzsche reads disinterest as a conscious, intentional state of mind in opposition to the more "natural" freeness of whim and desire, as if the will must become subservient to the larger goal of disinterest. If disinterest does indeed entail a suppression of the will and desire, this is problematic for Nietzsche.

He begins one passage from *On the Genealogy of Morals* by lamenting the emergence of concern for what would be the judging subject, rather than the artist who undergoes "vivid authentic experiences, desires, surprises, and delights in the realm of the beautiful."[18] This reading is tempered by an insistence that Kant's view of beauty depends on a deadening, a self-alienation that, furthermore, is disingenuous and even impossible. This can be seen in Nietzsche's example:

> If our aestheticians never weary of asserting in Kant's favor that, under the spell of beauty, one can *even* view undraped female statues "without interest," one may laugh a little at their expense: the experiences of *artists* on this ticklish point are more "interesting," and Pygmalion was in any event *not* necessarily an "unaesthetic man."[19]

Nietzsche's valorization of interest reveals that he considers it to be completely antithetical to disinterest, and to have a sort of gravitational pull: interest will impose itself if at all possible, for example, in the presence of undraped female statues. Given that Kant approaches the aesthetic from nature first, and works of art second, it is curious that Nietzsche enlists artists to validate his argument when spectators (whose introduction into the beautiful he decries in the lines preceding these) might seem to be the most "interesting" evidence for interested viewing. To be sure, neither artists nor museum-goers—nor, it also turns out, solitary figures with no audience at all—are invulnerable from critique in terms of affectation, and are susceptible to exhibiting interest at any time. However, the reference to Pygmalion helps articulate how exactly Nietzsche understands interest and what role it might play in a more vital conception of aesthetic experience.

Pygmalion is a sculptor who creates a female statue that he begins to desire, which is eventually granted life by Venus after Pygmalion prays that he might marry it. Pygmalion conceives a child with the statue, thereby giving proof of his desire and interest. But what is woven between the artist and his statue has to do with an aesthetic (and not necessarily, or not only, interested) encounter between the two:

> [...] The best art, they say,
> Is that which conceals art, and so Pygmalion
> Marvels, and loves the body he has fashioned.
> He would often move his hands to test and touch it,
> Could this be flesh, or was it ivory only?
> No, it could not be ivory [...][20]

We can agree with Nietzsche that Pygmalion is an aesthetic man, but I would argue that this is true only as far as his work remains uncanny to us—and to Pygmalion himself. For it seems that Pygmalion has succeeded in creating something uncanny, something indistinguishable from, but curiously proximate to, real human flesh. Pygmalion is also led to question the work's categorization as work or nature, with the suggestion that he is ultimately unable to decide between the two. In effect, the artist becomes a spectator of his own work, but in a way that does not in the least diminish the vitality of the work of art. Of course, Pygmalion's engagement with the statue is "interested," but he no longer seems to exercise the kind of mastery that we might typically imagine an artist has over the work. If Pygmalion is an interested spectator, Nietzsche's example, while it aims to elevate interest over disinterest, calls for a commentary that goes beyond the *Critique* in a different manner. Giorgio Agamben takes up Nietzsche's critique in a way that considers the two sides of the issue:

> It appears, in fact, that simultaneously with the process through which the spectator insinuates himself into the concept of "art" [...] we see

the opposite process taking place from the point of view of the artist. For the one who creates it, art becomes an increasingly uncanny experience, with respect to which speaking of interest is at the very least a euphemism, because what is at stake seems to be not in any way the production of a beautiful work but instead the life and death of the author, or at least his spiritual health.[21]

Agamben also foregrounds interest, though somewhat differently from Nietzsche. The increasing alienation of the artist is such that his well-being is in question as a result of the creative process. This is placed in opposition to the introduction of the spectator into the realm of art, which seems willful and inconsequential for Agamben, meaning in turn that the artist is as if possessed and compelled to create, and any "interest" taken in the work of art may in fact be considered a disinterested one. For if the work of art can have such an effect over its creator, who remains "*not* necessarily an 'unaesthetic man,'" does this not mean that art—like a natural object encountered out in the wild—can have a life of its own, separate from and alien to even its creator, not specific to the particular work itself, or even to the formal or legible aspects of the work? Is it not the case that what might be perceived as an interested relation to the work could in fact be motivated by disinterest, especially if we grant the same distinction to objects of beauty—that is, that there is no patently "beautiful" object before the moment of judgment? And in turn, does this not bolster the relevance of disinterest as far as it is related to the realm of the aesthetic?

It is true that Kant's four moments seem at first glance to excise any spontaneity from the beautiful, making it instead a calculated, effortful endeavor. They are difficult moments to achieve, especially all together in a single judgment. But at the same time, Kant is careful to associate the beautiful with spontaneity and novelty. Importantly, this novelty is not a categorical characteristic of objects—that is, one whereby only "new" or previously unseen objects can be beautiful—but rather a subjective qualification: the thing must be *experienced anew*, whether or not it has been experienced before, and its disinterest becomes closely associated with a kind of inability to anticipate the encounter in question. We might imagine an aficionado of flowers who eventually abandons them altogether, precisely due to his constant quest for beauty in them, which renders them sterile and tiresome. At the same time, we might imagine a different aficionado of flowers who is able to sustain his interest in them through patience and discipline. Before all of the requirements of the beautiful are secured there is an additional requirement: namely, the requirement that they are not secured in a calculated way by the subject, but arise spontaneously in (and as) the event of aesthetic experience itself.

Instead of being an absolute opposite of subjective interest, disinterest might be considered as a certain refinement of the subjective without the fetters of the merely personal. Considering the question in this way does not necessarily resolve the problem. Instead, we are brought to a deeper level of the issue. If we acknowledge that the aesthetic subject may become interested in aesthetic experience itself, a fundamental paradox of the aesthetic emerges. Arthur Schopenhauer's discussion of genius in *The World as Will and Representation* touches on this exact problem. For Schopenhauer, the genius and his attunement to the aesthetic depends upon a withdrawal from the will and a detached view on life; he calls this "an attitude that is fully disinterested."[22] Schopenhauer identifies aesthetic pleasure as a reprieve from suffering. As if that were not enough to prompt an "interest" in aesthetic experience, he also writes that the "pure, true and profound cognition of the essence of the world becomes a goal in itself" for the artist and genius.[23] Retaining a careful rhetoric while also being attentive to the paradoxes at play when the aesthetic itself becomes an object of interest, Schopenhauer falls somewhere in between Kant and Nietzsche in his articulation of aesthetic experience. The question can be stated threefold, once for each philosopher. For Kant, can we reach disinterest without effort, or does disinterest itself prompt interest? For Nietzsche, how can we uphold the vital, intense nature of the work of art and aesthetic experience when confronted with the growing threat of affectation and bad faith? For Schopenhauer, how can the will-less and disinterested aesthetic experience of the genius be squared with the genius's quest for further experiences of the same kind?

To turn the screw further, Schopenhauer also insists that "the nature of aesthetic pleasure is the same whether it is called forth by a work of art or directly through the intuition of nature and life. The artwork merely facilitates the kind of cognition in which the pleasure consists."[24] With Schopenhauer, the artist/spectator divide is less of a question, while interest and disinterest, as well as the looming question of what happens when we begin to thirst for the aesthetic, become ever more relevant. In basic terms, we might ask: what happens to the subject who, on a fundamental level, possesses knowledge, taste, and memory? What kind of problem does the remembering subject pose to aesthetic experience, and how is the possibility of such an experience therefore endangered by memory, taste, and knowledge? How, to use the example given above, can the second aficionado of flowers preserve his passion for his aesthetic object, while the first exhausts it entirely?

Marcel Proust: Writing Against Taste

Marcel Proust's writing responds in a unique way to what I described above as an aesthetic paradox. Though not a philosopher per se, his work has immense and complex philosophical implications, and he is in many ways the central figure of this book. He is preoccupied throughout his oeuvre with the question of how to recognize aesthetic experience in its many forms and how to immortalize some aspect of it—an impression, an image, a sensation, a thought—in a work of art. Gilles Deleuze argues that *À la recherche du temps perdu* [*In Search of Lost Time*] is not about memory, even involuntary memory, though the theme continues to loom large in interpretations of the work. Instead, Deleuze writes that the novel is "the narrative of an apprenticeship: more precisely the apprenticeship of a man of letters," and that "[l]earning is essentially concerned with *signs*."[25] For Deleuze, signs are emitted by things out in the world, and our encounter with them forces us to think. By elevating signs over memory (including even the earth-shattering phenomenon of involuntary memory), Deleuze makes a helpful distinction between the merely personal aspect of an experience and something else that is there, something not simply personal that must be recognized in the subjective dimension of aesthetic experience. While it may not necessarily be appropriate to consider this as objective, these experiences do have a certain force of truth behind them.

For Proust, aesthetic experience occurs involuntarily, accidentally, when the hero comes into contact with something, usually a material quality in the world, that prompts a reflection, a memory, or a creative impulse. Deleuze characterizes such moments as an encounter with a sign that does violence to the subject and forces it to think. In other words, the sign forces something upon the subject, which is violent because it upends the common understanding of how thought occurs (i.e., as an act of free will). This sort of relation is crucial for my understanding of aesthetic experience, and Deleuze's reading of Proust and of thought more generally will provide an undercurrent for the arguments that follow. Importantly, the encounter with a sign is never guaranteed, as Proust suggests in an early passage from *À la recherche*. After discussing "la croyance celtique que les âmes de ceux que nous avons perdus sont captives dans quelque être inférieur [the Celtic belief that the souls of those whom we have lost are held captive in some inferior being]" only to be activated and recaptured once we encounter that being, Proust writes:

> Il en est ainsi de notre passé. C'est peine perdue que nous cherchions à l'évoquer, tous les efforts de notre intelligence sont inutiles. Il est caché hors de son domaine et de sa portée, en quelque objet matériel (en la sensation que nous donnerait cet objet matériel), que nous ne

soupçonnons pas. Cet objet, il dépend du hasard que nous le rencontrions avant de mourir, ou que nous ne le rencontrions pas.[26]

And so it is with our own past. It is a labour in vain to attempt to recapture it: all the efforts of our intellect must prove futile. The past is hidden somewhere outside the realm, beyond the reach of the intellect, in some material object (in the sensation which that material object will give us) of which we have no inkling. And it depends on chance whether or not we come upon this object before we ourselves must die.[27]

In this philosophically dense passage, Proust touches on some central components of aesthetic experience: contingency, finitude, uncertainty, accident, discovery, and the intellect. The phenomenon of involuntary memory, whose accidental and unguaranteed nature serves here as shorthand for aesthetic experience at large, is framed as a question of life and death, not unlike the role played by the aesthetic for Schopenhauer's genius. The dynamics of involuntary memory, and the involuntary more broadly, also factor into Deleuze's discussion of thought. As he writes: "What forces us to think is the sign. The sign is the object of an encounter, but it is precisely the contingency of the encounter that guarantees the necessity of what it leads us to think. The act of thinking does not proceed from a simple natural possibility; on the contrary, it is the only true creation."[28] If, as Joseph Acquisto has noted, there is "an intimate relationship between thinking and a strong personal investment in thought by the thinker, with an important affective dimension,"[29] then there is a marked similarity between aesthetic experience and Deleuze's discussion of thought based on their intensity and weight for the subject, and therefore there are grounds for discussing them in the same breath, which I will occasionally do throughout this book. Furthermore, rather than being traceable back to a certain concept or category, such an understanding of aesthetic experience allows for an element that is truly creative, immanent to the moment itself, despite the paradox that arises due to the subject's own history, habits, and knowledge.

Proust's writing responds to this paradox by keeping it alive, by allowing it to remain as an aporia. This occurs on multiple levels, as the paradox itself has many intertwined dimensions. For just one example, as I will discuss in Chapter 2, Proust's text accounts for the hero's own mistakes, missteps, and corrections, which allow for a complex form of thinking about the aesthetic to unfold in various stages. The Proustian subject is one who has particular tastes and habits, and yet remains sensitive to the aesthetic in a way that values its novelty, while also constantly reflecting on his own aesthetic projects and concerns. Proust also preserves the phenomenological or experiential aspect of the aesthetic paradox by complicating the relationship between chance and necessity. He is aware of this paradox on a canonical level, or on the level of distinction, regarding the choice of aesthetic object. Proust's preface to his translation of John Ruskin's *Sesame and Lilies* (as *Sésame et les Lys*) begins with a rich description of childhood days spent reading. While Ruskin could be considered Proust's master in a certain sense, influencing his aesthetic theories to a large extent, Proust was not always in agreement with Ruskin's treatment of art and its role in our lives. In this preface, rather than focusing on the ways we engage with the content or plot of a book, or even its characters, Proust gives what might be called a phenomenology of reading that holds any idea of received taste in suspension. I will quote here the opening passage, with Proust the reader looking back on his childhood reading:

> Il n'y a peut-être pas de jours de notre enfance que nous ayons si pleinement vécus que ceux que nous avons cru laisser sans les vivre, ceux que nous avons passés avec un livre préféré. Tout ce qui, semblait-il, les remplissait pour les autres, et que nous écartions comme un obstacle vulgaire à un plaisir divin: le jeu pour lequel un ami venait nous chercher au passage le plus intéressant, l'abeille ou le rayon de soleil gênants qui nous forçaient à lever les yeux de sur la page ou à changer de place, les provisions de goûter qu'on nous avait fait emporter et que nous laissions à côté de nous sur le banc, sans y toucher, tandis que, au-dessus de notre tête, le soleil diminuait de force dans le ciel bleu, le dîner pour lequel il avait fallu rentrer et où nous ne pensions qu'à monter finir, tout de suite après, le chapitre interrompu, tout cela, dont la lecture aurait dû nous empêcher de percevoir autre chose que l'importunité, elle en gravait au contraire en nous un souvenir tellement doux (tellement plus précieux à notre jugement actuel, que ce que nous lisions alors avec tant d'amour), que, s'il nous arrive encore aujourd'hui de feuilleter ces livres d'autrefois, ce n'est plus que comme les seuls calendriers que nous ayons gardés des jours enfuis, et avec l'espoir de voir reflétés sur leurs pages les demeures et les étangs qui n'existent plus.[30]

There are perhaps no days of our childhood we lived so fully as those we believe we left without having lived them, those we spent with a favorite book. Everything that filled them for others, so it seemed, and that we dismissed as a vulgar obstacle to a divine pleasure: the game for which a friend would come to fetch us at the most interesting passage; the troublesome bee or sun ray that forced us to lift our eyes from the page or to change position; the provisions for the afternoon snack that we had been made to take along and that we left beside us on the bench without touching, while above our head the sun was diminishing in force in the blue sky; the dinner we had to return home for, and during which we thought only of going up immediately afterward to finish the interrupted chapter, all those things which reading should have kept us from feeling anything but annoyance at, it has on the contrary engraved in us so sweet a memory of (so much more precious to our present judgment than what we read then with such love), that if we still happen today to leaf through those books of another time, it is for no other reason than that they are the only calendars we have kept of days that have vanished, and we hope to see reflected on their pages the dwellings and the ponds which no longer exist.[31]

What Proust is pointing out engages the dual levels of experience and interpretation, as much of his writing does. On the one hand, this is an account of the ways that we internalize not only the text, but the very experience of reading, including those things that occur accidentally and atmospherically around us while we read. The fullness of these days of reading depends, oddly, on our reading being interrupted. The time of memory transforms the annoying interruptions of a friend, a bee, the sun, into a vibrant experience. In turn, the memory of this experience may stay with us to a greater degree and more vividly than the text itself, turning these books into calendars of times past. Something must be happening while we read, without our knowing it, that undoes every preconceived notion we have about reading as a linear and self-enclosed concern for plot, character, and even language. Reading takes place in time, over time, and life goes on around us. While the book is in our hands, we take in what is in our periphery, despite our best efforts to focus on the book. The benefit is a deep fondness that we have both for the text and for the time in which we had originally read it. Writing about the assessments of reading put forth by Proust and Virginia Woolf, Peter Schwenger writes: "These are memories of reading as an action once performed, but not of what was read in the book itself."[32] Reading itself is pleasurable, and has its own form that does not directly correspond to the form or the content of what is read.

Furthermore, the pleasure of reading does not solely depend upon the status of the text we are reading. Of course, this is not to say that any text goes, or that the canon should be abolished outright. But when a set of aesthetic objects, such as the texts that make up the literary canon, are allowed to become sedimented, detached from our actual encounters with them, it can be difficult to imagine them in their full potential; they become, like Deleuze writes of doxa, something that "everybody knows."[33] The vision of reading that Proust offers here, which pointedly does not name a particular text, suggests that it is incidental what text we might be reading when we find this pleasure, just as there cannot be a "beautiful" or "sublime" object outside of our experience of it. When this same principle is translated into *À la recherche du temps perdu*, it is George Sand's *François le champi*, not exactly a "canonical" text, that the narrator is reading.[34] Proust's hero finds it in the Guermantes library near the end of the novel, as part of the chain of involuntary memories that prompts the narrator to outline his aesthetic theory, and it is therefore one of the novel's most important encounters with a work of art. This distinction between aesthetic experience and work of art points more generally to a disconnection, or at least a crucial difference, between aesthetic experience and aesthetic object, and deepens a concern for contingency beyond what is explicit in Kant and Nietzsche. Considered alongside the idea that Proust wrote, in a certain way, against ideas of received taste, his aesthetics can be put into conversation with Kant's, Nietzsche's, and Schopenhauer's as a helpful intervention speaking to the phenomenon of aesthetic experience and how we might recognize it.

It is not by accident that these insights from Proust emerge from scenes of reading. The main project of this book is a philosophical one, and while Kant, Nietzsche, Schopenhauer, and others remain always at hand throughout, the rest of what is to follow centers largely on literature. So, why literature, rather than philosophy? Why literature, rather than some other form of art? It is my contention that literature's philosophical capacity—because still discursive—tends as a form of art to excel in providing accounts of experience. Especially for the reasons outlined by Proust above, the lines between the work of literature and the atmosphere surrounding us when we are reading are blurred; we do not take in literature all at once, as in a painting or sculpture, and its temporal qualities are not determined in the way that a film or piece of music might be. We pick up the novel, put it down, get lost in it and in our thoughts, and lose track of time, all while unconsciously forming the very memories that we will have of the work (if not exactly the text itself and its plot) in many years' time. And since this book is concerned first and foremost with aesthetic experience, literature is a fitting place to turn to, not least due to the fact that it can avoid the deterministic subsumption of examples under categories and concepts. It is here that the theory of aesthetic experience can benefit from literature's singularity: no one text or passage can serve as an example that would adequately circumscribe the field of aesthetic experience, just as no one philosophical example could, and yet the reflective nature of the literary text demands a rigorous look at aesthetic experience without the restrictions of a totalizing philosophical system.

Four Moments of Aesthetic Experience

With the above in mind, this book is structured according to four moments of aesthetic experience. I borrow this term and organizing principle from Kant, whose four moments of aesthetic judgment both describe the boundaries and characteristics of the beautiful, and structure its discussion in the *Critique*. I propose an alternate set of moments pertaining to aesthetic experience, in line with the paradox outlined above. These moments do not correspond to Kant's four moments, as they are not offered as determinations; instead, they are derived from a consideration of an array of literary texts and together pertain primarily to an understanding of aesthetic experience from the side of the subject. These moments are: curation, quietness, violence, and disconnection. Similar to Kant's moments, it is possible to see two pairs within these: curation and violence are interrelated, as are quietness and disconnection—though, in truth, all four are inseparable, and while each chapter highlights one at a time, each of my four authors can be said to display all four at various points. These moments are inseparable by way of a key difference from Kant's moments, which is that here, there are two negative and two positive moments. The instances of curation and violence that I will examine are negative examples in the sense that they provide limitations for the subject's ability to undergo aesthetic experience despite doggedly seeking after it, whereas the quiet and disconnected moments can be considered as positive examples not only because they involve an attunement to the vicissitudes of atmosphere and narrative that can only be achieved through patience and reflection, but also because of their proximity to the creative act of writing in the novels where I discuss them.

Again, although each chapter focuses on one author and one of the four moments, each author participates in all of them, and they are by no means mutually exclusive. But focusing on one moment per author has the benefit of highlighting the differences in their engagements with these moments, which tend to allow each author to give an exemplary view of their particular moment. One further consequence of this constellation is that, in addition to the pairings above (negative and positive moments), there is an additional pairing, as well as an additional dimension to the aforementioned pairing, since the chapters deal with two French authors from the turn of the century (Joris-Karl Huysmans and Marcel Proust) and two contemporary English novelists (Tom McCarthy and Rachel Cusk). My hope is that this grouping—albeit necessarily quite limited in scope—goes some way in showing that these concerns stretch across the literary landscape of at least the past century or so.

Chapter 1 draws upon Huysmans's *À rebours* [*Against Nature*] and its *curated moments* in response to the question of what happens when aesthetic experience itself, rather than any particular object, becomes the object of interest. Partly in response to a general distaste for his fellow man, the narrator Jean des Esseintes retreats to a secluded estate where he surrounds himself with works of art and other forms of artifice, including artificially concocted flowers, perfumes of his own making, and even a tortoise encrusted with precious gems. This chapter examines the ultimately negative effects of des Esseintes's curatorial impulse, which can be seen in the death of the tortoise, crushed under the weight of its gems, or even in des Esseintes's escalating illness. This illness forces him to return to society at the end of the novel, and this illness corresponds to his ingestion of too much of the aesthetic (though, importantly, perhaps not enough aesthetic experience). In other words, he has very clearly acquired a *taste* for the aesthetic, and in pursuing it to no end has made himself ill. Thus, the curatorial impulse can lead to a degeneration with respect to aesthetic experience, even to such an extent that actual illness results.

Chapter 2 deals with *quiet moments* in Proust's *À la recherche du temps perdu*. These moments are quiet for two reasons: first, they are largely overlooked in the scholarship, which tends to focus on involuntary memory and the iconic moments that herald the hero's aesthetic theory. Second, they are comparatively overlooked within the text itself, as they often pass by as brief scenes with little importance, do not present any explicit aesthetic theory, and are not recalled at other points in the text. Here, I examine two passages that can be deemed quiet in the above ways, bookended by discussions of two of the novel's major, well-known passages, in order to argue that within the novel (and within aesthetic experience more broadly) the process of selection (of passages, objects, examples) is undermined by instances that fall outside of that process or theory. Most importantly, the quiet moments offer some clarifications about the relationship between subject and object in aesthetic experience, both on a conceptual or theoretical level and on a subjective level.

Chapter 3 turns to the work of Tom McCarthy, largely his novel *Remainder*, to discuss what I am calling *violent moments*. *Remainder* features an unnamed narrator who, upon undergoing a striking aesthetic experience that he understands as strongly linked to his "memories," begins a series of increasingly complex, wasteful, and eventually physically violent reenactments of those moments as a means of recapturing the initial experiences. The narrator's project bears the mark of violence not only because it culminates in a number of violent encounters, but also because its very inception—not too differently from des Esseintes's project in *À rebours*—depends upon an identification of aesthetic experience with a specific scenario and set of objects. Like des Esseintes, he experiences diminished returns throughout the course of the novel, and as a result, he escalates his project always higher, taking it to the next level of extravagance and wastefulness. In short, his lack of control over aesthetic experience leads him to execute more and more precisely scripted measures. However, unlike in Huysmans's novel, he is not an aesthete and is not concerned with works of art in any identifiable way; instead, he recreates specific physical scenarios in hopes of also recreating feelings associated with those original scenarios. These violent moments illustrate some of the consequences of trying to control chance, as well as exploring some of the options (and challenges) faced by the subject who has become invested to such a degree in aesthetic experience.

Chapter 4 looks to Rachel Cusk's *Outline* trilogy and some of its many *disconnected moments*. This trilogy is largely concerned with conversations between writers, and the writer–narrator Faye is told many stories by her interlocutors. In this chapter, I discuss one passage from each volume in which the narrative being conveyed at the same time includes an awareness of a tension between narration and something that escapes it; often, in the novels, this takes shape as a feeling expressed by one character or another of being alienated from any sense of larger plot or narrative. These moments are, like the quiet moments in Proust, disconnected in two ways. First, they represent a break from the idea of straightforward, "realistic" narration, and second, this break is doubled in an experiential sense, whereby a moment of intensity (for a character) seems to be unrelated to a larger narrative. Beyond addressing urgent questions about the task of the writer in discussing or evoking aesthetic experience, these disconnected moments are another way of figuring the quiet intensity of aesthetic experience as it takes shape in Proust.

As stated above, all four moments of aesthetic experience are interconnected, despite having positive and negative valences. The reason for the negative value of curation and violence is not only due to the fates of each novel's respective protagonists. Although Huysmans's and McCarthy's protagonists each meet a grim fate and cause various amounts of destruction on their paths to aesthetic satisfaction, these are negative examples primarily because it is questionable whether they do attain such satisfaction in the first place—and if so, at what cost. On the other hand, I consider the examples of Proust and Cusk to be positive because they represent successful attempts to mediate aesthetic experience through writing, both because their narrators are also writers, but also and mainly because they are able to be reflective about their experiences without creating so much distance from them as to deaden them or overly abstract them. For all of these writers, and in all of these moments, however, aesthetic experience is alive—the stakes are high, and whatever the outcome happens to be, in each case the subject is invested. Taken together, these four moments show aesthetic experience as a dynamic, vital, dangerous, intense, unpredictable, mysterious instance of responding to the world around us.

End Notes

1 Christopher Prendergast, Living and Dying with Marcel Proust, 36.
2 Joseph Tanke, "Communicability Without Communication: Kant and Proust on Aesthetic Pleasure," 78.

3 Balzac, *La Peau de chagrin*, 29; *The Wild Ass's Skin*, 27. All subsequent references will be given parenthetically.
4 Peter Brooks, *Reading for the Plot: Design and Intention in Narrative*, 49.
5 Ibid.
6 In "Introduction to the Structural Analysis of Narratives," Roland Barthes writes: "Everything suggests, indeed, that the mainspring of narrative is precisely the confusion of consecution and consequence, what comes *after* being read in narrative as what is *caused by*; in which case narrative would be a systematic application of the logical fallacy denounced by Scholasticism in the formula *post hoc, ergo propter hoc*—a good motto for Destiny, of which narrative all things considered is no more than the 'language'" (*Image, Music, Text*, 94). If the temporal succession of events does not equate to causality, then it is at least in part due to the mediating factor of chance.
7 Warren Johnson, "That Sudden Shrinking Feeling: Exchange in *La Peau de chagrin*," 543.
8 Patrick Bray, "Balzac and the Chagrin of Theory," 68–69.
9 David F. Bell, *Circumstances: Chance in the Literary Text*, 157.
10 Immanuel Kant, *Critique of the Power of Judgment*, 92.
11 Ibid.
12 Ibid.
13 Ibid., 93–94.
14 Ibid., 94.
15 Ibid., 93.
16 Ibid., 129.
17 Ibid.
18 Friedrich Nietzsche, *On the Genealogy of Morals and Ecce Homo*, 103–104.
19 Ibid., 104.
20 Ovid, *Metamorphoses*, Book 10, lines 254–259.
21 Giorgio Agamben, *The Man Without Content*, 5.
22 Arthur Schopenhauer, *The World as Will and Representation*, Volume 1, 210.
23 Ibid., 295.
24 Ibid., 218.
25 Gilles Deleuze, *Proust and Signs*, 3–4.
26 Marcel Proust, *A la recherche du temps perdu*, Vol. I, 44. Hereafter, all page references to this text will be given parenthetically.
27 Proust, *Remembrance of Things Past*, Vol. 1, 47–48. Hereafter, all page references to this text will be given parenthetically.
28 Deleuze, *Proust and Signs*, 97.
29 Joseph Acquisto, *Thought as Experience in Bataille, Cioran, and Rosset*, 3.
30 Proust, "Préface. Sur la lecture," in *La Bible d'Amiens, Sésame et les Lys et autres textes*, 405–407.
31 Proust, *On Reading Ruskin*, 99–100.
32 Peter Schwenger, "Reading's Residue," 62.
33 For instance, Deleuze writes: "*Everybody knows, no one can deny*, is the form of representation and the discourse of the representative. When philosophy rests its beginning upon such implicit or subjective presuppositions, it can claim innocence, since it has kept nothing back—except, of course, the essential—namely, the form of this discourse" (*Difference and Repetition*, 130).

34 For a recent article on ways of reading that discusses Sand's work in particular, see Michael Lucey's "Conceptualizing Trajectories of Readability." As Lucey writes, with reference to Pierre Bourdieu's distinction between the "relation savante" and the "relation pratique" and the conundrum that arises when a reader trained on difficult or more demanding literature encounters a text that asks for a different kind of relation: "Perhaps the way that Sand's *François le champi* is incorporated into Proust's long novel might suggest an awareness on Proust's part of this difference" (33, fn. 5).

Chapter 1

CURATED MOMENTS IN JORIS-KARL HUYSMANS'S *À REBOURS*

Joris-Karl Huysmans's 1884 novel *À rebours* is concerned with chance and the struggle to navigate it—indeed, to control it outright. My aim in this chapter will be to explore the relationship between chance and control, and the extent to which each might play into aesthetic experience, by way of what I consider the novel's *curated moments*. This difficult and oddly structured novel follows the life of Jean Floressas des Esseintes, a reclusive misanthrope who has fled society to an aesthetic palace of his own making. There, he indulges in countless aesthetic fantasies, which is what we—the readers—receive, in painstaking detail, as the makeup of the text. Thus, in terms of genre conventions, the novel lies somewhere between decadent literature (with its disdain for nature and its fetishization of excess and the artificial) and naturalism (with its extreme, at times exhausting, reliance on description).[1] The result is a hallucinatory, and at times tedious, cataloging of des Esseintes's various ritualistic aesthetic activities, which range from overviews of literature and paintings to bizarre architectural innovations within his home.

In terms of its chapter-by-chapter makeup, the novel does not follow a linear plot in a conventional way. David Mickelsen suggests that the novel is "orange-structured," structured spatially rather than temporally, with "temporal change, though present, [having] no functional role in the action."[2] For Mickelsen, this means that "a number of similar episodes and chapters are arranged spherically, and therefore "[p]ortrait, not plot, is paramount."[3] Gail Finney disagrees and argues that "[c]ontrary to what many critics have claimed, *A Rebours* does have a plot. It is the plot of countless nineteenth-century novels […] that of 'lost illusions.'"[4] Rodolphe Gasché points out that, because of its adherence to naturalist principles, "*Against Nature* should border on historicity; however, the almost plotless novel seems to contradict such a conclusion."[5] Ellis Hanson writes that "Huysmans' meandering plotlessness, broken up by conversations, mired down by endless disgorgements of obscure information from his library, leaves us with a fin de siècle sensation of paralysis, of winding down or of getting wound up in the tangle of a text, the tangle of text upon text, as they come apart at the seams."[6]

Whatever one's ideas about the novel's plot, the scholarly controversy surrounding it is worth mentioning because, beyond affecting the experience of reading the novel, its structure also influences what answers we may find to the many questions raised by the novel, if answers are indeed possible. Before discussing the main themes that will be operative in my reading of the novel, I will address in advance an ambiguity or contradiction that might come into view when comparing this chapter with my final chapter on Rachel Cusk: namely, two different ways of conceiving plotlessness. In my final chapter on Cusk's fiction, I will discuss several moments in her *Outline* trilogy when characters explicitly note having experiences in which they *feel* disconnected from plot or narrative. These moments, I will argue, point to a disjunction between aesthetic experience and plot, in the sense that aesthetic experience is ultimately immanent to itself. While not plotlessness per se, there is a movement away from plot that, philosophically, is mirrored by an acknowledgment that aesthetic experience is not based on, or deduced from, concepts, categories, or conscious intention. Furthermore, in the context of Cusk's trilogy, this feeling is at least doubly narrative: descriptions of this phenomenon are not only contained within a novel but are oftentimes told to the narrator by somebody else, in the form of a story.

The alleged plotlessness of *À rebours* is a different matter and pertains to aesthetic experience in a different way. Because des Esseintes does not explicitly address plot as it pertains to his life, any plotlessness of the novel is more strictly a narrative matter, rather than a specifically experiential one. He is not concerned with plot in any substantive manner, and his actions waver between the lackadaisical and the calculated. In contrast to the *Outline* trilogy, the plotlessness of *À rebours* makes it difficult to paraphrase, and therefore requires a lot of quotation, as will shortly become clear. I would add that this is perhaps a mimetic function of how the aesthetic, in the form of objects and phenomena, is thematically disseminated throughout the novel. Whereas Cusk's writing is sparser and tends to focus on dialogue, with feelings being explained more directly through the speech of the characters, Huysmans at nearly every turn gives us rich description of the already artistically dense novelistic spaces (mostly of the narrator's home), meaning that where plot is lacking, description abounds—though this is not to say that every moment in the novel is elevated in this same manner. If, as Ruth Plaut Weinreb writes, the novel is "a work that explores abstract problems of aesthetics and is scarcely concerned with a vital presentation of reality,"[7] the vitality of the novel must be sought elsewhere than in its description, leaving us with the question of where exactly we must find it. As the said description is often laden with cultural and artistic references, the halting experience of the reader, especially today, both mirrors and is in tension with des Esseintes's experiences in his aesthetic palace.

Une arche immobile et tiède

Throughout *À rebours*, we mainly read des Esseintes's lengthy dissertations about literature and various other arts, extended reveries that are prompted by certain of his fleeting encounters with the sensory world, an abandoned attempt at travel, and several accounts of his various ailments. The inability to neatly situate the novel runs far deeper than the question of genre or plot, and far deeper than the question of its composition. A glance at its opening pages makes it clear that the field of aesthetics is a major concern for des Esseintes. But beyond his ruminations about literature, painting, music, horticulture, and aromachology, the novel stages an important problem that is often overlooked in contemporary discussions about aesthetics: the tension between the work of art and what more properly belongs to the domain of aesthetic experience. Des Esseintes embodies the tension between aesthetics as a field of inquiry and aesthetic experience as a fact of life: he is decidedly an aesthete, with rarefied tastes; but he is just as vitally invested in achieving certain experiences through the encounters driven by those tastes. However, the interrelatedness of aesthetics and aesthetic experience complicates matters even further, and has unexpected consequences, as we will see later on. It would not be an exaggeration to say that des Esseintes is somebody who has gotten a "taste" for the aesthetic itself, not simply in the sense that he has "good taste," or even in a Kantian sense that he has the ability to make judgments of taste—though both can be argued—but rather that he has gone beyond the philosophical question of taste altogether, and has begun truly to thirst for aesthetic experience. Des Esseintes's project throughout the novel, with the dual purpose of exiting society and sustaining a certain experience curated according to his tastes, pushes to the forefront a crucial philosophical problem pertaining to the idea of aesthetic taste and aesthetic experience in general. With its series of curated moments, *À rebours* allows for a deeper exploration of certain paradoxes brought up by Kant, and explored somewhat more directly by Schopenhauer: what happens when aesthetic experience itself becomes the object of our interest?

As a starting point for this question, Huysmans allows us to see, in very complex ways, how taste, chance, and plot are interrelated. I want to begin with Hanson's suggestion about decadence which, as a movement, raised the aesthetic dictum of 'art for art's sake' to the status of a cult, especially in the final decades of the nineteenth century. [...] Decadent style is characterized by an elaborate, highly artificial, highly ornamented, often tortuous style; it delights in strange and obscure words, sumptuous exoticism, exquisite sensations, and improbable juxtapositions; it is fraught with disruption, fragmentation, and paradox; it has a tendency to vague and mystical language, a longing to wring from words an enigmatic symbolism or a perverse irony.[8]

All of the above is fitting for describing Huysmans's style, and later in this chapter, I will touch in particular on the suggestion that des Esseintes's attitude toward art might be considered cult-like. For now, Huysman's strange prose stylings must be addressed. Robert Baldick describes Huysmans's style as "one of the strangest literary idioms in existence, packed with purple passages, intricate sentences, weird metaphors, unexpected tense changes, and a vocabulary rich in slang and technical terms."[9] While I will be more concerned with the ideas expressed in the novel than in its style, Huysmans's strange way of writing is crucial for the experience of reading *À rebours*, which is at turns hilarious, tedious, disgusting, terrifying, and ecstatic and, again, nearly impossible to summarize or paraphrase. It is worth noting that, above all, decadent literature is both "commonly defined by its thematic preoccupation with art,"[10] as Hanson writes, but also with a form of aesthetic hedonism that often (but not necessarily) implicates works of art. This hedonism is marked by a particular attunement to the senses and perception, including works of art that champion the senses, and it is no surprise that Huysmans was an early proponent of impressionist painting.[11] If Huysmans's writing provides a kind of shock to the senses, it is primarily in service of heightening the stakes of what his protagonist undergoes throughout the novel. Furthermore, it is only through his bizarre, obscure, at times stilted form of writing—very different from that of the other novelists discussed in this book—that Huysmans describes des Esseintes's own brand of aesthetic experience.

The groundwork for our protagonist's personality and temperament, as well as his habits, aesthetic and otherwise, is laid in the prologue. This prologue begins with an account of the portraits that depict the des Esseintes bloodline: "A en juger par les quelques portraits conservés au château de Lourps, la famille des Floressas des Esseintes avait été, au temps jadis, composée d'athlétiques soudards, de rébarbatifs reîtres [Judging by the few portraits that have been preserved in the Château de Lourps, the line of the Floressas des Esseintes consisted, in bygone days, of muscular warriors and grim-looking mercenaries]."[12] The tale begins with a two-fold focus:

genealogy and portraiture, thereby joining the two deeper themes, which each point back at one another: nature and art. These portraits—and the apparent gap, the missing portraits in between these more robust men and their descendants—are cited as evidence for the decay of the bloodline, which has degenerated over time. This brings us to the narrative's real beginning with des Esseintes himself, "un seul rejeton vivait, le duc Jean, un grêle jeune homme de trente ans, anémique et nerveux, aux joues caves, aux yeux d'un bleu froid d'acier, au nez éventé et pourtant droit, aux mains sèches et fluettes [one solitary descendant, the Duc Jean, a frail young man of thirty, nervous and anaemic, with hollow cheeks and cold, steel-blue eyes, a straight nose with flaring nostrils, and dry, slender hands]" (78/3).[13] Des Esseintes is introduced and compared to the likenesses of his forebears by way of portraiture, and these lines read like a description of a portrait. Even frozen in time, his frailty bears traces of decline and is a constant burden to him both in his day-to-day existence and in the long-term trajectory of the novel, where it takes shape in numerous ways. In comparison with his ancestors, des Esseintes seems like a deviation within nature itself.

In an essay dealing with history and aesthetics in *À rebours*, Gasché sees a link between the decline of des Esseintes's bloodline and ill health on the one hand, and the decay of language that informs the decadent aesthetics loved by des Esseintes himself on the other hand. In particular, Gasché argues that while "genealogy and its correlative, the theory of degeneration, was a major preoccupation of the second half of the nineteenth century," the novel is unique in its focus on one single character in particular, and "it is as a whole turned backwards in an attempt to explore origins, beginnings, and memories, thus receiving whatever meaning it has from its past."[14] The novel's preoccupation with tracing origins, even as des Esseintes's decadent tastes may seem to break apart from a certain artistic lineage or create a new lineage, will be offset by Tom McCarthy's *Remainder*, whose narrator's quest for authenticity has an origin that is troubled beyond the impossibility of such tracing.

Gasché goes on to note des Esseintes's "irretrievably divided, double" ancestry, split into "good seed" and "evil seed."[15] The prologue's description of des Esseintes's lineage is notable for being an early instance where the text raises the question of nature, and perhaps already complicates this question beyond its status in Balzac: "La décadence de cette ancienne maison avait, sans nul doute, suivi régulièrement son cours [It was obvious that the decline of this ancient house had followed an inevitable course]" (78/3). In anticipation of the distinction the text eventually makes between nature and artifice, I will pose a further question: is the suggestion here that this unnatural degeneration is, because inevitable, natural? If so, what role does chance have in this degeneration? And how would this relate to the protagonist's *particular* decline? That these unanswered—perhaps unanswerable—questions come up so early on in the novel highlights, however baffling they may be, the fact that the question of what exactly is natural lingers throughout the entire novel in some form or another. Despite des Esseintes's decadent disavowal of nature in favor of artifice, his "project," so to speak, seems to engage this question in an aporetic way, as he never quite allows himself to settle on the ideal object.

After introducing des Esseintes, the prologue details his upbringing and the formation of his disposition, including, in large part, his growing disappointment in his fellow man. After suffering a childhood described as "funèbre [dismal]" (78/3), plagued by sickness and frailty, he is educated at a Jesuit college: "Les Pères se mirent à choyer l'enfant dont l'intelligence les étonnait; cependant, en dépit de leurs efforts, ils ne purent obtenir qu'il se livrât à des études disciplinées [The Fathers pampered this child whose intelligence amazed them; but, despite their efforts, they could not make him settle down to any systematic programme of study]" (79/4). The brilliant young man rejects a systematic education, perhaps foreshadowing his rejection of systems altogether. Combined with the indifference of his parents, his uneven education—tempered by his brilliance—sets the stage for the formation of his habits and tastes, which will be out of step with those of the people around him. "Il lisait ou rêvait, s'abreuvait jusqu'à la nuit de solitude; à force de méditer sur les mêmes pensées, son esprit se concentra et ses idées encore indécises mûrirent [Reading or dreaming, he would soak himself in solitude until nightfall; by dint of always mulling over the same thoughts his mind became more concentrated and his as yet indeterminate ideas matured]" (80/5). Early on, des Esseintes develops a penchant for solitude, reading, and reverie—with an emphasis on waking dreams rather than what we usually understand by the term—which will be indispensable once he sets his aesthetic project into motion. For instance, in the first chapter, as des Esseintes is readying his Fontenay lodgings, he turns his attention to the colors in each room, with a particular attention to how they look by lamplight:

> Ce qu'il voulait, c'étaient des couleurs dont l'expression s'affirmât aux lumières factices des lampes; peu lui importait même qu'elles fussent, aux lueurs du jour, insipides ou rêches, car il ne vivait guère que la nuit, pensant qu'on était mieux chez soi, plus seul, et que l'esprit ne s'excitait et ne crépitait réellement qu'au contact voisin de l'ombre; il trouvait aussi une jouissance particulière à se tenir dans une chambre largement éclairée, seule éveillée et debout, au milieu des maisons enténébrées et endormies, une sorte de jouissance où il entrait peut-être une pointe de vanité, une satisfaction toute singulière, que connaissent les travailleurs

attardés alors que, soulevant les rideaux des fenêtres, ils s'aperçoivent autour d'eux que tout est éteint, que tout est muet, que tout est mort. (91) What he sought were colours that increased in intensity by lamplight; little did he care if they appeared insipid or harsh by daylight, for it was at night that he really lived, believing that you were more completely at home, more truly alone, that the mind was only aroused and kindled into life as darkness drew near; he found too that there was a particular pleasure in being in a well-lit room, in being the only person up and about amid the shadowy, sleeping houses, a kind of pleasure which perhaps included a touch of vanity, a most unusual kind of satisfaction, like that experienced by people working late at night when, drawing aside the window curtains, they realize that round about them everything is dark, everything is silent, everything is dead. (12–13)

This single long sentence, with its evocation of nocturnal solitude, further solidifies des Esseintes's approach to aesthetic encounters. These habits will return in the next chapter with the preoccupations of Proust's narrator, though in a markedly different fashion and to quite different ends. In the present case it is important to note the link between this solitude, however poignant, and des Esseintes's burgeoning misanthropy as it develops into a strict requirement for his aesthetic satisfaction. It is not only that he wants to be alone, away from those he deems unworthy; this solitude in fact *enhances* his aesthetic pleasures, and becomes tied up with them as he continues to form his habits.

Des Esseintes's upbringing and education having instilled these tendencies in him, what comes next in the prologue is not exactly surprising. After leaving the Jesuit college, he sets forth on a series of associations with various communities. First, he visits the family of his cousin, the Comte de Montchevrel, only to find the company boring, petty, and frozen in time. In an early instance of the novel's many botanical metaphors, the text reads thus with reference to the bland repetition he finds here: "De même que dans la tige coupée d'une fougère, une fleur de lis semblait seule empreinte dans la pulpe ramollie de ces vieux crânes [As happens in the snapped-off stem of a fern, a fleur-de-lis seemed the only thing imprinted in the decaying pulp of those ancient brain-pans]" (82/6). In distinction from the deadheading of a flower to promote new growth, des Esseintes finds his aristocratic relatives feeble, uninteresting, and intellectually stunted, with only their royalty on the mind. They are not up to his standards, have nothing of value to offer, and after swearing them off he decides to circulate among his peers, "les jeunes gens de son âge et de son monde [young men of his own age and his own class]" (82/6). He finds these men divided into two general camps: otherwise devout believers who hid their various transgressions from one another, and libertines, those who "étaient moins hypocrites et plus libres, mais ils n'étaient ni plus intéressants ni moins étroits [were less hypocritical and more free and easy, but they were neither more interesting nor less narrow in their views]" (82–83/6). It is worth pausing to consider this distinction, especially the latter group and des Esseintes's distaste for them.

It is easier to understand des Esseintes's disappointment with the first group of his peers, about whom the text reads: "C'étaient, pour la plupart, des bellâtres inintelligents et asservis, de victorieux cancres qui avaient lassé la patience de leurs professeurs, mais avaient néanmoins satisfait à leur volonté de déposer, dans la société, des êtres obéissants et pieux [They were, for the most part, obtuse, obsequious dandies, successful dunces who had tried the patience of their teachers but had, nevertheless, fulfilled the latter's aim of peopling society with submissive believers]" (82/6). This is simple enough: these men are essentially hypocrites unwilling or unable to commit to the pleasures that they indulge in but never speak of. Given that their education has been absorbed by them but has not pierced beyond the surface, they are no better than the common man. It seems that they have digested the "études disciplines" encouraged by the Jesuit fathers, and as a result they "avaient gardé de cette éducation une marque spéciale [still bore the special stamp of that education]" (82/6). For our protagonist, education is but one metric among others by which one's fellow man can be assessed, and it must be worked with, employed in some way, in order to mean anything at all. Intelligence on its own is not enough; it must be supplemented by a desire to exercise one's will and the conviction to stand by one's project. More surprising is des Esseintes's scorn for the libertines:

> Les autres, élevés dans les collèges de l'État ou dans les lycées, étaient moins hypocrites et plus libres, mais ils n'étaient ni plus intéressants ni moins étroits. Ceux-là étaient des noceurs, épris d'opérettes et de courses, jouant le lansquenet et le baccarat, pariant des fortunes sur des chevaux, sur des cartes, sur tous les plaisirs chers aux gens creux. Après une année d'épreuve, une immense lassitude résulta de cette compagnie dont les débauches lui semblèrent basses et faciles, faites sans discernement, sans apparat fébrile, sans réelle surexcitation de sang et de nerfs. (82–83)

> Others, educated in the state colleges or at lycées, were less hypocritical and more free and easy, but they were neither more interesting nor less narrow in their views. These men were libertines, devotees of musical comedy and of horse-racing, who played lansquenet and baccarat, and bet fortunes on horses, on cards, on every diversion dear to the

empty-headed. After a year's trial of these companions, Des Esseintes was filled with an immense weariness by their excesses, which struck him as petty and facile, pursued with no discrimination, with no feverish involvement, with no genuine, intense excitement of blood and nerves. (6–7)

These lines, as early as they come in the text, are rich in terms of laying out des Esseintes's aesthetic—and, for that matter, ethical—discriminations. Whereas the first group was made up of sheep, perhaps intelligent but basically run-of-the-mill young men with no courage and no ability to make anything of themselves and their education, he finds the libertines lacking in their heedless, thoughtless adherence to the doctrine of excess, which is unable to locate something worth truly investing in. It is as if these libertines represent a swing of the pendulum to the extreme opposite side. Furthermore, even the investments they do manage to make are weak, without true enthusiasm or real stakes. Here we see a gesture toward a higher level of chance, as we do in *La Peau de chagrin*: it is nothing meaningful in itself to bet a fortune on horses or cards. These men are going through the motions just as much as the previous group, raising some doubt as to the text's claim that they are "less hypocritical." In fact, this group's lack of virility in their pleasures may be taken as a sign that they are involved in the same kind of familial decay as des Esseintes, further deepening the question of what is proper, respectively, to art (or humanity) and nature. One way to describe these two groups is that neither of them is attempting to pose or solve any real (aesthetic) problems the way that des Esseintes will constantly be doing throughout the bulk of the novel.

Much the same happens when he next seeks out another group, one who on the face of it would seem more in line with his tastes:

> les hommes de lettres avec lesquels sa pensée devait rencontrer plus d'affinités et se sentir mieux à l'aise. Ce fut un nouveau leurre; il demeura révolté par leurs jugements rancuniers et mesquins, par leur conversation aussi banale qu'une porte d'église, par leurs dégoûtantes discussions, jaugeant la valeur d'une oeuvre selon le nombre des éditions et le bénéfice de la vente. (83)
>
> men of letters with whom his mind would surely find more common ground and feel more at ease. This was yet another delusion: he was revolted by their spiteful mean-spirited opinions, by their conversation which was as trite as a weekday sermon, by their sickening discussions which measured the value of a work by the number of editions and the profit on the sales. (7)

In this case, the prospect of finding himself in good company—despite or perhaps because of how true it may seem—is an illusion. The problem is that these men are superficial, notwithstanding their intelligence and their supposed vocation as men of letters. It turns out that they are not as devoted to letters as such a vocation would seem to entail, meaning in particular that they are just as petty in their literary bad faith as his cousin's family and the libertines. Finally, des Esseintes is also disappointed in "les libres penseurs, les doctrinaires de la bourgeoisie, des gens qui réclamaient toutes les libertés pour étrangler les opinions des autres, d'avides et d'éhontés puritains, qu'il estima, comme éducation, inférieurs au cordonnier du coin [the free-thinkers, the doctrinarians of the bourgeoisie, people who claimed the right to every freedom in order to stifle the opinions of others, rapacious and insolent puritans whose breeding he considered inferior to that of the neighbourhood bootmaker]" (83/7). These free thinkers claim the right to their opinions, but to what end? To what purpose? What, in short, do they *do*? In sum, then, taking action—as hermetic and sedentary as he will later seem—is of prime importance for des Esseintes.

Thinking back for a moment to his Jesuit education, each of these groups represents merely one particular system that des Esseintes rejects. This series of rejected brethren indicates a serious refusal to associate himself with systems that cannot bear their full weight, rather than a categorical distaste for certain ideas on a moral level. If, after all of these failed encounters, he "comprit enfin que le monde est, en majeure partie, composé de sacripants et d'imbéciles [realized that, for the most part, the world is made up of scoundrels and half-wits]" (83/7), it should be understood that his estimation of others, as well as of ideas, comes about from a process of examining the entire situation in a way that might be considered extra-ethical; he is more concerned with the aesthetic consistency of any perspective or way of life than what could be called its "objective" truth or morality. He imagines each of these groups as being overly concerned with appearances and with how they are perceived by others rather than with their avowed interests. His early habit of inwardness, of solitary reading and dreaming—oddly, since these pursuits tend to be so aimless—seems to have also instilled in him a code of ethics that disdains any deviation from a stated goal, or any misrepresentations, intentional or otherwise.

Des Esseintes's distaste for all of these men is overwhelmingly based on what he considers to be their laziness or complacency. "Son mépris de l'humanité s'accrut [His contempt for humanity increased]" (83/7), and in conjunction with this he begins to experience a heightened sense of the stupidity of others, as well as the symptoms of the illness that will haunt him throughout the novel. His illness is first brought on by an attempt to engage in his own licentiousness and libertinism. Once he recovers somewhat, he begins fantasizing about his escape from society: "Déjà il rêvait à une thébaïde raffinée, à un désert confortable, à une arche immobile et tiède où il se réfugierait loin de l'incessant déluge de la sottise humaine [Already he was dreaming of a peaceful, civilized retreat, a comfortable desert, a snug, immovable ark where he could take refuge, far from the incessant deluge of human folly]" (84/7). The biblical overtones of these lines foreshadow Huysmans's eventual conversion to Christianity, but they also hint at des Esseintes's religious or "cult-like" devotion to his aesthetic tastes, which are spoiled by the necessity of interacting with his fellow man. The end of the prologue sees our hero on the way to fulfilling this dream; he sells the Château de Lourps and finds his "ark" in a secluded property at Fontenay-aux-Roses. The remainder of the book, the book proper, consists mainly of his seclusion in this aesthetic palace.

La marque distinctive du génie de l'homme

The prologue hints at des Esseintes's decadent ranking of artifice over nature and does so largely by way of certain comments about his lineage that problematize the status of nature in genealogical decline, as well as his dealings with his fellow man. I will now turn briefly to a passage from the second chapter where this attitude is explored in further detail. These lines come in the midst of a still-introductory moment in the text where des Esseintes's existence is likened to "un rigide silence de moines claustrés, sans communication avec le dehors [the unvarying silence of the cloistered monk who lives without communication to the outside world]" (97/16). At this point, his dwellings have been prepared and he is in the midst of his project—not unlike, as we will see in Chapter 3, what first happens with the narrator's initial apartment reenactment in Tom McCarthy's *Remainder*. Not only does he hardly see or interact with the two servants he keeps on, but the floors they inhabit are laid with thick carpeting so that he does not have to hear their footsteps.[16] He lives a highly regimented life, with a meticulously planned meal schedule due to his poor digestion, and his other sensations are controlled to the highest degree possible. He has a false dining room built inside of the house's original dining room, and, by way of an aquarium in the window which filters the incoming light, is able to change the colors and overall "weather" of the room by dispensing dyes into the water:

> s'offrant, à sa guise ainsi, les tons verts ou saumâtres, opalins ou argentés, qu'ont les véritables rivières, suivant la couleur du ciel, l'ardeur plus ou moins vive du soleil, les menaces plus ou moins accentuées de la pluie, suivant, en un mot, l'état de la saison et de l'atmosphère. (100)

thus creating for himself, at his own pleasure, the various shades displayed by real rivers, green or greyish, opaline or silvery, depending on the colour of the sky, the greater or lesser intensity of the sun, the more or less imminent threat of rain, depending, in a word, on the stage of the season and the state of the atmosphere. (17–18)

Like in *Remainder*, des Esseintes is invested in operating a situation according to his designs, in view of awakening and sustaining a certain feeling. This project employs artifice to recreate natural occurrences, like the actual colors that rivers may take on. But this passage, which also anticipates the way that weather works in Proust, is careful to specify (with its earlier description of the architecture of the room (99/17)), that the atmosphere in the dining room still depends on the atmosphere outside, which the narrator is ultimately unable to control. This is an early intimation that atmosphere, and nature more generally, contains an element of chance that des Esseintes cannot fully account for. There is something in the natural that even the most skilled artist cannot grapple with, much to his eventual chagrin.

The dining room description rapidly shifts into an account of des Esseintes's obsessions with travel. As the room "ressemblait à la cabine d'un navire [resembled a ship's cabin]" (99/17), and since his adjustments to the aquarium produce various water-like effects of light, he uses this room to sustain a fantasy of being aboard a ship on a journey. Foreshadowing his later "trip" to London—wherein he simply visits an English-style restaurant in Paris, and then, satisfied, returns home—this section elaborates a particular theory of travel that, while in part arguably true, is an instance of des Esseintes attempting to short-circuit experience or override chance:

> Il se procurait ainsi, en ne bougeant point, les sensations rapides, presque instantanées, d'un voyage au long cours, et ce plaisir du déplacement qui n'existe, en somme, que par le souvenir et presque jamais dans le présent, à la minute même où il s'effectue, il le humait pleinement, à l'aise, sans fatigue, sans tracas [...]. Le mouvement lui paraissait d'ailleurs inutile et l'imagination lui semblait pouvoir aisément suppléer à la vulgaire réalité des faits. (101)
> In this manner, without ever leaving his home, he was able to enjoy the rapidly succeeding, indeed almost simultaneous, sensations of a long voyage; the pleasure of travel—existing as it largely does only in recollection and almost never in the present, at the actual moment when it is taking place—this pleasure he could savour fully, at his ease, without fatigue or worry [...]. Besides, he considered travel to be pointless, believing that the imagination could easily compensate for the vulgar reality of actual experience. (18)

Perceptively, des Esseintes pinpoints the aspect of travel that is so enjoyable: looking back on it after the fact, in memory. This function of memory can be credited with many pleasures, as Proust shows us, such that the work of memory itself becomes pleasurable. Certain things fall away from our moment-to-moment experience when it becomes memory; but certain things come to be experienced only through memory, or, following Deleuze's discussion of Proust, only by passing through memory.[17] If our memories of travel give us joy, it is not necessarily that memory simply fills in the gaps, but rather that the intervening time has afforded us a distilled image of the travel, and possibly even a clearer sense of the place we have visited. Just as Mickelsen argues for a spatial—that is, simultaneous—conception of *À rebours*, the takeaway from the above description of virtual travel is an idea of simultaneity. However, what falls away in des Esseintes's idea of travel here—which is named as a "captieuse déviation [devious kind of sophistry]" (102/19)—is precisely time, as well as the accidental and the unpredictable experiences that come with it, which are crucial to the workings of memory, just as the atmosphere is crucial to the artificial weather in the room itself.

The insurmountable difficulties of time and atmosphere notwithstanding, des Esseintes holds man's capacity for artifice in far higher regard than the forces of nature. Shortly after explaining how he is able to manipulate the state of his dining room to suit his travel needs, the text launches into an impassioned diatribe against nature:

[L]'artifice paraissait à des Esseintes la marque distinctive du génie de l'homme.

Comme il le disait, la nature a fait son temps; elle a définitivement lassé, par la dégoûtante uniformité de ses paysages et de ses ciels, l'attentive patience des raffinés. Au fond, quelle platitude de spécialiste confinée dans sa partie, quelle petitesse de boutiquière tenant tel article à l'exclusion de tout autre, quel monotone magasin de prairies et d'arbres, quelle banale agence de montagnes et de mers! (103)

Des Esseintes considered [...] that artifice was the distinguishing characteristic of human genius. As he was wont to remark, Nature has had her day; she has finally exhausted, through the nauseating uniformity of her landscapes and her skies, the sedulous patience of men of refined taste. Essentially, what triteness Nature displays, like a specialist who confines himself to his own single sphere; what small-mindedness, like a shopkeeper who stocks only this one article to the exclusion of any other; what monotony she exhibits with her stores of meadows and trees, what banality with her arrangements of mountains and seas! (20)

For des Esseintes, artifice is not only better than nature, it is in fact what distinguishes man's genius. Nature is "dégoûtante," that is, not only "nauseating" but more literally distasteful, contrary to man's taste. But is this necessarily the taste of the genius? Kant writes that "**Genius** is the talent (natural gift) that gives the rule to art. Since the talent, as an inborn productive faculty of the artist, itself belongs to nature, this could also be expressed thus: **Genius** is the inborn predisposition of the mind (*ingenium*) **through which** nature gives the rule to art."[18] Genius communicates between nature and art, and troubles our ability to distinguish between the two, while at the same time giving us the injunction of doing so. As is clear from the difficulty of fully circumscribing its boundaries, beauty is without rules. If we take nature in a broad sense as meaning anything apart from human activity or intention, then it cannot so easily be avoided. And if genius is the ability to create beautiful art—and, for Schopenhauer, the ability to recognize beauty, and even the very impulse to seek out beauty—then genius cannot be learned. It is something inborn. This makes it difficult to accept the connection made by des Esseintes between artifice and genius, insofar as it posits for him an alignment with artifice and control.

What des Esseintes means by nature can be detected in the ways that he describes it, all of which tend to confine it to a kind of static simplicity, something very different from the force of genius that would give the rule to art. Two things are at work in imagining that the tastes of refined men would be contrary to uniform landscapes and skies, meadows and trees, mountains and seas. First, we might say that des Esseintes is reacting to what he perceives as a more dogmatic, common idea of taste. As Baudelaire writes,

> from time to time there come forward righters of wrong, critics, amateurs, curious enquirers, to declare that Raphael, or Racine, does not contain the whole secret, and that the minor poets too have something good, solid and delightful to offer; and finally that however much we may love *general* beauty, as it is expressed by classical poets and artists, we are no less wrong to neglect *particular* beauty, the beauty of circumstance and the sketch of manners.[19]

By lauding underappreciated artists, Baudelaire is in part praising the accidental nature of aesthetic experience over, in a museum, the tendency to flock directly to what everybody "knows" is the essential work of art. He suggests, correspondingly, that it is worth thinking against taste, that what can be considered minor will often bear just as much fruit as what we already know deserves our aesthetic esteem. But des Esseintes is not content with this, and his "against the grain" taste reaches the point of caricature. Instead of being open to finding beauty in artifice as well as nature, des Esseintes reverses the entire structure, deeming nature totally spent, boring, exhausted, and exhausting to men of good taste. (As a brief side-note, it is worth mentioning how different Proust's narrator's unconventional conception of taste is from des Esseintes's, and especially how these ideas of taste develop throughout the respective novels.)

Second, des Esseintes is imagining nature as mediated through the image, in particular the landscape, which also names a kind of painting—just like the portrait with which the novel begins. There is another, perhaps more hidden, reversal at play in des Esseintes's attitude, this time with respect to the relationship between nature and the work of art. As Kant writes in the third *Critique*, "Nature was beautiful, if at the same time it looked like art; and art can only be called beautiful if we are aware that it is art and yet it looks to us like nature."[20] What is beautiful is purposive without purpose, meaning that there is no determinate concept for the object, yet it seems as if it were fashioned according to one. Beautiful art, on the other hand, is like nature because it must seem to us like the result of some natural process. The circular relation between nature and art in Kant is delicate; as explained above, genius is its mediating factor. Instead of considering this relation, which necessarily involves much indeterminacy and chance, des Esseintes prefers artifice due to what he perceives as nature's shortcomings, its triteness, small-mindedness, monotony, banality—all because, it seems, her consistency has tried the patience of the well-cultivated man.

To ponder the question of why he dislikes the landscape, the painting, and the image in general, we should consider that when a specific painting is positively evoked in *À rebours*, namely, Gustave Moreau's *Salomé*, it is in the fashion of a hallucinatory vision, the object of des Esseintes's obsession. The "highly erotic"[21] description of this painting is of an entire scene and its surrounding atmospheric phenomena, replete with the movements of Salomé's dance and even the smell of incense, and occasions what can only be described as an essayistic reflection on the figure of Salomé more generally. If des Esseintes dislikes the landscape as an image, it is as a specifically *still* image, one that merely represents rather than brings into being. However, the way to discern how this can be recognized is far from clear and seems to involve a highly subjective encounter with particular works, especially works that appeal to des Esseintes's peculiar and carefully cultivated tastes.

The above passage about nature continues, and moves from nature's uniformity—considered, it should be noted, in a quite one-dimensional way—to artifice's ability to replicate any of her inventions at will:

> Il n'est, d'ailleurs, aucune de ses inventions réputée si subtile ou si grandiose que le génie humain ne puisse créer; aucune forêt de

> Fontainebleau, aucun clair de lune que des décors inondés de jets électriques ne produisent; aucune cascade que l'hydraulique n'imite à s'y méprendre; aucun roc que le carton-pâte ne s'assimile; aucune fleur que de spécieux taffetas et de délicats papiers peints n'égalent!
>
> A n'en pas douter, cette sempiternelle radoteuse a maintenant usé la débonnaire admiration des vrais artistes, et le moment est venu où il s'agit de la remplacer, autant que faire se pourra, par l'artifice. (103)
>
> Moreover, there is not one single invention of hers, however subtle or impressive it may be thought to be, that the human spirit cannot create; no forest of Fontainebleau or moonlit scene that cannot be produced with a floodlit stage set; no waterfall that hydraulics cannot imitate so perfectly as to be indistinguishable from the original; no rock that papier-mâché cannot copy; no flower that specious taffetas and delicately painted papers cannot rival! There is no doubt whatever that this eternally self-replicating old fool has now exhausted the good-natured admiration of all true artists, and the moment has come to replace her, as far as that can be achieved, with artifice. (20)

Nature is again characterized in picturesque terms—moonlight, a waterfall, rocks, and flowers—as if already considered in its "artistic" capacity. The contrast from *La Peau de chagrin* is noteworthy in that Raphaël's engagement with nature late in the text takes an entirely different approach, where nature is understood as a force, an intensity beyond any concern for image or artifice. In fact, Raphaël's encounter with nature is predicated on a flight from will and, therefore, from any artifice that he himself might engage in or concern himself with. Des Esseintes, instead, understands nature in terms of an "aesthetic" (in quotations because held at a distance) problem, as something to be resolved by any means. The means, of course, is artifice, which is apparently able to replicate all of nature's effects to a higher and more appealing degree, perhaps because it requires less than the bare minimum of patience, just as his imaginary travels described above. The difference between these two figures might provisionally be understood in terms of a division between the sublime (Raphaël) and the beautiful (des Esseintes), especially given des Esseintes's drive to control and select what he engages with, as opposed to Raphaël's abandonment to chance. Des Esseintes, with his curatorial impulse, apparently does not heed Baudelaire's question: "Who would dare assign to art the sterile function of imitating Nature?"[22] Or perhaps he has misunderstood the emphasis of terms in this question, taking the sterility of this enterprise to apply to nature more than to the gesture of replicating it through art.

Au hasard des rues

The fourth chapter of *À rebours* contains one of its most well-known passages, wherein des Esseintes orders himself a tortoise and has its shell decorated with precious gems. Throughout this chapter as well as elsewhere in the novel, the places where des Esseintes is searching for aesthetic experience are not necessarily where he will find it, nor is it necessarily where the reader will find it. Partly in anticipation of my claim about Proust in the following chapter, I want to argue that aesthetic experience is located in the moments not explicitly emphasized by the text—for example, in the tense shifts and certain subtle aspects of how objects and scenes are described—rather than in the hero's stated attempts to engage with works of art (in this case, with the tortoise which he has made into a work of art).

The chapter begins as follows:

> Une voiture s'arrêta, vers une fin d'après-midi, devant la maison de Fontenay. Comme des Esseintes ne recevait aucune visite, comme le facteur ne se hasardait même pas dans ces parages inhabités, puisqu'il n'avait à lui remettre aucun journal, aucune revue, aucune lettre, les domestiques hésitèrent, se demandant s'il fallait ouvrir; puis, au carillon de la sonnette, lancée à toute volée contre le mur, ils se hasardèrent à tirer le judas incisé dans la porte et ils aperçurent un Monsieur dont toute la poitrine était couverte, du col au ventre, par un immense bouclier d'or.
>
> [...] Le Monsieur salua, déposa, dans la salle à manger, sur le parquet de pitchpin, son bouclier qui oscilla, se soulevant un peu, allongeant une tête serpentine de tortue qui, soudain effarée, rentra sous sa carapace. (127)
>
> Late one afternoon a carriage drew up in front of the house at Fontenay. Since Des Esseintes received no visitors, since the postman dared not even set foot within those unfrequented precincts, having neither newspaper, nor journal, nor letter to deliver there, the servants hesitated, uncertain whether or not to open the door; then, on hearing the ringing of the bell as it clanged vigorously against the way, they ventured to uncover the spyhole cut into the door and saw a gentleman whose entire chest, from neck to waist, was concealed by a huge golden shield.
>
> [...] The gentleman bowed and placed his shield upon the pitchpine parquet of the dining-room. Rocking itself and rising up a trifle from the floor, it stretched forth a tortoise's serpentine head; then, suddenly taking fright, retreated into its shell. (35)

The tortoise's presence in the novel begins in metaphor, as "un immense bouclier d'or." Even its introduction as a shield in the first place comes only at the end of a meandering sentence that emphasizes not only the seclusion of des Esseintes at Fontenay, but also his lack of mail—meaning the written word, and specifically the contemporary written word—perhaps mirroring des Esseintes's slowness to remember just who exactly might be visiting him in this moment. He has cut himself off from communications from others, but also from writing more broadly, a point that is not unimportant for the overall structure and concerns of *À rebours*, which can be seen in the odd manner that literary devices are employed throughout. For instance, the tortoise arguably remains a shield even once it is revealed as being a tortoise since it simply *has* "une tête serpentine de tortue." Two instances of *hasard* show up in these lines—first negatively, with reference to the postman's avoidance of the house, and second to describe the servants peering through the spy-hole to see who is there. *Hasard* is all around, even when our protagonist struggles against it. Besides drawing our attention to *hasard* as a general theme that, to recall Bell's gloss of it, "suggests [...] that chance is primordial, that it precedes order,"[23] the importance of this will become clear in a moment, as the passage unfolds.

The text continues with an explanation of the reason for this tortoise's arrival:

> Cette tortue était une fantaisie venue à des Esseintes quelque temps avant son départ de Paris. Regardant, un jour, un tapis d'Orient, à reflets, et, suivant les lueurs argentées qui couraient sur la trame de la laine, jaune aladin et violet prune, il s'était dit: il serait bon de placer sur ce tapis quelque chose qui remuât et dont le ton foncé aiguisât la vivacité de ces teintes.
>
> Possédé par cette idée il avait vagué, au hasard des rues, était arrivé au Palais-Royal, et devant la vitrine de Chevet s'était frappé le front: une énorme tortue était là, dans un bassin. (127–128)
>
> This tortoise was the consequence of a whim of Des Esseintes's, which antedated his departure from Paris. One day, while gazing at a shimmering oriental carpet and following the sheen of the silvery lights darting about on the woven woollen threads, plummy purple and golden yellow in colour, he had thought: it would be a good idea to place upon this carpet something that moves, and is dark enough in hue to set off the brilliance of these tones.
>
> Wandering haphazardly through the city streets in the grip of this idea, he had reached the Palais-Royal, and in front of Chevet's shop-window had struck himself upon the forehead: an enormous tortoise was there, in a tank. (35)

The tortoise is the solution to a fairly straightforward aesthetic problem: how best to compliment or highlight the carpet's hues. Interestingly, des Esseintes arrives at this solution *au hasard*: he comes fortuitously upon the tortoise in a store-front while walking about the Palais-Royal, the very same area where Raphaël finds the magical skin after wandering through the streets once he casts what should have been his final bet. This passage nicely portrays how, on the one hand, an aesthetic question is formulated through concentration and critical thinking, and, on the other hand, may be solved by accident. Perhaps it is better to say that its "solution" may be discovered by accident, for at this point in the text the solution has not yet been implemented, and the results of its implementation remain to be seen. As we will see in Chapter 3, the *Remainder* narrator has a remarkably similar idea vis-à-vis randomness and irrationality as methods of solving an aesthetic problem.

The initial test run of the tortoise is a failure, since "la couleur tête-de-nègre, le ton de Sienne crue de cette carapace salissait les reflets du tapis sans les activer; les lueurs dominantes de l'argent étincelaient maintenant à peine, rampant avec les tons froids du zinc écorché, sur les bords de ce test dur et terne [the dark brown and raw Sienna shades of that shell dimmed the play of colours in the carpet without bringing them to life; the overwhelmingly silvery lights now barely even gleamed, deferring to the chill tones of unpolished zinc that edged the hard, dull carapace]" (128/35). The tortoise in this first attempt does not have the expected effect due to the dull tones of its shell, and therefore it does not enliven the colors of the carpet.[24] To mitigate his disappointment, des Esseintes decides to have the shell gilded, so that the tortoise stands out against the carpet rather than the other way around:

> Une fois rapportée de chez le praticien qui la prit en pension, la bête fulgura comme un soleil, rayonna sur le tapis dont les teintes repoussées fléchirent, avec des irradiations de pavois wisigoth aux squames imbriquées par un artiste d'un goût barbare.
>
> Des Esseintes fut tout d'abord enchanté de cet effet; puis il pensa que ce gigantesque bijou n'était qu'ébauché, qu'il ne serait vraiment complet qu'après qu'il aurait été incrusté de pierres rares. (129)
>
> Once back from the gilder's where it had been lodging, the creature blazed like a sun, shining triumphantly over the subjugated tones of the carpet, radiant as a Visigoth's shield inlaid with scales by an artist of barbaric tastes.
>
> At first, Des Esseintes was enchanted with this effect; then it struck him that this gigantic jewel was still unfinished, and would not be truly complete until it had been encrusted with precious stones. (36)

In a shift back to metaphor, this passage recalls us to the tortoise's original appearance as a shield, as it first likens it to a sun, and then to a jewel. This highlights an important question about this passage's temporality, a localized version of the temporality of the novel as a whole, whose chapters—aside from the early and late ones—could arguably be read in any order. While it is quite different and possibly even the inverse of it, this technique anticipates Proust's use of the iterative in some of his most interesting passages on aesthetic experience, which I will address in the next chapter. With three instances of the tortoise's delivery now revealed, and three different states of the tortoise itself, the opening paragraphs of this chapter cannot be solidly situated within a determined time frame, *even within this very chapter.* The flashback that immediately occurs after the "shield" is placed on the floor and reveals its tortoise's head introduces a complex timeline, as I have tried to show with reference to the quotations above. In short, the gilded tortoise is delivered, reminding des Esseintes that he has bought a tortoise, at which point the narrative moves backward to detail his process of buying it, and then shows not one but two distinct alterations that require the tortoise to be sent off again (and redelivered). This is worth elaborating not only because time is an important factor in aesthetic experience (as I will discuss more at length in my chapter on Proust), but also because the assisted travels of the tortoise entail more (and more noticeable) movement than we see when it is finally placed on the floor at Fontenay-aux-Roses. This passage is one example of an instance in which the muddled nature of the plot in *À rebours* is an effect of the prose changing speed and register in service of description.

Like the reader, des Esseintes himself seems to lose track of time during this chapter. Following his realization that the tortoise requires precious stones for its full effect, he decides to select a bouquet pattern in which the gems will be fitted, and there is a detailed explanation of his process of selecting the appropriate stones. This explanation is essayistic and lengthy, and I will limit myself to including only one brief quotation from it that is emblematic of the thinking behind his aesthetic tastes and his personality more generally. Needless to say, he is dissatisfied with most of his options:

> Décidément aucune de ces pierreries ne contentait des Esseintes; elles étaient d'ailleurs trop civilisées et trop connues. Il fit ruisseler entre ses doigts des minéraux plus surprenants et plus bizarres, finit par trier une série de pierres réelles et factices dont le mélange devait produire une harmonie fascinatrice et déconcertante. (130)
> None of these gems at all satisfied Des Esseintes; they were, in any case, too civilized and too well known. He ran some stones that were more unusual, more bizarre, through his fingers, finally selecting a series of both real and artificial gems, which in combination would produce a harmony at once fascinating and unsettling. (37)

In the preceding paragraph, he runs through the precious stones—diamonds, emeralds, topazes, amethysts, sapphires—and finds fault with each one. The sapphire is unique in being discarded for purely aesthetic reasons, as it does not sparkle under artificial light; all of the others are avoided for their popularity with certain types of people deemed vulgar by des Esseintes—in other words, for their place in the matter of sociological distinction. Hannah Freed-Thall suggests that nuance in *À rebours* signifies "as a rarified or delicate quality perceptible only to a privileged minority," and the description of gem selection is an appropriate example of this, with des Esseintes going one step further in including a concern for what is perceptible to others in his selection.[25] Some lines down, discussing the stones that he winds up choosing, this line of reasoning is continued: "il repoussa formellement cette turquoise orientale qui se met en broches et en bagues et qui fait, avec la banale perle et l'odieux corail, les délices du menu peuple [he rejected out of hand that Oriental turquoise which is used on brooches and rings and which, along with the humdrum pearl and the odious coral, delights the hearts of the humbler classes]," choosing instead Western turquoises whose colors are described as "engorgé, opaque, sulfureux, comme jauni de bile [clogged, opaque, sulphurous, as though yellowed with bile]" (130–131/37). Especially emblematic of decadence, this description of the winning jewel is marked by obscurity and disgust, a perverse reveling in the bodily, but primarily due to its deviance from the norm and its excessive nature. Bile in particular can also be associated with impermanence, as it is the fluid that breaks down molecules in the process of digestion. The turquoise is chosen because it gives a sense of disintegration, and this impermanence also foreshadows the end of the chapter, as well as the trajectory of the novel as a whole.

The tortoise is finally "complete" some pages into the chapter, after its various shipments and fittings, leaving it to gleam "dans la pénombre [in the semi-darkness]" of des Esseintes's dining room (132/38). What happens next takes up the rest of the chapter and proceeds from his pleasure at finally seeing his vision come to life. The text's description of this pleasure seems somewhat simplistic: "Il se sentit parfaitement heureux; ses yeux se grisaient à ces resplendissements de corolles en flammes sur un fond d'or [He felt perfectly happy; his eyes were intoxicated by those resplendent corollas blazing on a golden ground]" (132/38). This straightforward way of representing des Esseintes's affect anticipates McCarthy's *Remainder*, which, among its many similarities to Huysmans's novel, tends at times to describe intense aesthetic feelings in a straightforward and almost childish way. The narrator of *Remainder* launches his project in response to a "tingling," a "mixture of serene and intense [...] so serene and intense that I felt almost real."[26] While the entire building that McCarthy's unnamed narrator has constructed according to his specifications is not exactly an aesthetic palace, he embarks on a series of "re-enactments" of increasing complexity, expense, and danger, as part of an aesthetic endeavor that blurs the lines between rehearsal and reality, which can be seen as another dimension or iteration of des Esseintes's concern for distinguishing between the artificial and the natural.

In the present context, placed in the midst of a chapter so temporally complex that the timeline of any identifiable events (the arrival of the tortoise, its multiple trips back and forth to be gilded and set with stones, not to mention des Esseintes's visits to various shops, and so on) is dizzying, the basic description of feeling "parfaitement heureux" offers a striking stylistic contrast to the surrounding text and arguably indicates a kind of listlessness despite all of des Esseintes's fervent enthusiasm for the aesthetic. Writing about the innovation and novelty typical of modernism, Elizabeth Goodstein suggests that boredom is a "tangle of word and experience: a subject in crisis, a vacuous world, interchangeable losses. [...] It appears as both cause and effect of this universal process—both as the disaffection with the old that drives the search for change and as the malaise produced by living under a permanent speedup."[27] As both cause and effect of the conditions of modernity, boredom is unavoidable. It is linked intimately to aesthetic experience, but how exactly they are linked is difficult to explain. Helpfully, Goodstein calls boredom "a form of reflective distance that becomes a new attitude toward experience altogether."[28] Boredom complicates experience, launching the subject into a critical mode; but the subject's response to what is seen while in this mode is not predetermined. Reflective distance does not, in other words, necessarily lead to predictable outcomes. In des Esseintes's case, as we have seen above, boredom sometimes leads to the formation of an aesthetic problem through careful reasoning and deliberation, and other times it leads to a chance encounter in the streets of Paris whereby that problem is solved. Goodstein's analysis also provides some insight into the strangeness of prose that we may encounter in cases like this, where a possibly unspeakable feeling is described in almost mundane terms. "The experience without qualities is the plague of the enlightened subject, whose skeptical distance from the certainties of faith, tradition, sensation renders the immediacy of quotidian meaning hollow or inaccessible."[29] We have already raised the question of des Esseintes's cult-like adherence to the aesthetic, and perhaps it can be traced in part to this very same skepticism, whereby any experience worth noting must be mediated through a highly cultivated set of aesthetic tastes. I would add, borrowing a term from Proust, that his admiration for the aesthetic can be called *idolatry*.

In the preface to his translation of John Ruskin's *Bible of Amiens*, Proust writes: "Il n'est pas dans la nature de forme particulière, si belle soit-elle, qui vaille autrement que par la part de beauté infinite qui a pu s'y incarner: pas même la fleur du pommier, pas même la fleur de l'épine rose [There is not in nature any particular form, no matter how beautiful, that is worth anything in any other way than by the hint of infinite beauty incarnated in it: not even the blossom of the apple tree, not even the blossom of the pink hawthorn]."[30] Echoing Kant's aesthetics, what Proust means is that the beauty found in an object is not, strictly speaking, proper to that object. He takes this sentiment one step further, writing also that "la beauté d'un tableau ne dépend pas des choses qui y sont représentées [the beauty of a painting does not depend on the things represented in it]."[31] He makes these remarks to substantiate his discussion of idolatry, of which he accuses Ruskin, and of which we can also accuse des Esseintes. Proust gives a striking example to explain how idolatry can pervade one's aesthetic tastes in specific cases. Idolatry can be operative even beyond a concern for any kind of canon—in fact, one can be idolatrous even in terms of one's own particular habitual tastes. Proust's love of hawthorns helps him clarify the above statement by touching on the particular hint of beauty incarnated in them:

> même envers elles, envers elles si peu littéraires, se rapportant si peu à une tradition esthétique [...] je me garderai toujours d'un culte exclusif qui s'attacherait en elles à autre chose qu'à la joie qu'elles nous donnent, un culte au nom de qui, par un retour égoïste sur nous-mêmes, nous en ferions « nos » fleurs, et prendrions soin de les honorer en ornant notre chambre des oeuvres d'art où elles sont figurées.[32]
> even for them, so nonliterary, so unconnected with an aesthetic tradition [...] I shall always guard against an exclusive cult that would attach to them anything but the joy they give us, a cult in the name of which, by an egotistical inward movement, we would make of them "our" flowers, and would take care to honor them by adorning our rooms with works of art in which they figure.[33]

Proust's intervention is to distinguish on the one hand between canonical aesthetic objects and ones more personal to us, and on the other hand between ways of appreciating something aesthetically. Proust writes that he would go to smell the hawthorns despite his allergies, but populating a room with depictions of them is, for him, out of bounds: to do so would be a mark of idolatry. This is a difficult and multi-tiered distinction, and I do not wish to claim that des Esseintes is simply replicating the kind of behavior that Proust cautions against here. However, I do think it is fair to call him a cult-like idolator for one key, if more general reason, which is his identification and classification of objects as the material for his search for aesthetic experience. In other words, if he has gained the "taste" for the aesthetic as I have suggested above, he does so in a way that reads objects, and especially particular objects, as containing the ability to evoke aesthetic experience, and therefore multiplies the "aesthetic" objects around him in his endeavor. He becomes a collector. The gilded, bejeweled tortoise embodies this tendency, which we might name as des Esseintes's conscious aesthetic project.

Un silence profond

As des Esseintes's project unravels, however, it tends toward aesthetic experience despite itself. Beyond this point in the fourth chapter, the narrative is occupied largely with des Esseintes's reveries and shifts back and forth a number of times between the text's present moment and memories of his past. The text picks up after the tortoise is placed on the floor, and there is a brief, beautiful description of the weather outside:

> Le neige tombait. Aux lumières des lampes, des herbes de glace poussaient derrière les vitres bleuâtres et le givre, pareil à du sucre fondu, scintillait dans les culs de bouteille des carreaux tiquetés d'or.
> Un silence profond enveloppait la maisonnette engourdie dans les ténèbres. (133)
> It was snowing. In the lamplight, blades of ice were growing on the outside of the blue-tinged window-panes and the hoarfrost, like melted sugar, glittered on the gold-spangled bottle-glass of the windows. Absolute silence enveloped the little house as it slumbered in the shadows. (38)

These short lines give a sense of calling back to the prologue and the formation of des Esseintes's habits of solitude. The absence of reference to taste—not only des Esseintes's taste, but the tastes of others against which he is reacting, and indeed any preference at all—contrasts with the rest of the chapter, which is concerned with his enthusiastic attempts to curate his experience. This truly feels like an accidental, unforeseen moment of beauty: there is silence, attention to nuance (rather than the flashy brilliance of the tortoise's gems), and to anticipate Proust one more time, there is an attunement to nature and atmosphere, though here there is no explicit subjective resonance since there is no mention of des Esseintes or any other subject at all. In this moment, we are being given a glimpse of the atmosphere as it carries on beyond des Esseintes's purview, as it escapes his impatient, controlling urge to curate. The moment simply exists in silence.

Following this brief passage, we return to des Esseintes while he seems to be distracted: "Des Esseintes rêvassait [Des Esseintes let his mind wander]"

(133/38). Unlike what comes later in the chapter, we do not get the contents of his reverie; he soon closes the window and decides to take something to drink to warm himself against the cold. This leads to the introduction of his "orgue à bouche [mouth organ]" (133/39), a series of liqueur casks connected to an intricate tap system designed to simultaneously pour the selections of his choosing. In this particular instance, the text reads: "Les tiroirs étiquetés « flûte, cor, vox céleste » étaient tirés, prêts à la manoeuvre. [...] [C]haque liqueur correspondait, selon lui, comme goût, au son d'un instrument [The stops labelled 'flute, horn, vox angelica' were pulled out, ready for use. [...] [T]he flavour of each cordial corresponded, Des Esseintes believed, to the sound of an instrument]" (134/39). Indeed, each liqueur is likened to a section of an orchestra, from the clarinet-like curaçao to the tuba-like brandy. This mouth organ is testimony to the aesthetic capacities of the gourmand and, in turn, des Esseintes's incorporation of all of the senses in service of his aesthetic endeavors. But its metaphorical cross-pollination with music also points to the ubiquity of art throughout the novel and his attention to artifice more broadly, while revealing that the position des Esseintes imagines himself to have relative to aesthetic experience depends upon the homonymy of the two meanings of taste. As Paul Fox has written, "[t]he synesthetic medleys that are performed on the palate of des Esseintes are, it is vital to note, aligned to *his* tastes, just as they are to his *sense* of taste."[34] These lines lay bare des Esseintes's instrumentalization of the object as an aesthetic object, as a work of art, in his attempt to incite certain experiences at will. And these experiences depend on a direct link between sensation and aesthetic cultivation. Otherwise, his project would be totally bankrupt, without any grounding at all.

Fox also points out how others have found des Esseintes's aesthetic project to be a failed, perhaps self-sabotaging endeavor. But taking the strangeness of this text into account, and especially the temporal jumps and repeated calls to memory in this particular chapter, it is clear that things are not so simple. Following the description of the "orgue à bouche" is a passage that reads as an instance of Proustian involuntary memory where des Esseintes recalls the sensation of having his gums worked on by dentists.[35] This passage plays out across a few pages and carries the narrative to the end of the chapter. The bulk of its import is to portray a horrible toothache that resulted, sometime in the past, in des Esseintes having a tooth removed. After the extraction and the ensuing relief, he feels "joyeux, rajeuni de dix ans, s'intéressant aux moindres choses [full of joy and ten years younger, feeling an interest in the most trivial little things]" (139/42).

Strangely, perhaps signaling the disavowal or even the fleetingness of this relief, the memory ends when, in the present, des Esseintes again feels and comments upon the cold. Strictly speaking, it is of course a different reverie from the one earlier when he lets his mind wander before closing the window, but each instance of daydreaming essentially amounts to the same thing in terms of narrative and even description. The only difference is a certain definitive marker of narrative time. The final lines of the chapter, picking up from his daydream, read as follows:

> —Brou! fit-il, attristé par l'assaut de ces souvenirs. Il se leva pour rompre l'horrible charme de cette vision et, revenu dans la vie présente, il s'inquiéta de la tortue.
> Elle ne bougeait toujours point, il la palpa; elle était morte. Sans doute habituée à une existence sédentaire, à une humble vie passée sous sa pauvre carapace, elle n'avait pu supporter le luxe éblouissant qu'on lui imposait, la rutilante chape dont on l'avait vêtue, les pierreries dont on lui avait pavé le dos, comme un ciboire. (139)
>
> 'Brrrr!' he muttered, depressed by the onslaught of these recollections. To free himself from the vision's horrifying spell he rose to his feet and, returning to the present, began to worry about the tortoise.
> It was still quite motionless and he felt it with his fingers; it was dead. Accustomed, no doubt, to an uneventful existence, to a humble life spent beneath its poor carapace, it had not been able to bear the dazzling splendour thrust upon it, the glittering cope in which it had been garbed, the gems with which its back had been encrusted, like a ciborium. (42–43)

The tortoise, after a few consecutive digressions, reappears at the very end of the chapter. What is more, the tortoise—the work of art around which this chapter is ostensibly structured—returns and is returned to as a distraction from an intense experience of memory. Besides its first appearance as a shield, its journeys back and forth to be prepared as an art object, and its death here, the tortoise is only mentioned in a line conveying that des Esseintes was "perfectly happy" to see it on the carpet. This is mirrored by the tortoise's trajectory from metaphor, to actual tortoise, and back again (in death). It begins as a shield and is by turns likened to a sun and to a jewel, is a tortoise while it is in the process of becoming an ornamental artwork, and reverts once again to metaphor, as a ciborium, the decorated receptacle for the consecrated Eucharist—yet another marker of des Esseintes's religious or cult-like adherence to the doctrine of the aesthetic. Hanson writes that the tortoise's jewels "kill it into art and dispel into the past the spark of life that once might have distinguished the ornamental shell from organic tissue."[36] The tortoise's death by being killed into art is also a figure for the way that the vitality of aesthetic experience on the one hand, and works of art on the other, can be deadened by one's attempt to harness or control them for curation and habitual use. Des Esseintes pronounces the tortoise dead due not to the weight of the gems, but rather its previously humble existence and inability to metaphorically "bear the weight" of its splendor. The irony here is not just that the tortoise, neglected, dies. The irony is that des Esseintes does not quite heed the warning of this tortoise if it does indeed perish from too much brilliance, too much of the aesthetic.

This does not mean that everything in the novel is killed into art; despite des Esseintes's attempts to curate and control his experiences, moments of beauty shine through, as with the description of silent snowfall cited above, because certain things refuse to be reined in under an aesthetic project. Large portions of *À rebours* read, like the tortoise's shell, as a gilded text, with decadent, glittering language. But, like the tortoise, it is difficult to tell whether it is moving or not—that is, whether or not des Esseintes is experiencing aesthetic pleasure.

The domestication of works of art is remarked upon by Adorno, who writes in "Valéry Proust Museum" that "[t]he German word, '*museal*' ['*museumlike*'], has unpleasant overtones. It describes objects to which the observer no longer has a vital relationship and which are in the process of dying."[37] If the museum domesticates works of art—that is, if it allows us to encounter works on our own time and according to our own wishes, placing them at our mercy—then it surely complicates any direct approach that we might take to works of art and aesthetic experience. The museum allows us to subsume works according to our tastes, whatever they may be.

Near the end of *À rebours*, des Esseintes becomes seriously ill, to the point where he no longer recognizes his own reflection in the mirror. This prompts him to call on his doctor, who gives him a grave ultimatum: "il fallait quitter cette solitude, revenir à Paris, rentrer dans la vie commune, tâcher enfin de se distraire comme les autres [he must abandon this solitary existence, return to Paris, get back into ordinary life, and try to enjoy himself, in short, like other people]" (336/173). In spirit, des Esseintes rebels: he is not like others, his illness cannot possibly be due to his solitude, and he is fine where he is. For him, dealing with art is nothing but a vital, life-giving matter. And yet, it destroys his health, so that he must do the unthinkable and return to society.

To read *À rebours* simply as a case of a hero who brings art to his own "museum" to die would do the text a disservice. On the one hand, he is guilty through his acts of curation of "killing into art" certain aesthetic objects and a certain otherwise animate tortoise. However, to take this as an absolute failure of aesthetic experience would be to identify aesthetic experience with works of art just as much as the curator-protagonist does. Gail Finney writes: "In light of the ultimate frustration of des Esseintes' escapist enterprise, much speaks in favor of reading *A Rebours* itself 'à rebours.' Viewed in this way—against the grain—the novel emerges as a critique of the aestheticist doctrine it appears to espouse."[38] This reading holds because, crucially, des Esseintes strays from the work of art (here, the tortoise) that he expends so much time and effort preparing. It is "killed into art," to be sure, but never quite experienced *as* art, since he falls almost immediately into a daydream that, however painful and disturbing, gives him an experience of no small intensity. Despite himself and his project, des Esseintes remains sensitive to aesthetic experience in a way that will occupy the following three chapters.

End Notes

1 The novel's troubled relationship to naturalism in particular can be evidenced from Emile Zola's famous comment berating Huysmans for having dealt with his novel a "coup terrible" to naturalism. Ellis Hanson, in a different context, writes that "Zola was convinced that his former disciple had literally gone off his head." Ellis Hanson, *Decadence and Catholicism*, 128.
2 David Mickelsen, "*A Rebours*: Spatial Form," 48.
3 Ibid., 48, 54.
4 Gail Finney, "In the Naturalist Grain: Huysmans' 'A Rebours' Viewed through the Lens of Zola's 'Germinal,'" 76.
5 Rodolphe Gasché, *The Stelliferous Fold: Toward a Virtual Law of Literature's Self-Formation*, 147.
6 Hanson, *Decadence and Catholicism*, 124.
7 Ruth Plaut Weinreb, "Structural Techniques in *A rebours*," 226.
8 Hanson, *Decadence and Catholicism*, 2.
9 Robert Baldick, Introduction to Huysmans, *Against Nature*, 14.
10 Hanson, *Decadence and Catholicism*, 2.
11 He wrote several articles on the impressionists, and developed friendships with some of them. See George A. Cevasco, "J.-K. Huysmans and the Impressionists."
12 Joris-Karl Huysmans, *À rebours*, 77; *Against Nature*, 3. Hereafter, all citations will be provided in text.
13 Dominique Bauer notes: "*Rejeton* indicates perhaps even more the important fact that Des Esseintes is fundamentally a 'reject', a position that results from his own repulsion towards the world" (*Beyond the Frame*, 51, fn. 101). If des Esseintes is a "reject," it is largely due to the extent of his hatred of nature and his obsession with art, and the interconnectedness of these twin impulses.
14 Gasché, *The Stelliferous Fold*, 154–155.
15 Ibid., 155.
16 This reaches comic proportions, as even the female servant's silhouette, on occasions when she has to walk by his window, disturbs him: "il voulut que son ombre, lorsqu'elle traversait les carreaux de ses fenêtres, ne fût pas hostile, et il lui fit fabriquer un costume en faille flamande, avec bonnet blanc et large capuchon, baissé, noir, tel qu'en portent encore, à Gand, les femmes du béguinage [he wanted her silhouette, as she passed his windows, not to seem inimical, and he had made for her a costume of Flemish faille, with a white cap and a large black cowl pulled down over it, such as the lay sisters of the *béguinage* still wear today in Ghent]" (98/16). Des Esseintes

uses artifice to make the presence of his servant feel more natural—in other words, to make them feel less like a supplement necessary for upkeeping his aesthetic palace.
17 In *Proust and Signs*, Deleuze makes the case that the instances of involuntary memory in *À la recherche du temps perdu* allow the narrator to experience something as it was not experienced in the time being remembered. Rather than a memory of Combray, for instance, the narrator accesses the essence of Combray.
18 Kant, *Critique of the Power of Judgment*, 186.
19 Charles Baudelaire, *The Painter of Modern Life and Other Essays*, 1.
20 Kant, *Critique of the Power of Judgment*, 185.
21 Ruth Antosh, *J.-K. Huysmans*, 44.
22 Baudelaire, *The Painter of Modern Life and Other Essays*, 34.
23 Bell, *Circumstances*, 157.
24 Though they are eliminated in Margaret Mauldon's translation, the description of the tortoise's shell has problematic undertones—*nègre*, while not considered as offensive in French as certain other slurs in English, is an informal and racist term for a black person—an example of Huysmans's use of slang in his prose that lines up here with des Esseintes's disappointment at this obstacle to his project.
25 Hannah Freed-Thall, *Spoiled Distinctions: Aesthetics and the Ordinary in French Modernism*, 70.
26 Tom McCarthy, *Remainder*, 44. All references to the novel hereafter will be given parenthetically.
27 Elizabeth S. Goodstein, *Experience Without Qualities: Boredom and Modernity*, 1.
28 Ibid., 3.
29 Ibid., 4.
30 Proust, preface to *La Bible d'Amiens* in *La Bible d'Amiens, Sésame et les Lys et autres textes*, 96; *On Reading Ruskin*, 56–57.
31 Ibid., 96; 57.
32 Proust, preface to *La Bible d'Amiens*, 96.
33 Proust, *On Reading Ruskin*, 57.
34 Paul Fox, "Dickens À La Carte: Aesthetic Victualism and the Invigoration of the Artist in Huysmans's *Against Nature*," 65.
35 "Peu à peu, en buvant, sa pensée suivit l'impression maintenant ravivée de son palais, emboîta le pas à la saveur du whisky, réveilla, par une fatale exactitude d'odeurs, des souvenirs effacés depuis des ans. Ce fleur phéniqué, âcre, lui remémorait forcément l'identique senteur dont il avait eu la langue pleine au temps où les dentistes travaillaient dans sa gencive [Little by little, as he drank, his thoughts followed the impression that had been evoked on his palate, closely pursuing the taste of the whiskey and awakening, by a fatal conjunction of odours, memories that had long since vanished. That bitter carbolic aroma inevitably reminded him of the identical savour which had saturated his palate on those occasions when dentists had worked on his gums]" (136/40). The sentiment of memories "long since vanished" is especially close to how certain scenes of involuntary memory are written in the *Recherche*, though unlike in Proust it involves a painful medical procedure conducted by a "quenottier du peuple [poor man's tooth-puller]" (137/41).
36 Hanson, *Decadence and Catholicism*, 123.
37 Theodor Adorno, *Prisms*, 175.
38 Finney, "In the Naturalist Grain," 76.

Chapter 2

QUIET MOMENTS IN MARCEL PROUST'S *À LA RECHERCHE DU TEMPS PERDU*

Proust's *À la recherche du temps perdu* has been the subject of countless scholarly studies. It has even made its way into everyday life, with film adaptations and endless references in popular culture. Two notable examples of this come to mind from the Anglophone world: the evocation of a certain "Proustian memory" when talking about sense memories, and Starbucks brand madeleine cookies. Thomas Baldwin has referred to this phenomenon as "the Proust brand."[1] In coining this phrase, Baldwin points out that such references, while they easily proliferate through society, merely graze the surface of Proust's text in a superficial way; they are branding. Sense memories are not something that Proust single-handedly invented, nor are madeleines. Yet, both examples are linked to the question of Proust's aesthetics, meaning not only the style of his writing, but more importantly the way that aesthetic experience is deployed throughout the novel. In short, the Proust brand is shorthand for the most obvious and identifiable aspects of the *Recherche*, insofar as these aspects and references tend to be identified with the novel, influencing the way that we recognize its instances of aesthetic experience, as well as what we understand as its contribution to the theory of aesthetic experience. And this Proust brand is not limited to popular culture, but has also affected the way that his work is studied.

To be sure, involuntary memory has a key place in the novel, but the situation is far more complicated than any particular example or structure can convey, not least because involuntary memory also occasions the novel's major and most well-known theoretical passages. These passages have often served for critics as the hermeneutic key to the work itself, and it is not hard to see why. But at the same time, these passages, which are prompted by instances of involuntary memory, also incite theorizations of involuntary memory itself, as well as prefacing the narrator's exposition of his "aesthetic theory." The madeleine scene from early in the novel, for one, is preceded by a short comment laying out the narrator's unique understanding of the relationship between object and impression. And later, in the very portion of the novel where the narrator's aesthetic theory is revealed, his digression about this theory is prompted by a series of involuntary memories, one after the other. While involuntary memory is demonstrably central to the narrator's theory, I argue that this is only part of the story, and furthermore that his theory must be read critically instead of taken straightforwardly as a cohesive philosophy. Involuntary memory—for the scholars, and perhaps even for Proust himself—is the closest analog for the aesthetic theory that serves as the undercurrent and organizing principle of the work. Because of this, we must be cautious of overlooking the novel's other potential contributions to the idea of aesthetic experience. In other words, the proximity between involuntary memory and its theorization is also a narrative tactic, and its effect has been to amplify the status of involuntary memory in the criticism, which should be kept in mind when reading the novel as a whole.

What I will argue in this chapter is that even if we grant that they reflect Proust's own thoughts about aesthetic experience, and not just the narrator's, the iconic moments of *À la recherche du temps perdu*—which are equally important for its narrative trajectory—should not be accepted wholesale as articulating the totality of a so-called "Proustian aesthetic theory." Instead, as I will suggest, Proust's overlooked contribution to the discussion of aesthetic experience lies precisely in the moments of the novel that fall outside of and perhaps even undermine the narrator's aesthetic theory as it is articulated near the end of the novel. The narrator's (and the critics') preoccupation with involuntary memory, while fruitful, has resulted in a lack of attention to what strictly speaking is *involuntary*, which is a separate phenomenon altogether, given that in isolation from memory it loses any concern for an origin and gains its own force. What about those instances where what is at play is simply the involuntary, without the interference of memory, without an "original" back to which we might trace the sensation?

I have drawn attention to the phenomenon of Proustian involuntary memory (with the madeleine as the most iconic and, perhaps not unrelatedly, the earliest instance in the narrative of a discrete trigger object) as a counterpoint for what I wish to discuss under the heading of *quiet moments* in Proust. In contrast to the madeleine scene—which everybody seems to know about, which has received ample scholarly treatment, and which is a reference point for the narrator's theoretical musings, both contemporaneously and retrospectively—what I will hereafter call quiet moments are those passages in the novel that remain virtually unread, both in the criticism and within the text itself. This means that they garner little or no critical attention by scholars *and* occur without much commentary by the narrator—at least, without explicit theorization such as may be found in the "major" moments of the text. The examples that I will offer provide further insight as to Proust's aesthetics beyond what is explicitly stated by the narrator in his more essayistic moments. Furthermore, these passages even undermine the narrator's aesthetic theory as it is laid out in the final volume of the novel.

My purpose here is not necessarily to downplay the importance of involuntary memory, either in the narrative itself or in Proust's aesthetics; nor is it to completely overturn the narrator's aesthetic theory. Instead, I argue that the role of the involuntary in Proustian aesthetic experience is far from limited to the text's instances of involuntary memory, and furthermore that the involuntary should not be read exclusively in terms of the narrator's theory, which carries a kind of systematic quality that threatens to erase the singularity of discrete aesthetic experience, both within the text and in a more general philosophical sense, not unlike what I have suggested in the introduction regarding the relationship between literature and philosophy. In the quiet moments that I will discuss, aesthetic experience seems to hinge on a particular subjective attunement that cannot be mistaken for the sort of engineering or curation that des Esseintes engages in, for instance. In my first example of such a moment, there is not an aesthetic experience as such, but rather a failed attempt to bring one about, followed by a later recognition of this error that points out, in a negative manner, the limitations of subjective intention in aesthetic experience. In my second example of a quiet moment, the narrator experiences "a particular state of soul" that he wishes to sustain at any cost, as a result of atmospheric forces that lie beyond his control, thus highlighting the crucial aspect of contingency in aesthetic experience. In different ways, both passages highlight a crucial and often neglected dimension of aesthetic experience: it cannot be brought about by conscious will, but instead requires patience and something bordering on passivity. In these passages, this fact is simply shown, without recourse to essayistic exposition. These passages simply remain as moments in the text, without any commentary or theorization following them. They must be read, interpreted, and even happened upon, just as the narrator happens upon these moments themselves, and thus they mimic the actual occurrence of aesthetic experience in the midst of life. Additionally, they do not necessarily stem from any original or originary experience; they are not experiences of involuntary memory, though they do raise the question of the involuntary. Taken together, the above facts indicate that these passages undermine the narrator's systematic theory of aesthetic experience to show that it occurs involuntarily, and even without an origin. Rather than making it any less remarkable, this renders the force of aesthetic experience all the more potent. However, it is both understandable and notable that these passages are not included alongside the "classic" passages from the *Recherche*. They fly under the radar, so to speak, and are largely overshadowed by those passages that more self-consciously tend to announce and theorize themselves.

In sum, I am responding to an injunction proffered by Baldwin by way of Roland Barthes: the injunction to read Proust *against* the Proust "brand," to read Proust *otherwise*, particularly where the question of aesthetic experience is concerned. The course of this chapter will be as follows. First, to set up my pair of quiet moments, I will discuss the most famous moment of the novel: the madeleine scene. This is perhaps the single moment of the novel that has gained the most attention, both critically and culturally, and serves as the first moment in the novel where involuntary memory is explicitly evoked and, furthermore, theorized. Following this, I will introduce and discuss my two main examples, both of which fall outside of the narrator's theory of involuntary memory, but which nevertheless speak directly to aesthetic experience. As quiet moments, they serve this purpose in different ways. Finally, I will briefly consider another major moment, near the end of the novel, where the narrator delivers his ultimate aesthetic theory. My purpose for ending on this point is to show how the quiet moments might actually challenge his theory, in addition to exceeding or escaping it.

Il dépend du hasard

It has been noted that the novel's instances of involuntary memory serve to organize its structure. Leo Bersani writes: "The profound connection between literature and sensation is suggested [by] Proust's use of his body's involuntary memories as a principle of narrative organization in the novel."[2] While one may be wary of conflating Proust the writer with the narrator of his novel, as well as of the directness with which Proust's own involuntary memories structured the text, Bersani adds to the case for why these particular moments within the text are so well-known: not only are they striking and relatable, but they furthermore propel the text forward, allowing it to unfold. The madeleine scene is what most immediately comes to mind, since it comes in the early pages of the novel and allows the description of the hero's childhood at Combray to unfold. Though not as verbose as the passage near the end of the novel in which the narrator expounds his aesthetic theory amidst several instances of involuntary memory, the iconic madeleine scene nevertheless involves a theory of involuntary memory, however brief or minimal.

As I have noted already, my reason for discussing this passage has to do with its critical legacy. Much has been made of this passage in service of constructing the narrator's—and Proust's—aesthetics. As a consequence of this, the novel has attracted the attention of numerous scholars wishing to claim that it is a philosophical text. Beyond any actual philosophical import that it may have, the relationship of the *Recherche* to philosophy remains an urgent topic. Besides *Proust and Signs*, in which Deleuze analyzes the *Recherche* according to the several regimes of signs that the narrator encounters throughout his "apprenticeship," Vincent Descombes has carefully read the *Recherche* alongside the idea of philosophy; as he comments, the novel in general, and Proust's novel in particular, cannot "be considered the illustration of a philosophical proposition," and "[t]he philosophy of the novel is not to be sought in this or that thought content, but rather in the fact that the novel requires of the reader a *reformation of the understanding*."[3] Maurizio Ferraris writes that the *Recherche* "is a philosophical work precisely because it rivals philosophy."[4] Even more recently, James Dutton has claimed that the *Recherche* "famously blurs the distinction between philosophy and literature," because while it is formally literary, "its initiating strangeness [...] points towards something more difficult," something involving a "reading-through that is different upon every re-reading, offering ever-new, richly forgettable details."[5] Each of these responses to the novel entails a different approach, and indeed a different understanding of what makes a text philosophical. But regardless of how one decides to articulate the relation between Proust's writing and philosophy, what is undeniable is that the novel is doing something philosophical.

The instance of the madeleine comes early in *Du côté de chez Swann*, at the end of the first section of "Combray," translated as "Overture" in the Moncrieff/Kilmartin translation. This first section, with its iconic opening line centered around sleep, can be situated stylistically somewhere between an essay and an interior monologue. In fact, in addition to giving context to what follows, this "Overture" can be considered as containing the entire work in miniature, and not only because the bulk of the text is written in this same unique style. Above all, this section touches on several themes that are, more slowly and with varying degrees of subtlety, then brought to bear throughout the rest of the novel. To give a short list, these pages include a sort of phenomenology of sleeping and waking; a theory of reading; a social theory of subjectivity; digressions about dreams and memory; and, most importantly, the division of memory into voluntary and involuntary memory.

In the pages leading up to the madeleine scene, the narrator is already engaged in reverie. However, because it is narrated in the imperfect tense, and because it does not seem to involve the same sort of effort required of him in the madeleine scene, this initial passage more likely involves voluntary memory than involuntary memory. But what happens is much the same as what happens with the madeleine scene: the narrator unlocks a further narrative by way of memory. In the passage in question, after musing on sleep, waking, dreaming, and the many different bedrooms that one inhabits throughout one's lifetime, the older narrator launches into a long digression about his childhood at Combray, ending with the drama of kissing his mother goodnight. Thereafter, the narrative returns to the writing "present," and, after commenting on the effect that the scene just recounted has had upon him over the years, the narrator begins an essayistic treatment of the forms of memory. After explaining the Celtic belief by which the souls of the departed are held within inanimate objects and can be accessed only by chance, one relevant paragraph reads, and I quote again:

> Il en est ainsi de notre passé. C'est peine perdue que nous cherchions à l'évoquer, tous les efforts de notre intelligence sont inutiles. Il est caché hors de son domaine et de sa portée, en quelque objet matériel (en la sensation que nous donnerait cet objet matériel), que nous ne soupçonnons pas. Cet objet, il dépend du hasard que nous le rencontrions avant de mourir, ou que nous ne le rencontrions pas. (1: 44)
> And so it is with our own past. It is a labour in vain to attempt to recapture it: all the efforts of our intellect must prove futile. The past is hidden somewhere outside the realm, beyond the reach of intellect, in some material object (in the sensation which that material object will give us) of which we have no inkling. And it depends on chance whether or not we come upon this object before we ourselves must die. (1: 47–48)

In a concise way, here is where we have what is perhaps the first instance of the narrator's theory of involuntary memory. The various aspects and moments of our past leave traces in objects, or, as Deleuze would say, in *signs*.[6] When—*if*—we make contact with one of these objects, it may proceed to give us access to something otherwise beyond our capacities, at least beyond the capacities of conscious thought. If this encounter is involuntary, it is also remarkable for its affective force: as we will see later in this chapter, the involuntary nature of aesthetic experience has its own intensity.

Notably, this theory precedes the famous madeleine scene, which begins in the very next paragraph. The madeleine scene, it must be stressed, is only a few pages long. For this reason, its proliferation throughout popular culture is surprising, but at the same time, its popularity makes sense, since the passage is quite transparent about announcing its importance for the novel as a whole. The narrator's mother brings him tea and madeleines, and, as he writes:

> Mais à l'instant même où la gorgée mêlée des miettes du gâteau toucha mon palais, je tressaillis, attentif à ce qui se passait d'extraordinaire

en moi. Un plaisir délicieux m'avait envahi, isolé, sans la notion de sa cause. Il m'avait aussitôt rendu les vicissitudes de la vie indifférentes [...] (1: 44)

No sooner had the warm liquid mixed with the crumbs touched my palate than a shudder ran through me and I stopped, intent upon the extraordinary thing that was happening to me. An exquisite pleasure had invaded my senses, something isolated, detached, with no suggestion of its origin. And at once the vicissitudes of life had become indifferent to me [...] (1: 48)

Coming right after the theory of involuntary memory, then, is a prime example of it. The reversal of theory and example should be taken into consideration, as it can be seen as situating the theory *before* the example, as a novelistic or essayistic touch intended to guide the reader through the scene. But it can also be seen as coming temporally *after* the scene, according to the time of writing, simply placed earlier to preface it. Either way—and in truth, it is undecidable—we are left to understand that the tea and the cake together make up the "object" (or sign) that prompts the narrator to recapture some aspect of his past (or, as Deleuze would have it, some essential aspect of Combray as it was not experienced during his childhood). The rest of the passage is devoted to dramatizing the narrator's struggles to meet this object halfway—that is, to locate the "origin" of his sensations that the object refuses to reveal. After taking a few more sips, he continues:

> Il est temps que je m'arrête, la vertu du breuvage semble diminuer. Il est clair que la vérité que je cherche n'est pas en lui, mais en moi. Il l'y a éveillée, mais ne la connaît pas, et ne peut que répéter indéfiniment, avec de moins en moins de force, ce même témoignage que je ne sais pas interpréter et que je veux au moins pouvoir lui redemander et retrouver intact, à ma disposition, tout à l'heure, pour un éclaircissement décisif. (1: 45)

> It is time to stop; the potion is losing its magic. It is plain that the truth I am seeking lies not in the cup but in myself. The drink has called it into being, but does not know it, and can only repeat indefinitely, with a progressive diminution of strength, the same message which I cannot interpret, though I hope at least to be able to call it forth again and to find it there presently, intact and at my disposal, for my final enlightenment. (1: 48–49)

Within this passage, a major aesthetic problem is already highlighted: the addictive quality of the aesthetic object, complete with its diminishing returns.

Even as the narrator realizes that what he is seeking lies within him rather than in the object, he is nevertheless hard-pressed to put the object down, though he sees that its repetitions will have decreased effects and diminishing returns.

As I have suggested thus far, the realm of the aesthetic tends to be troubled by a contradiction between its singularity on the one hand and its penchant for creating connoisseurs on the other: subjects who become, as it were, addicted to aesthetic experience, thus spoiling it for themselves. This aesthetic paradox involves thinking the novelty of the experience alongside the subject's always-growing *taste* for the experience, a taste that is often displaced onto the particular object—whether a work of art or a "sign" more broadly—thus revealing an error in judgment or recognition whereby the object is taken as that which "causes" the experience. In the above passage, we see this both in the narrator's repeated effort, and in the sensation's "progressive diminution of strength." What is at issue here is not the presence of an object altogether, but rather the subjective relation to the object whereby that object would be sufficient to prompt and even sustain the experience being sought, as if the madeleine *causes* the experience.

Despite the paradox I have isolated, the narrator continues in his endeavor: "Je veux essayer de le faire réapparaître. Je rétrograde par la pensée au moment où je pris la première cuillerée de thé. Je retrouve le même état, sans une clarté nouvelle [I decide to attempt to make it reappear. I retrace my thoughts to the moment at which I drank the first spoonful of tea. I rediscover the same state, illuminated by no fresh light]" (1: 45/1: 49). This attempt not only prolongs the narrator's state, but also gestures toward its limits, and he comes to see that further effort is not enough to bring about further results. Despite this, but also because of this, something does eventually happen:

> Et tout d'un coup le souvenir m'est apparu. Ce goût c'était celui du petit morceau de madeleine que le dimanche matin à Combray (parce que ce jour-là je ne sortais pas avant l'heure de la messe), quand j'allais lui dire bonjour dans sa chambre, ma tante Léonie m'offrait après l'avoir trempé dans son infusion de thé ou de tilleul. La vue de la petite madeleine ne m'avait rien rappelé avant que je n'y eusse goûté [...] (1: 46)
> And suddenly the memory revealed itself. The taste was that of the little piece of madeleine which on Sunday mornings at Combray (because on those mornings I did not go out before mass), when I went to say good morning to her in her bedroom, by aunt Léonie used to give me, dipping it first in her own cup of tea or tisane. The sight of the little madeleine had recalled nothing to my mind before I tasted it [...] (1: 50)

If his repeated efforts give way to the insight he is seeking, it is apart from—again, perhaps *despite*—those efforts. This is why he notes the suddenness of the revelation. He is able to trace the origin of this sensation back to his childhood at Combray, to "the little piece of madeleine." In my reading, the origin of this feeling, while important, is merely supplementary to the way that this kind of aesthetic experience works; what is important for what will follow in this chapter is the feeling's force, and its involuntary nature. In this light, I wish to highlight the narrator's comment that only the taste of the madeleine—and decidedly not its appearance—is what allows for this experience.

While appearance and vision are thematized throughout Proust's novel, their role is often metaphorical, to aid the narrator in his sociological discussions of, for example, how to distinguish one person from a group of people or recognize them for who they truly are.[7] The other senses are often called upon throughout the novel for various purposes, but they largely concern discrete experiences, among which aesthetic experience numbers. Here, the taste of the madeleine, the actual *experience* of it, without the identificatory distance that sight may afford, is the minimum requirement for involuntary memory. As the narrator continues,

> seules, plus frêles mais plus vivaces, plus immatérielles, plus persistantes, plus fidèles, l'odeur et la saveur restent encore longtemps, comme des âmes, à se rappeler, à attendre, à espérer, sur la ruine de tout le reste, à porter sans fléchir, sur leur gouttelette presque impalpable, l'édifice immense du souvenir. (1: 46)
> taste and smell alone, more fragile but more enduring, more unsubstantial, more persistent, more faithful, remain poised a long time, like souls, remembering, waiting, hoping, amid the ruins of all the rest; and bear unflinchingly, in the tiny and almost impalpable drop of their essence, the vast structure of recollection. (1: 50–51)

As a response to the predominance of sight and appearance as themes and perceptual modes in philosophy, the senses of taste and smell (as well as sound and touch) are at the heart of involuntary memory. This is, in miniature, a view of Proust's attitude toward aesthetic experience, namely, to identify and take up an alternative logic that is seemingly counterintuitive and that requires us to read against our habitual tendencies.[8] Of course, this impulse is not simply contrarian, and Proust is not presuming to advance a "new" aesthetics; instead, he takes on what I argue is a much more difficult endeavor: to think aesthetics otherwise, in a way that we might consider subjective, but not necessarily personal. In the present context, the narrator's preference for taste and smell does exactly this. Taste and smell are more fleeting, more fragile, and indeed (to once again evoke Deleuze) literally *without image*, meaning that they may be harder, in principle, to recognize. However, for Proust, this difficulty of recognition means that our access to them remains singular and involuntary, which has as its corollary the fact that they preserve "l'édifice immense du souvenir." If this is true, it is because smell and taste are, unlike appearance, unchanging. When we recognize a smell or a taste, we are experiencing something without the aid of visual recognition; while we may see a table and recall a different table, or see a person and recall them at a different time in their life, the taste of the madeleine dipped in the tea is the very same taste, whether we are speaking of the taste in childhood or the taste that launches the *Recherche*. Of course, one's sense of taste or smell is subject to change over the course of one's life, as is one's sense of sight. But this only points out a more salient and relevant fact of these senses: what is tasted and smelled is, each time, actually something new, even while it remains the same. Involuntary memory is already on the road to being immaterial if this madeleine and cup of tea can fully recall a different madeleine and a different cup of tea from years before.

Through a brief reading of the most well-known Proustian moment, I hope to have convincingly argued that this "major" scene is more complicated than its popular reception allows us to think—that, perhaps, it has its own quietness. Besides its beautiful turns of phrase and its sensitive evocation of aesthetic experience, what makes this passage shine forth as an iconic moment in literature is its unique role in the overall trajectory of the novel. As we have seen, it both sets up the chronological "beginning" of the hero's narrative and touches on several of the work's main themes. But I have also tried to show something that this larger-picture perspective misses out on: the crucial contribution that Proust makes to the idea of aesthetic experience as both singular and iterable. Reading this passage apart from the larger picture of the work and apart from its critical reception, what it gives us is a nuanced depiction of aesthetic experience, one that can only be recognized and assessed after the fact—whether this entails the passage of many years, or only mere moments. It also gives us a more nuanced, experiential basis for the narrator's theory that will come near the end of the novel. In that sense, this makes it especially fitting that the two "quiet moments" I will now discuss come in between the two major scenes.

Peut-être aurais-je dû penser

To set the scene for the first quiet moment, which comes partway through *Le Côté de Guermantes*, we find the narrator with his friend Robert de Saint-Loup and Robert's mistress Rachel. From the start, the narrator's experience in this passage is cast in an unfavorable light: it is off-putting and tiresome for him, especially as the revelation of Rachel's identity leads him to make a long digression about the various and often seemingly contradictory "sides" that one might see of a single person. The very same Rachel, whom the narrator knows as "Rachel quand du Seigneur [Rachel when from the lord]" from his visits to a brothel earlier in the text, is Saint-Loup's beloved (1: 567/1: 621). In the scholarship, the phenomenon of Proust's so-called "perspectivism," specifically around his perception of others, has been read in a number of different ways. For Descombes, Rachel's "nature" is bifurcated along the lines of the two perspectives from which she is seen: "Robert de Saint-Loup saw Rachel as a woman of great worth. Marcel knows better, having declined to enjoy her favors for twenty francs. [...] If these are two perspectives, each of them sees one *aspect* of Rachel. Neither of them is either right or wrong."[9] On the other hand, and in response, Joshua Landy writes that even "to claim that Rachel is 'really' a prostitute is [...] to give in to a certain recent bias according to which a person's most vicious trait is exclusively allowed to define her identity. Marcel's own view runs counter to such bias."[10] Landy points out that, contra Descombes (who is interested "in alleging that the novel's examples undermine its own claims" on this matter), the narrator explicitly calls into question the idea that one of these points of view is "correct" and the other "incorrect": "All that the episode proves is that people display various sides of themselves at various times and in various situations, and that those who meet them are accordingly susceptible to misjudgments, taking the part for the whole."[11] I would like to extend Landy's point beyond Proust's perspectivism, at least as far as the novel's other characters are concerned. I suggest that we can apply it to the novel as a whole, encompassing roughly the two levels that I began this chapter by discussing: the narrator's experiences and his understanding of them on the one hand, and the novel's critical reception on the other hand. With this in mind, what is at stake in the dilemma surrounding Rachel is what is at stake in my reading of the novel's and Proust's aesthetics. We are guilty of "taking the part for the whole" if we pass judgment on the aesthetics of the novel based solely on the narrator's stated aesthetic theory.

In the present passage, the narrator winds up in a state that might be characterized as "ill will." As Rodolphe Gasché writes in an exposition of Deleuze's new image of thought, "Relinquishing the assumptions that everybody has a natural inclination to thinking and that thought has an affinity to truth is to disconnect thought from any love for truth and to have it begin with the individual, who is full of ill will."[12] This is crucial for Deleuze, who in Gasché's words also holds that "there is only *involuntary thought*, aroused but constrained within thought, and all the more absolutely necessary for being born, illegitimately, of fortuitousness in the world."[13] My point in highlighting this state is that it throws him off guard in a way that is itself already somewhat involuntary, and therefore prepares him for what happens next, including even what happens beyond the lines I am discussing here. Finding himself in a private room in the restaurant where he dined with Robert and Rachel, and observing his companions stretched out on a sofa, drinking champagne and kissing, he bitterly recounts:

> J'avais mal déjeuné, j'étais mal à l'aise, et sans que les paroles de Legrandin y fussent pour quelque chose, je regrettais de penser que je commençais dans un cabinet de restaurant et finirais dans des coulisses de théâtre cette première après-midi de printemps. (2: 468)
> I had had little lunch, I was extremely uncomfortable, and, though Legrandin's words had no bearing on the matter, I was sorry to think that I was beginning this first afternoon of spring in a back room in a restaurant and would finish it in the wings of a theatre. (2: 173)

Irritable, and sickened not only by his empty stomach but also by weariness, by the cloying scene to which he is a witness, the narrator thus bemoans his state.[14] In his self-awareness, he regrets in advance the very *prospect* of spending his day in such a way—which also means of *having spent* his day in such a way, or even of *appearing to have spent* his day in such a way. His tone is already marked by anticipation, as if he were already exposed to an audience (or reader) and therefore vulnerable to judgment from the outside, and he regrets what he is experiencing as if from a space outside of or beyond his current experience. At this stage, he is oriented in his self-conscious thinking by his own particular understanding of what is proper for him to experience, of what sorts of engagements or encounters are fitting for him, and are therefore worth undergoing, as if he already has a particular model of experience in mind.

Here, we should also note that the narrator's disqualification of Legrandin's words should not necessarily be taken at face value; in fact, this expression, as forceful as it is, may justifiably be met with suspicion. On the way to see Saint-Loup sometime before the main passage I am concerned with here, the narrator runs into the snobbish Legrandin, who launches into an aesthetically oriented polemic against "l'atmosphère nauséabonde, irrespirable pour moi, des salons [the for me nauseating, unbreathable atmosphere of the salons]":

> Pendant que vous irez à quelque *five o'clock*, votre vieil ami sera plus heureux que vous, car seul dans un faubourg, il regardera monter dans

le ciel violet la lune rose. La vérité est que je n'appartiens guère à cette terre où je me sens si exilé; il faut toute la force de la loi de gravitation pour m'y maintenir et que je ne m'évade pas dans une autre sphère. Je suis d'une autre planète. [...] [J]'ai le tort de mettre du coeur dans ce que j'écris, cela ne se porte plus; et puis la vie du peuple, ce n'est pas assez distingué pour intéresser vos snobinettes. (2: 452)

While you are on your way to some tea-party your old friend will be more fortunate than you, for alone in an outlying suburb he will be watching the pink moon rise in a violet sky. The truth is that I scarcely belong to this earth upon which I feel myself such an exile; it takes all the force of the law of gravity to hold me here, to keep me from escaping into another sphere. I belong to a different planet. [...] I make the mistake of putting my heart into what I write: that is no longer done; besides, the life of the people is not distinguished enough to interest your little snobbicules. (2: 156)

As his extravagant language here might suggest, Legrandin, who appears earlier in the novel as a neighbor and friend of the narrator's family, is a writer. Therefore, it makes sense that the literature-loving narrator would take his words to heart, especially at this stage in the novel's trajectory. For René Girard, desire in literature is always mediated by a third party; in his words, "[a] *vaniteux* will desire any object so long as he is convinced that it is already desired by another person whom he admires."[15] One of Girard's examples of this principle is Proust's narrator, of whom he writes that "[t]he snob is also an imitator. He slavishly copies the person whose birth, fortune, or stylishness he envies."[16] As we will see in the following pages, Legrandin's words seem to impact the narrator, and the latter's gesture of distancing himself from those words can be read as an awareness of this influence and an attempt to disavow it. However, what the narrator perhaps misses in his idolization of Legrandin is that Legrandin himself is following a certain model idolatrously, and so on *ad infinitum*. In addition to the over-enthusiasm for the aesthetic based on a kind of object or scenario, such as we might find in *À rebours* or later in *Remainder*, idolatry can also apply more directly to the principle of influence as a straightforward and direct adoption of another's aesthetic tastes and sensibilities.

Legrandin has put something in the narrator's mind, a model to aspire to. For the narrator, Legrandin takes up the role of the enlightened aesthete, the one who can choose to forego society to enjoy the aesthetic pleasures of "watching the pink moon rise in a violet sky," while the narrator wastes his time with, at best, "friends." Returning to his day with Saint-Loup and Rachel, the narrator—with Legrandin's words in mind—attempts to salvage his day through what he understands to be aesthetic means. Taking hold of his surroundings, he reshapes them by narrating to himself:

> Après avoir regardé l'heure pour voir si elle ne se mettrait pas en retard, elle m'offrit du champagne, me tendit une de ses cigarettes d'Orient et détacha pour moi une rose de son corsage. Je me dis alors: « Je n'ai pas trop à regretter ma journée; ces heures passées auprès de cette jeune femme ne sont pas perdues pour moi puisque par elle j'ai, chose gracieuse et qu'on ne peut payer trop cher, une rose, une cigarette parfumée, une coupe de champagne. » Je me le disais parce qu'il me semblait que c'était douer d'un caractère esthétique, et par là justifier, sauver ces heures d'ennui. (2: 468–469)
>
> Looking first at the time to see that she was not making herself late, Rachel offered me a glass of champagne, handed me one of her Turkish cigarettes and unpinned a rose for me from her bodice. Whereupon I said to myself: 'I needn't regret my day too much, after all. These hours spent in this young woman's company are not wasted, since I have had from her—charming gifts which cannot be bought to dear—a rose, a scented cigarette and a glass of champagne.' I told myself this because I felt that it would endow with an aesthetic character, and thereby justify and rescue, these hours of boredom. (2: 173–174)

Most immediately, we see an explicit mention of "an aesthetic character" and a conscious effort to employ such a character to redeem an otherwise unpleasant experience. Beyond this, however, several points should be noted. First, at this stage of the novel, the narrator has already received several "lessons" about the aesthetic, both related and unrelated to actual works of art. The most obviously relevant lesson here is Legrandin's brief speech about spending time in solitude enjoying beauty rather than wasting it in society, but there are many others. These lessons have a number of consequences for the narrator, beyond mere education, and they occur in the midst of life rather than being confined to a classroom. They arouse certain desires, they indicate certain objects of desire, and they suggest an aesthetic hierarchy. At the same time, they impart to the narrator the knowledge that works of art will not necessarily be sufficient to satisfy his desire for, and the conditions of, aesthetic experience. Looking at the previous volume, for instance, we find the narrator's excitement about, and disappointment at, seeing la Berma in *Phèdre*, a performance that he had greatly anticipated.[17] According to Bryan Reddick, these passages "represent in little a development in the narrator's thinking about the imagination which is analogous to his 'education' in the novel as a whole."[18] Importantly, this "education" is dialectical rather than simply cumulative: disappointment and correction are just as important as straightforward education, or even clear-cut aesthetic experiences, and the entire education takes place on the stage of life.

If we consider Girard's remarks for a moment, the narrator's impulse begins to make more sense: though in this passage he denies any influence from Legrandin's speech, Legrandin's status as a writer (and therefore as somebody who, in the narrator's mind, must have *taste*, must be attuned to the aesthetic) makes him a prime candidate for the role of Girardian mediator—at least, if we understand desire here more abstractly, in the sense that one of the narrator's long-standing desires is to become intimate with the aesthetic dimension of life. Despite their obvious differences, Legrandin can be said to hold a similar place for the narrator as Ruskin did for the young Proust. In both cases, the influence of an older and more experienced writer instructs the younger reader, who wishes to become a writer himself. However, the successive stages of this education each carry a certain weight, at times verging on what might be deemed enthusiasm or idolatry. This means that the writer's words may be taken to heart without their subtlety being fully accounted for, and indeed without being fully understood—which also means without being fully *experienced*. The narrator's error in understanding is particular to his own context, and will become clear in the analysis that follows.

In the present passage, the narrator's dissatisfaction with how he is spending his day is a naïve echo of Legrandin's endorsement of solitude on the one hand. We might say that, less directly, it echoes des Esseintes's obsession with solitude as well. Without passing judgment on Legrandin's or des Esseintes's ideas about solitude, the danger is that the narrator might agree with him for the wrong reasons, without properly understanding the implications of this solitude or the steps that lead to it. For Proust's narrator, reading is undoubtedly an education, but this education is far from a one-way endeavor, whether he knows it or not. Instead, it is an ever-shifting process whose conclusions are rarely certain and are always subject to revision. This is not to say that what in this passage reveals itself as an error (i.e., the added value that influence, whether from reading or otherwise, grants to particular objects or situations) cannot be productive or provocative. In fact, the opposite is true, and it is only by moving through such errors and understanding *why* they are errors that the narrator's apprenticeship truly takes flight.

Reddick notes the novel's "consistent concern with the fusion of artistic experience with all experience."[19] Throughout its entire trajectory, the novel is engaged in establishing the question of the experience of the work of art within life, as well as the influence of mediating figures on the understanding of art. Each of these aspects is crucial for understanding the "aesthetic character" evoked in the present passage, especially as far as its role in the narrator's education is concerned. With Legrandin in mind, among others, it is not hard to see that the narrator at this stage is clinging to a received notion of the aesthetic and of aesthetic taste. He is prone to equate a work of art with aesthetic experience (among other things), so it is only a small leap to believing that qualities deemed to align with aesthetic taste are markers for or signposts toward aesthetic experience, whether those qualities are found within works of art or as other kinds of signs out in the world. So, even as it seems that the narrator has already discovered that aesthetic experience finds its proper field far beyond the work of art per se, he still exhibits the belief that certain objects could be qualified as *aesthetic* objects, a belief that betrays his naïve adherence, at this stage, to examples or models, and his inability to pull apart object and experience.

Perhaps what is most complex about this passage, however, is its inclusion of a narration of the scene *within the scene*. After a description of the scene, we read the narrator's re-narration to himself of what he is concurrently undergoing. Between the narration of the scene and the narration within it, there are small but significant differences: the order and presentation of the objects are changed, and any reference to the narrator's misgivings about being in the company of a woman of Rachel's status, about his feelings of awkwardness at the knowledge of her two "sides," or even any mention of Saint-Loup at all, disappear as Rachel becomes simply "this young woman." In his narration within the scene, which is pointedly motivated by a will to not have wasted his day, the narrator seems to strive for a kind of de-differentiation, a removal of things from their origins and associations. For example, "a rose [...] from her bodice" becomes, simply, "a rose." This alteration in particular should give us pause, as Kant mentions the rose when discussing judgments of the beautiful in the third *Critique*, rendering this revision at least doubly intriguing. The rose famously appears in Kant's discussion of the singularity of aesthetic judgments, versus the repeatable nature of logical judgments:

> by means of a judgment of taste I declare the rose that I am gazing at to be beautiful. By contrast, the judgment that arises from the comparison of many singular ones, that roses in general are beautiful, is no longer pronounced merely as an aesthetic judgment, but as an aesthetically grounded logical judgment.[20]

In the context of the present passage from *À la recherche du temps perdu*, this seems to be exactly the problem: the narrator, whether he has heard somewhere that roses are beautiful or has experienced the beauty of a particular rose at some point, is motivated to act as if the rose he has received from Rachel is indeed beautiful in a singular way, even though, as we will see shortly, the very need to recast his experience in this manner is revealed to be proof that this is likely not the case. Furthermore, the rose in his case decidedly does have an origin or an ancestor, whether it is Kant's example in particular, or its general status in culture (as a symbol of beauty, love, etc.) more broadly. It is being treated as a rose "in general," meaning that his judgment would, in Kantian terms, be merely a logical one.

At the same time, the narrator is under the impression that this act of reiterating, combined with its distancing gesture, will truly lend to his experience an aesthetic dimension and thus save his day from boredom and oblivion. In part, this means that he is taking up the bad-faith attitude of Nietzsche's spectator, willing himself into "disinterest." In this sense, despite his education up to this point, he displays a misguided enthusiasm for the aesthetic. He has not yet had enough time to *live* with the aesthetic, to learn the patience and interpretation that it requires, and yet it seems that he imagines himself to be an aesthete—as if that were even sufficient in the first place to guarantee aesthetic experience, and as if being an aesthete simply meant bestowing upon certain things (a rose, a cigarette, or some champagne) the designation "aesthetic." Furthermore, since his re-narration bears a resemblance to the process of writing—since it involves highlighting certain details over others—this passage can be seen as a more literal, albeit incipient, stage of the narrator's apprenticeship to writing.

At this point, there is an intervention, ostensibly by the narrator in his more advanced age, which would also be the age of writing—the age, that is, in which the narrator is finally ready to write or already writing, and finally understands something vital about aesthetic experience. He points out his former error, retrospectively, stating: "Peut-être aurais-je dû penser que le besoin même que j'éprouvais d'une raison qui me consolât de mon ennui, suffisait à prouver que je ne ressentais rien d'esthétique [I ought perhaps to have reflected that the very need which I felt of a reason that would console me for my boredom was sufficient to prove that I was experiencing no aesthetic sensation]" (2: 469/2: 174). Tellingly, this does not give us any positive definition of the aesthetic or even of "aesthetic sensation," though we are pointed in its direction. At first glance, the narrator is correct in that an aesthetic experience would, as an involuntary encounter, obviate the need for any such consolation. As I have already argued in the introduction, this is implicit in Kant's aesthetics: we do not, cannot, will ourselves into such an experience. But what is happening here is more complicated because it concerns the workings of a narrative. The narrator is calling his earlier self into question not based on the material of the scene, or the fact that he was not having an aesthetic experience. Rather, he is calling his earlier *reading* of the scene, and his place within it, into question. This is tantamount to questioning the role of the subject in the aesthetic more broadly. It is worth emphasizing that he does not question his earlier reading based on any particular aspect of the scene—in other words, it is not the case that its setting, or the objects or people involved, disqualify this in advance as a potential scene of aesthetic experience—nor does he disqualify this scene from being an aesthetic experience based on his ennui or "ill will." It is not the case that either Rachel's presence or her "true being" prohibit this scene from being an aesthetic one—such concerns are wholly beside the point. Instead, the problem is his motivation in re-narrating this scene to himself, of consciously rearticulating his experience with view to the outcome of aesthetic experience: in short, of trying to curate his experience like des Esseintes, even virtually, in narrative form.

Recalling for a moment the question of who exactly Rachel is, Descombes holds that Marcel's "mistake" about her nature is an example of "novelistic error," an error that "one person makes regarding another."[21] For Descombes, "the important point is that error as optical illusion can be corrected only by a change of vantage point, a change of position. The novel, which not only depicts errors but shows how they are, little by little, corrected, is the story of the circumstances in which the character makes the painful discovery that he has been wrong. What sort of change of position makes possible the correction of a novelistic error?"[22] The novelistic error, which consists simply of what Descombes refers to as an illusion, requires a shift in viewpoint. However, as Descombes notes, the metaphorization of error in optical terms obfuscates the mystery not only of what position is necessary, but of how one might move toward it if one is already occupying a position vulnerable to illusion. This is even more complicated in Proust's novel since it is a novel involving a writer—and doubly so, since it is a novel concerning the becoming of a writer from one who simply wants to write. The connection between literature and life is always in the foreground for Proust's narrator. Miguel de Beistegui writes: "Literature, then—and this is, after all, the novel's real subject—doesn't take us out of the real world, thereby leaving life behind; rather, it transfigures life, reversing it, not into its opposite but into its other or its flip side. Literature is the flip side of the side that coincides with reality, the wrong side or the inside of the real and the sign of another meaning of experience."[23]

Reading the above quotations from Descombes and de Beistegui alongside one another, the philosophical stakes of Proust's novel become clearer. If there is a "philosophy" at work in *À la recherche du temps perdu*, it is akin to a Platonic dialogue in that it involves the entire trajectory of the text, all of its twists and turns, as well as its concern for how one is to become oriented (within the text, but also narratively, within life) in the first place. It is not just that we only gain insight at the end, but rather what insight there is comes, gradually, on every page. But insight is also absent from any particular page, even the final page: it does not simply come at the end of the novel, fully formed, but is the result of a process. Insight cuts across the temporal jump that takes place in involuntary memory, meaning that any error on the part of the narrator is just as important and just as productive as its correction. This is what prevents what Deleuze calls "signs" from being simply ideals out in the world that must be sought out and studied. And, since I am attempting to consider these passages apart from the novel as a whole, perhaps the insight I am concerned with here takes place interstitially, with an unusual temporality. Between any two (or more) moments of aesthetic experience within the novel, there will be a certain shift in consideration, in interpretation, such as between the madeleine passage and the present one, or this one and the next one. Charting this aesthetic insight requires a constellation of aesthetic encounters, rather than an articulated and self-enclosed theory, whether we are working with several novels or several moments within a single novel.

With the above in mind, the mature narrator's intervention indicates that the aesthetic cannot be employed to combat ennui (or, we can assume, any other state), which also means that it will not be "found" where we would seek it. Attempting to do so is part of the error that he makes and subsequently corrects. With Huysmans, we have already seen the misfortune that might befall one who seeks to curate the aesthetic within his daily life, and remains mostly unchecked in his endeavor. Here, Proust problematizes, from within, the role of discursive thought and intention in aesthetic experience, as well as the very possibility of seeking out the aesthetic at all. Discursive thought is especially difficult to deal with in this context, since we are generally trained to "think critically" as if this were a straightforward and voluntary endeavor. Interestingly, the correction is itself discursive, and the question remains of what exactly allows for the narrator's change of position. In general, though—and we see this here and elsewhere—aesthetic experience poses a question to discursive thought, and perhaps even stops it in its tracks, before allowing for a reorientation of the thinker. As de Beistigui writes, "[m]emory doesn't just go back in time and writing doesn't just run around in search of lost time."[24] Something else intervenes, under the guise of the aesthetic, and this is only possible due to the narrator's early reliance on intention and interest.

In light of this reading, and with all of the questions that it raises only to leave them in abeyance, one further reflection on the narrator's re-narration of the scene is in order. In particular, what motivates the alterations that occur in this re-narration? What holds this re-narration together? I would suggest that Rachel's "[l]ooking [...] to see that she was not making herself late" can be understood as a markedly "unaesthetic" gesture in the eyes of the narrator, both evidenced from and leading him to its omission from his re-narration. His main error here is to assume that there would be a legible distinction between "aesthetic" and "unaesthetic" objects, "aesthetic" and "unaesthetic" gestures—in either direction, positively or negatively—and to allow this assumption to motivate and shape his re-narration. Therefore, Rachel's impatience anticipates his own, and in his re-narration, he effaces any mark of either. As begins to emerge here, but will become clearer in what follows, aesthetic experience knows no distinction between "aesthetic" and "unaesthetic" objects, and cannot be anticipated ahead of time based on such distinctions, but our narrator has not yet learned this.

Pour cet état si particulier

My second example of a quiet moment comes much later on, in *La Prisonnière*. Here, the narrator is alone in his bedroom, and the main factor influencing his experience is the atmosphere surrounding him. In the opening pages of this volume, the narrator's meditations about his life with Albertine are set in the context of the weather, to which he is particularly sensitive. The very first sentence of the volume reads: "Dès le matin, la tête encore tournée contre le mur et avant d'avoir vu, au-dessus des grands rideaux de la fenêtre, de quelle nuance était la raie du jour, je savais déjà le temps qu'il faisait [At daybreak, my face still turned to the wall, and before I had seen above the big window-curtains what tone the first streaks of light assumed, I could already tell what the weather was like]" (3: 519/3: 1). Here, the weather is not merely an object or a condition of the outside world, something to be observed safely from indoors, but part of an all-encompassing atmosphere that reaches into the home. It is the first thing impacting the narrator upon his waking. Significantly, given the discussion of the senses in the madeleine passage, before he *sees* what is outside, and before he even catches a glimpse of the light that enters through the window, he can sense the weather.

In the context of the history of aesthetic philosophy and what he calls, in distinction from that history, a "new aesthetics," German philosopher Gernot Böhme writes that "[a]esthetics so far has been an aesthetic of judgment; that is, it is not so much about experience, let alone sensuous experience," meaning that aesthetics has gotten away from its original sense of being rooted in experience.[25] Böhme's aesthetics of atmosphere, besides running counter to philosophical aesthetics and other recent trends in aesthetics, explicitly distances experience from subjective intention: "*that* something is experienced is not in the subject's control."[26] Böhme's argumentation here is similar to the basis on which Deleuze claims that Proust's writing "vies with philosophy" by "set[ting] up an image of thought in opposition to that of philosophy."[27] If philosophy's advance has brought it farther away from its origins, the same can be said of aesthetics. Importantly, Böhme holds that atmosphere is neither subjective nor objective. In his words, atmospheres

> are not conceived as something objective (i.e., as properties of things), and yet they are something thing-like, belonging to the thing—insofar as things articulate their spheres of presence through their qualities, conceived as ecstasies. But atmospheres are nothing subjective, like determinations of a state of mind, either. And yet, they are subject-like, they belong to subjects insofar as they are sensed by humans in bodily presence, and insofar as this sensing is simultaneously the subject's bodily being-located in space.[28]

Insofar as it tends to weaken subject/object distinctions and upend our normal conception of the corresponding active and passive roles, atmosphere offers us a different way of understanding the aesthetic encounter. With this second quiet moment, I will argue that the arbitrary, contingent nature of the atmosphere allows Proust to illuminate the simultaneous contingency and intensity of aesthetic experience. First, I should note that because this passage features what can quite accurately be called an aesthetic experience, especially when compared to the previous passage, this is more of a positive example of the subjective receptivity characteristic of aesthetic experience. As such, the atmospheric disruption of the active and passive roles should not be taken as an absolute erasure of those distinctions (nor is there a total erasure of the boundary between subject and object). Instead, this particular encounter with atmosphere is exemplary of the way that aesthetic experience productively challenges both the subjective and philosophical aspects of the subject–object relation, as well as how we generally conceive of what is entailed by the active and passive roles, both within and beyond aesthetics.

In *La Prisonnière*, the narrator's initial meditation on the weather develops into an explanation of his preference to stay in while Albertine goes out for the day, for reasons that he is reluctant to share. He lies to Albertine, telling her that the doctor had ordered him to stay home. But then he explains to himself and us the wish to ease his own jealousy by absenting himself from a situation where he might worry about inconveniencing her by his presence; this explanation opens further onto what he calls "les exaltantes vertus de la solitude [the exhilarating virtues of solitude]" (3: 535/3: 17), which turn out to be his real motivation for staying home. Legrandin's earlier words may also remain an influence for this bout of solitude, even as far on in the text as we are. Either way, it is here that a further complication can be noted: the narrator's habit folds in on itself. In this context, it is his habit to be jealous, so he develops or wills himself into a new habit of staying home alone when

Albertine goes out. In turn, underlying this is necessarily his lack of knowledge about or control over his habit, as well as habit's general disconnection from the more vital experiences that it is designed to control. As Samuel Beckett writes with reference to Proustian involuntary memory: "This accidental and fugitive salvation in the midst of life may supervene when the action of involuntary memory is stimulated by the negligence or agony of Habit, and under no other circumstances, *nor necessarily then*."[29] What is involuntary cannot simply be brought about by the absence or interruption of habit and, as we will see, the incalculable and unpredictable nuances of habit are crucial to the dynamic nature of aesthetic experience.

From its beginning, the passage I am referring to is concerned with contingency, which becomes a third force mediating between habit and will, and is ultimately aligned with neither. Throughout Proust's writing, will is oftentimes evoked as what the hero calls upon in an attempt to stave off habit, but will and habit are not diametrically opposed. In fact, both habit and will in Proust are quite complex, each operating in different capacities and at different times. Richard Moran notes a tension between different employments of the will, whereby "[t]he Proustian enterprise" is "the story of the narrator's recovery of will," while also noting that, conversely, "the exclusion of the will comes to be a positive characterization of the terms of success for the *Search* itself."[30] Moran also touches on the concerns of my larger argument, writing that "[t]he very fame of the Proustian fascination with something called 'involuntary memory,' for instance, has tended to deflect attention from the question as to why its specifically involuntary character should matter at all, should be the index of a kind of value."[31] And, as he continues, "the meaning of the *exclusion* of the will from the process [of involuntary memory] can be no simple thing when we reflect on the fact that it is nothing other than the restoration of his own *will* and the calling to his infinitely laborious *task* that these experiences provide him with."[32] Habit, as evidenced from Beckett's words above, may be punctured or disrupted by the involuntary, but this is not the sufficient condition for the involuntary to occur. Will can be harnessed to break free from habit, but just like habit's absence, will is not sufficient for bringing about an involuntary aesthetic experience; we have seen as much from Huysmans and the first of Proust's quiet moments.

At any rate, what the narrator desires in this passage is something beyond his control entirely:

Je prenais ma part des plaisirs de la journée commençante; le désir arbitraire—la velléité capricieuse et purement mienne—de les goûter n'eût pas suffi à les mettre à portée de moi si le temps spécial qu'il faisait ne m'en avait non pas seulement évoqué les images passées, mais affirmé la réalité actuelle, immédiatement accessible à tous les hommes qu'une circonstance contingente et par conséquent négligeable ne forçait pas à rester chez eux. (3: 535)

I took my share in the pleasures of the new day; the arbitrary desire—the capricious and purely solipsistic impulse—to savour them would not have sufficed to place them within my reach, had not the particular state of the weather not merely evoked for me their past images but affirmed their present reality, immediately accessible to all men whom a contingent and consequently negligible circumstance did not compel to remain at home. (3: 17)

First of all, this passage recalls two ideas that have been mentioned already: arbitrariness and "le temps qu'il faisait." Here, arbitrariness refers to the narrator's desire; above, I have used the term in relation to the weather. As far as the reference to weather, we see a progression from "le temps qu'il faisait" to "le temps *spécial* qu'il faisait," which is already a signpost for what will follow. As I have already suggested, the particular is intimately linked—in this passage and elsewhere—to aesthetic experience and is crucial for understanding how it comes about. Focusing on the lines quoted immediately above, it is clear that the experience in question is not merely a matter of enjoying "the pleasures of the new day." Instead, it concerns the present reality of desires. However, the narrator is not seeking an object that could be placed before him, but something that could be experienced atmospherically, something experienced apart from the normal subject–object distinction—something that acts on him, something that, in a way, *experiences* him. This is therefore something that cannot be sought, properly speaking. Furthermore, this passage introduces and emphasizes the contingency of atmosphere. Though always experienced as a particular state, what is "particular" about this weather is not quite its particulars, so to speak; what exactly this means will become clear in the following pages.

Narrated in the imperfect tense, this passage cannot quite be in reference to any one specific time, but rather to a type of singular experience that the narrator can only categorize from the point of view of narration, retrospectively. It is an example of what Gérard Genette calls the iterative. Speaking of a different passage, Genette writes: "The *return* of the hours, the days, the seasons, the circularity of the cosmic movement, remains both the most constant motif and the most exact symbol of what I will readily call *Proustian iteratism*."[33] In a way, the iterative can be understood as a narrative mode that suspends the normal position of the narrator-hero in service of the unique position afforded by atmospheric attunement, and if circularity gives rise to the iterative on a large scale, the more subtle details of a passage such as this carry all the more weight. If the narrator's whim, his arbitrary desire, is not enough to bring aesthetic experience about, what *does* bring it about is instead "le temps spécial qu'il faisait," which is precisely what cannot be called upon by any intentional act of the narrator, whether linked to habit or to will. The atmospheric quality of these pleasures, dependent on the weather (*temps*) is also, to the extent that he can only retrospectively recognize their (indirect) cause, dependent on time (*temps*), a homonymy that Genette notes as well. I would add that, in terms of time, this experience also depends on the narrator's patience, which can be contrasted with his initial impatience in the first quiet moment where he calls preemptively on narration to change the course of his experience.

In short, aesthetic experience is not something that can be made into a goal, because it is precisely an experience of specificity and nuance, an experience that demands a certain degree of perceptual relaxation. In this way, it is largely accidental and incidental to any intentional project. As Freed-Thall notes, "nuance draws our gaze toward the periphery and the accessory."[34] As the periphery denotes the limits of the gaze, and shifts along with the gaze, our gaze can only be drawn *toward* the periphery, but it cannot settle there. The periphery is ambient, atmospheric, shifting in ways that we cannot control. Nuance causes our gaze to hover there, without settling, and the singularity that emerges from an iterative passage like the one in question here is something peripheral to any one material detail or aspect of the weather.

Weather, in its arbitrariness and indifference to human affairs, escapes the struggles of habit and desire; because of its nuances, it also resists our direct attention, though we might comment what sort of weather a day holds in store. As it is only very sparsely characterized throughout this passage, the bulk of what we can say about "le temps spécial qu'il faisait" concerns the narrator: it affects him in a certain way. The relationship of subject and object is anything but a normal relationship of observer and observed; rather, this relationship might be considered in terms of what Böhme calls a "modified thing-ontology," sensitive to atmosphere as something neither objective nor subjective, but nevertheless both "thing-like" and "subject-like."[35] As the passage continues, the atmosphere of the weather seems to open up the narrator's room and enter into it, allowing for communication between inside and outside centered primarily on hearing and sound:

> Certains beaux jours, il faisait si froid, on était en si large communication avec la rue qu'il semblait qu'on eût disjoint les murs de la maison, et chaque fois que passait le tramway, son timbre résonnait comme eût fait un couteau d'argent frappant une maison de verre. (3: 535)

On certain fine days, the weather was so cold, one was in such full communication with the street, that it seemed as though the other walls of the house had been dismantled, and, whenever a tramcar passed, the sound of its bell reverberated like that of a silver knife striking a wall of glass. (3: 17–18)

This relationship with the sounds of the street is marked by a confusion of distance and even of the boundary between inside and outside. As the walls of the house open up, allowing outside sounds to come in, rather than simply separating the inside from the outside, they act like "as eloquent a membrane as if [they] demarcated the chambers of [a] single ear, or heart," to quote Eve Kosofsky Sedgwick in her discussion of the narrator's stay with his grandmother in Balbec.[36] Furthermore, the walls seem to act as a translator; not only do the sounds permeate the narrator's bedroom, but they are transformed and take on new connotations because of the weather, so that the sound of the tramcar gains the resonance "of a silver knife striking a wall of glass," a sound that might ring out if uninterrupted.

The connection between sound and weather is already noted in the second sentence of the volume: "Les premiers bruits de la rue me l'avaient appris, selon qu'ils me parvenaient amortis et déviés par l'humidité ou vibrants comme des flèches dans l'aire résonnante et vide d'un matin spacieux, glacial et pur [The first sounds from the street had told me, according to whether they came to my ears deadened and distorted by the moisture of the atmosphere or quivering like arrows in the resonant, empty expanses of a spacious, frosty, pure morning]" (3: 519/3: 1). The narrator's attunement again involves the iterative nature of these passages. The weather and the sounds from the street present two sets of variables for the narrator to experience, and the repetitive nature of such an experience is what allows for him to become sensitive to their various combinations. With this in mind, what he is experiencing is in a way chance itself; what is novel with such an experience is the singularity of his *sensation*, rather than any "new" or unheard-of object, concept, or set of variables. The singularity of this sensation cannot be reduced to any particular combination of aspects of the weather.

The inward motion that had begun in the previous section of our main passage continues, moving further inward, until the narrator becomes attentive to something else, namely, a new sound within himself. It is here that we finally have an explicit description of his inner experience, which is notable for the typically Proustian way in which it engages metaphor:

Mais c'était surtout en moi que j'entendais avec ivresse un son nouveau rendu par le violon intérieur. Ses cordes sont serrées ou détendues par de simples différences de la température, de la lumière extérieures. (3: 535)

But it was above all in myself that I heard, with rapture, a new sound emitted by the violin within. Its strings are tautened or relaxed by mere differences in the temperature or the light outside. (3: 18)

Discussing the narrator's sensitivity to the weather—which is such that, elsewhere in the text, he feels himself to be "un baromètre vivant [an animated barometer]" (3: 586/3: 73)—Sedgwick notes the importance of "a change in the weather" for him in that it brings about other important changes.[37] However, his internal violin is perhaps a more fitting instrument than a barometer for dealing with the indirect, nuanced, and creative aspects of aesthetic experience. Unlike a barometer, a violin is not a scientific instrument and does not render a measurement of atmospheric pressures, though such pressures can undoubtedly affect its performance. The violin has a degree of autonomy not held by the barometer because it does not respond *directly* to the weather according to a rule of measurement fixed in advance. In short, the violin, like the barometer, does not take orders from the narrator. But it is set apart from the barometer because it is creative in a way the barometer is not: a violin can produce a note, sounds, even a song, as a way of responding to the atmosphere.

The narrator is aware that the violin exists within him, yet it is only occasionally awakened and is seemingly beyond his control. The sound that it makes varies with the weather; it is not subject to his "arbitrary desire." What the sounds of the violin and the sounds of the street share in common is that they are beyond his control. While this points toward a kind of sonic harmony, this also puts him in the position of the unlucky auditor who, according to Kant, is irritated because he cannot close his ears against the invading sounds. For Kant, music as an art form is at a disadvantage for spectators, because we have less choice in the matter than we do with a painting. We cannot "look away," and might unwillingly hear the music of our neighbors, Kant claims, unfavorably comparing this quality of music to the circulation of a perfume throughout the air.[38] As Pascal Quignard writes in *The Hatred of Music*, expressing a similar sentiment, "[w]hat is heard knows neither eyelids, nor partitions, neither curtains, nor walls."[39] But for Proust's narrator, this is not a bad thing. It is this very characteristic—common to both sound and weather—that allows for the violin's new sound as a positive and creative engagement with the world, as well as highlighting the distinct role of chance in aesthetic experience. Instead of harboring a distaste for sound based on his inability to control it, he is receptive, attuned to the internal violin and its changes in sound based on the "mere differences in the temperature or the light outside." These factors, being entirely beyond his purview, render him passive and, because they can lead to the emergence of a certain unpredictable feeling in him, facilitate the kind of affect that we might characterize as disinterest, especially because the sounds of the street and the sounds of the violin do not have any direct correspondence. That is, in the sense that it is only possible to narrate this passage retrospectively, as an index of pleasurable experiences that he can only be aware of after the fact—precisely because, as a series of quiet moments, these experiences slip by without necessarily impacting the course of the narrative— the narrator can be described as disinterested in the moment of the violin's awakening. There is no object, nothing he can identify beforehand, that can guarantee this experience; he is not curating his experience, whether materially or narratively. And it goes one step further: he has experienced the atmosphere and the sounds of the street enough times to be aware that this feeling will not correspond to any particular arrangement of weather and sounds that he has experienced before.

If the sound of the internal violin changes based on external factors, then both the sound and the instrument are beyond the narrator's control, and even opposed to the workings of both habit and will. This sound is heard and noted by the narrator himself "avec ivresse," with rapture or intoxication, a fact that is worth pausing to consider. For Nietzsche, intoxication is a state held in common by the artist and the beholder of the work of art, perhaps in response to the focus on the spectator in Kantian aesthetics as he imagines it. In particular, Nietzsche associates this state with "extreme subtlety and splendor of color, definiteness of line, nuances of tone"—that is, with an enhanced attention to detail.[40] However, given its association with a state of intoxication, there is something mysterious about this attention, something at least partly irrational. This means that it cannot properly be controlled, and may verge on a transformation or even distortion of perception, perhaps even danger or illness. But if there is a danger to this intoxication, it is a very different danger from the danger of des Esseintes's curatorial impulse.

Genette also remarks upon a certain Proustian intoxication: "une sorte d'*ivresse de l'itération* [a sort of *intoxication with the iterative*]."[41] Following the discussion of Nietzsche above, if Proust is intoxicated with the iterative, then it is doubly significant that the passage in question is able to articulate a certain intoxicating aesthetic experience by way of the iterative. In other words, and somewhat counterintuitively, the narrator's ability to characterize such experiences—and the passage does suggest that there have been many—*only after the fact* seems to safeguard the validity of them *as* aesthetic experiences. Contrary to the previous example, where his attempt to discursively bring about an aesthetic experience in the moment leads directly to the disqualification of any such experience, we only get a summary here of the circumstances allowing for a certain feeling after, presumably, that feeling has passed. In keeping with Nietzsche's vision of intoxication, this can be likened to a kind of creative or aesthetic possession, whereby the narrator is unable to catalog his feelings either discursively or categorically until the moment has passed.

Iterability and repetition should be distinguished insofar as they factor into aesthetic experience. I have been arguing that Proustian aesthetic experience, especially when it involves the atmosphere, is iterative, on the basis that the present passage seems to suggest the occurrence of many such experiences, some of which may have involved aesthetic experience. Championing the iterative nature of this passage may seem contradictory when considered alongside the insight that any attempt to bring about aesthetic experience, especially attempts that involve repeating a previous experience, often end in disappointment, a claim that will be further explored in the next chapter through a reading of Tom McCarthy's *Remainder*. But there is an important difference between the iterability of experience and the subjective attempt to repeat it. Aesthetic experience participates in the iterative because it involves various forces beyond the subject's control that may be considered variables (as we have seen above with the different aspects of atmosphere: weather, sound, temperature). The narrator speaks of *certain days*, which means that these days are pulled from countless other days, and, as *days*, they themselves are plural. Yet, as I have also already noted, there is no indication that these days are iterated exactly, down to the particular arrangement of atmosphere. Instead, two days with otherwise quite different weather might each be numbered among these certain days in the sense of involving this intoxicating atmospheric experience, and conversely, two days with the same exact weather may bring about two different subjective responses. The will to repeat such experiences, on the other hand, works in opposition to the iterative (though, of course, one can imagine a passage narrated in the iterative tense describing several attempts to repeat a certain experience, such as the narrator's re-enactments in *Remainder*). This impulse is a result of the cultivation of taste, interest, or—to keep with the theme of intoxication—even addiction for aesthetic experience itself. What is notable about the iterative aesthetic experiences described by Proust is their accidental, contingent, and singular nature, which they share with the atmosphere that is so instrumental in bringing them about.

These factors that act on the narrator's internal violin enliven him in a reckless way, with a loss of reason, and even a loss of concern for anything outside of the present moment. At the core of the violin's awakening is the overcoming of habit:

> En notre être, instrument que l'uniformité de l'habitude a rendu silencieux, le chant naît de ces écarts, de ces variations, source de toute

musique: le temps qu'il fait certains jours nous fait aussitôt passer d'une note à une autre. Nous retrouvons l'air oublié dont nous aurions pu deviner la nécessité mathématique et que pendant les premiers instants nous chantons sans le connaître. (3: 535)

Within our being, an instrument which the uniformity of habit has rendered mute, song is born of these divergences, these variations, the source of all music: the change of weather on certain days makes us pass at once from one note to another. We recapture the forgotten tune the mathematical necessity of which we might have deduced, and which for the first few moments we sing without recognizing it. (3: 18)

In the first instance, the awakening by sound of this instrument, silenced by habit, further emphasizes the ability of sound to place the listener in a passive position. Roger Foster comments on this passage, writing: "Proust's narrator speaks of the 'interior violin' [...] It is this instrument, the subject's very responsiveness to the significance of the world, which 'the uniformity of *habitude* has rendered silent.'"[42] Foster picks up on the emphasis on habit, which has over time allowed the instrument to fade into the background. The violin responds to the world around the narrator, and thus it can be reawakened or amplified on occasions when the atmosphere strikes him in a particular way. In the context of what he calls "the perfect Proustian day, where it crosses over from the ordinariness of the quotidian into the domain of the magical," Christopher Prendergast briefly mentions this same passage, calling it "a variant of the impressionist day, the weather outside attuned to a music within."[43] Prendergast's reversal of direction between outside weather and internal music is striking and highlights the difficulty of assigning a true temporal or causal progression from one to the other. Furthermore, his reference to impressionism recalls the iterative nature of a painter like Monet, whose countless versions of one and the same scene could be likened to a peeling apart of the unnumbered days contained in this single passage from Proust.

It is worth lingering on one line in particular, which I repeat here with added emphasis: "le temps qu'il fait certains jours *nous* fait aussitôt passer d'une note à une autre [the change of weather on certain days makes *us* pass at once from one note to another]." The solitude of this passage opens onto a curious sense of community in which this experience is collective, implying that anybody might hear the sounds of their internal violin if only the weather is right, and anybody might slide into the passive position of listening for and to this sound. However, this also suggests that the narrator is identifying with the violin—for, is the violin not, perhaps even more properly than the narrator, what is "pass[ing] from one note to another"? As suggested above, atmospheric changes could literally detune a violin, but it is unlikely that this is the real issue here. Rather, the violin is an internal instrument or organ that responds to the weather by way of the narrator, in a sort of chain effect.

The emergence of the new sound, paired with the fact that it seems to result from a concatenation of other sounds, indicates that this is primarily an experience of resonance. There is no longer the clausal form of a judgment, but instead a dissolution of boundaries and hierarchies; in addition to the overcoming of habit, will is overcome—or, more precisely, both habit and will are put out of work. Importantly, though, they are not put out of work by some other act of will. Instead of passing judgment on an object, the narrator responds through experience to his surroundings by recapturing a tune. At first glance, this may seem like nothing more than a case of recognition, but the narrator himself states that it occurs for some time "without recognizing it," which lends this experience structural similarity to the madeleine episode, an echo that belongs, precisely, to the involuntary. The difference this time is that it is not a memory being recalled: it is merely a sensation. The variation itself, the divergence, the change of weather, the jump from note to note—*this* is precisely what is recaptured, and the tune is picked up where it was left off, as if it had never ceased. Metaphorically, this should be understood to mean that the narrator resumes the tune, the feeling, from time to time, instead of remembering or repeating a song exactly, the way that Swann does with the sonata, to the point that he becomes dependent upon it in the formation of his love for Odette. And despite its communal nature, this tune does not involve a performance the way that Vinteuil's sonata or septet would. The narrator finds this sense of community in solitude, and what is mathematically necessary according to this passage is not the progression of a string of notes in the composition of a song, but the return itself of the tune, which comes about indirectly and unpredictably along with the return of a certain unforeseeable state of the weather.

Again, it is a question here of both weather and time. Because habit silences "the forgotten tune" over time, we might rediscover it by chance, just as we might fall into a resonance with the atmosphere. Whether or not we have recognized the inevitability of this tune, it brings us to a point where contingency and necessity are somehow brought closer together, as are inside and outside, conscious and unconscious self. In turn, this allows for a new purchase on the outside world:

> Seules ces modifications internes, bien que venues du dehors, renouvelaient pour moi le monde extérieur. Des portes de communication depuis longtemps condamnées se rouvraient dans mon cerveau. La vie de certaines villes, la gaieté de certaines promenades reprenaient en moi leur place. (3: 535)

> These modifications alone, internal though they had come from without, gave me a fresh vision of the external world. Communicating doors, long barred, reopened in my brain. The life of certain towns, the gaiety of certain excursions, resumed their place in my consciousness. (3: 18)

Here, space is cleared for the encounter with and communication between inside and outside. In particular, we can hear the repeated prefix *re-*: the exterior world is *remade, renewed, reiterated*; the boarded-up doors of communication are *reopened*; the joy of certain trips or walks *retakes, resumes* its place, or its place is *revived*. There is an overall reinvigoration that makes reference to certain aspects of the past, but it is important to remember that this passage is itself narrated iteratively—both retrospectively and collectively—rendering this reference to the past cumulative and perhaps even metaphorical. If certain towns and excursions regain their place in the narrator's mind, what is of interest here is not a case of involuntary memory as in the madeleine or the paving stones. Rather, it is the feeling of renewal itself—the always novel and singular nature of aesthetic experience—instead of what in particular is being renewed. In this way, it is like the violin's resumption of the tune, rather than the direct repetition of the specific notes of a song. The condition for this is that habit be put out of work by the state of the weather, that is, by a contingent event.

The narrator is in harmony with his inner violin, moving as it moves, without destination or final resting point. Rather than simply recognizing the movement, the tune, from a perspective of mastery, he himself is inseparable from the violin that makes the movements and jumps from one note to another: he is recognizing it from within the experience. Notably, this marks a zooming in from the narrative or iterative perspective toward the particular affect at hand. Regarding this movement, he states:

> Frémissant tout entier autour de la corde vibrante, j'aurais sacrifié ma terne vie d'autrefois et ma vie à venir, passées à la gomme à effacer de l'habitude, pour cet état si particulier. (3: 535)
> With my whole being quivering around the vibrating string, I would have sacrificed my former existence and my life to come, erasing them with the india-rubber of habit, for such a unique state of soul. (3: 18)

This is notable for several reasons, concerning both the mechanics of a violin and the sentiment of self-sacrifice as it relates to narrative and time. First, the vibration of a violin string is, for the most part, only perceptible sonically and tactilely—not visually, at least not with the naked eye—which fixes vibration to a present moment, and furthermore eliminates any concern for vision as far as this experience is concerned. The vibration is made possible and is translated into the familiar sound of the violin by way of the violin's resonant body, which receives and amplifies the sound. This is in accord with the previous acknowledgment of Proust's concern for senses other than vision. But furthermore, there is no mention in this passage of a bow, meaning that this analogical violin is not being "played" in any way that would correlate to the situation otherwise described. The only possible "player" would be the weather, which also has the metaphorical task of tuning (which also means retuning or detuning) the violin. In a way, the violin is being performed by the atmosphere, and the same is true of the narrator.

The narrator states that he *would have* sacrificed his past and future life, his life of other times (*d'autrefois*) and his life to come (*à venir*). He is necessarily narrating from these other times because, from the perspective of this sentiment of sacrifice, his narration—all of his possible narration—is to come, and his sacrifice is impossible in a strict sense. In turn, this suggests that the narrated experience is impossible to narrate concurrently, from within its present moment. Though this may be true in principle of all narration in general, here this split has high stakes for the narrator, who tells us that he would have sacrificed his past and future to remain in the interior of his narrative, to sustain his movement. "Frémissant tout entier autour de la corde vibrante," he wishes only to sustain this state in a way similar to how the Kantian state of free play in the beautiful wishes only to sustain itself. This prompts a consideration of the relation between narrative and aesthetic experience, a consideration that is also upheld in Rachel Cusk's novels, as we'll see in Chapter 4. If it is possible to experience without will, in a passive or disinterested way, would it be possible to passively narrate? Is aesthetic experience a particularly unnarratable kind of experience? What would it mean to exchange the condition of narrative for the ability to live *within* what is being narrated?

Setting these questions aside for now, we also see that this sacrifice would cause these other times to be erased by habit. The text itself refers to "la gomme à effacer de l'habitude [the india-rubber of habit]." Hypothetical as it is, the erasure of any time but this present time is curiously presented as passive, overdetermined, and ambiguous. The narrator's past life and life to come would be submitted to the eraser of habit—but what does this "de" or "of" refer to? Is habit the object of erasing, or the subject? Or both?[44] How exactly is habit related to "cet état si particulier [such a unique state of soul]," with its singular resonance with "le temps spécial qu'il faisait [the particular state of the weather]"? We know that the exclusion of habit is not sufficient to bring about such a state; at best, habit is excluded alongside the emergence of this state, as is will. Yet the question remains of how to orient oneself in the face of an apprenticeship that, in general, retains a deep investment and interest in such experiences.

The modalities of habit—which can be involved in both silencing and, it seems, erasing, even if this means self-erasure—open up to new modalities of experience. Through a leveling of oppositions brought about by the atmosphere, the narrator reaches a state attuned to *le temps*, both weather and time, a state for which he "would have sacrificed" everything else, every possibility and impossibility, every path available to choose, every path already closed off through prior choice. Over the course of this passage, we see the narrator's agency gradually disappear: "Je prenais ma part des plaisirs de la journée commençante [I took my share in the pleasures of the new day];" "j'entendais avec ivresse un son nouveau rendu par le violon intérieur [I heard, with rapture, a new sound emitted from the violin within];" "j'aurais sacrifié ma terne vie d'autrefois et ma vie à venir [I would have sacrificed my former existence and my life to come]" (3: 535/3: 17–18). Across these three statements—taking, hearing, willing (in the weak sense), the passage's only instances of the active first person—the expressions become progressively impersonal as he recedes into the surrounding atmosphere. First, he feels the subjective state of pleasure; then, he hears a sound from within himself; and finally, he makes a contradictory or impossible statement that breaks up the temporal dimension of the scene and points to the necessary distance of narration. Were he able to succeed on the final count, we would hear no more from him—except, perhaps, for an echo of this "new sound."

What causes this experience in him? What clears the space for this sound to resound, and what are the limits of its resonance? How can such an experience, bounded in time and yet unbounded by virtue of its intensity, be understood within the trajectory of a narrative or a life? The experience recounted by the narrator is not caused by a work of art: not a sonata, a novel, or a painting by Vermeer. Nor, strictly speaking, is it caused by memory. Freed-Thall claims that this represents a strain in Proust's writing that moves away from a traditional or formalist aesthetics:

> Proust is fascinated by the paradox of an everyday aesthetics. On the one hand, he works to transform the detritus of the ordinary into aesthetic riches [...]. But there is also a current in the *Recherche* that pulls us toward objects that the text itself seems unable to appropriate.[45]

One might call upon any number of scenes in Proust that cannot easily be squared with the predominant critical trend of understanding his novel to encompass a cohesive aesthetic theory. But if Proust transforms the ordinary or the everyday into an aesthetic object, it is not simply a case of creating a new, personal aesthetic theory, nor is it a case of simply appreciating or preferring what is marginal to traditional Western aesthetics. These "everyday" objects are not judged as if they were pieces of art, according to traditional standards of taste. They retain a certain degree of inaccessibility, and furthermore do not fall under the narrator's subjective theory by which he draws meaning from, and makes use of, the text's classic objects—the madeleine, the paving stone, the steeples, and so on. In Freed-Thall's words, "alongside this assemblage of decipherable objects, a secondary, shadow constellation is perceptible."[46] The narrator's "unique state," in Proust's words, is caused neither by a work of art nor by one of *his* objects. Such would be a case of the idolatry Proust cautions against in his Ruskin preface. Moreover, it is not caused by an object at all, and the text stages this tension on its own terms in a way that speaks to the question of the aesthetic object at large, all the while complicating the very ability to discuss the experience in terms of objects.

Whereas Freed-Thall tends to focus on moments where the narrator's "aesthetic disorientation" quite literally concerns his voice, I have chosen to focus on experiences that are borne out more specifically through encounters with weather and narration. In the passage I have just discussed at length, Proust deftly refrains from an essayistic, theoretical explication of his experience, such as may be found in *Le Temps retrouvé*. Rather than indicating a failure on the part of the narrator to live up to his stated vocation, this passage is crucial for understanding how Proust's concern with an everyday aesthetics extends beyond the object-choice of a personal aesthetics, shedding light on the nature of aesthetic experience itself, and destabilizing the role of subjective intention in such an experience.

In the novel's several instances of what Freed-Thall calls "aesthetic disorientation," the narrator encounters objects or scenes that bear "[t]he marker of unmarkedness," "the de-individuating space of the 'quelconque'—the ordinary, undistinguished, or 'whatever.'"[47] If these scenes happen to include unusual objects—unusual precisely for the fact that, with respect to what we might imagine as an exemplary aesthetic object, they are so mundane, so ordinary—they are as unique in their effects as they are unusual in their aesthetic context. The narrator's tendency to interact with these everyday objects and scenes does not mean that they have simply replaced, for his aesthetic eye, aesthetic objects that may be considered more appropriate or canonical. These objects' *quelconque*, ordinary nature, as exceptional as it may be in the context of Western aesthetics, should not obfuscate the real stakes of these scenes. These scenes point to something that would stand up to the analysis of aesthetic experience despite destabilizing any objective, formal, or social guidelines for the appropriateness of the aesthetic object. It is precisely because they do this that these scenes are so crucial to an understanding of Proust's aesthetics, and of aesthetics in general. This kind of aesthetic experience stubbornly questions the possibility of a presupposed theoretical framework, or even a set of aesthetic examples, and thus introduces a counterintuitive, subtle logic into Proust's understanding of the aesthetic. On a smaller scale, these scenes also disrupt the sort of theoretical maneuvering that the narrator is apt to engage in during the text's most well-known moments, including the gesture of tracing the meaning of an experience back to its source through association or memory.

The aesthetic object, Proust shows us, refuses to be domesticated. A look at Swann's attachment to the Vinteuil sonata is evidence enough of the results of attempting to do so, and recalls des Esseintes's trajectory of dissipation. This begins to erase the distinction between the *quelconque* and the work of art not only in order to imagine a new aesthetics, but in order to imagine aesthetics anew. Because any object has the potential—and indeed threatens—to be domesticated, in the sense of becoming familiar and incorporated into one's habit, and to thus have its aesthetic status placed into jeopardy, so might anything be removed from habit and made unfamiliar. And yet, this occurs outside any tradition or canon of aesthetic objects, before any glance at an index of aesthetic examples. Rather than being the cause of an aesthetic experience, and thus suggesting a kind of taxonomy of aesthetic objects, the unmarked object gains its mark only through a discrete aesthetic experience, which equalizes and renders useless and impossible any such taxonomy. The aesthetic object remains unmarked: it is not labeled as an "aesthetic object," even for one and the same subject, even when the subject cultivates a taste for such experiences and therefore such objects. The aesthetic experience in question is one where distinctions between subject and object break down, until we are brought to the point of sacrificing life-time as *autrefois* and *à venir* ("my former existence and my life to come") in exchange for *le temps*, the passive, uncontrollable, impersonal time of weather. This is the aspect shared in common between weather and the aesthetic, which, like rain, can always fall on us whether or not we are prepared or appropriately attired.

What is especially notable in this passage is an inner feeling of life, "cet état si particulier," without any concern beyond sustaining itself. This feeling emerges from a context of habit, and what prevails is a kind of resonance brought about by the weather, which runs on its own schedule, indifferent to any measure of habit or will. This resonance calls into question the ability to narrate, and leads narration to its limit. By expressing a wish to sacrifice all other times for the present moment of his resonant state—by all accounts an absurd gesture, given that it would defeat the possibility of achieving its goal—Proust's narrator reveals a difficult problem at issue in the aesthetic, a problem connected to the idea of disinterest. This is the problem of what the subject of the aesthetic is, where this subject might be situated in time, and how the subject is involved in aesthetic experience. Instead of being oriented toward judgment, the narrator's internal state mirrors the very state of the weather, through the new note sounding within him. In such a state, he is alive to the scene, alive to himself, and he wishes (without quite wishing, without even being able to wish) to remain in this state, nearly to the point of not being able to give an account of it. Yet, since we have the text, we know that this does not happen; he does continue on, in life and in narration. Narrated in the imperfect, this account indicates what Freed-Thall, in the context of French literature and its relationship to Kant's aesthetics, calls "a way of experiencing the particular without subsuming it under the general."[48] By dealing with both particular and general, singular and repetitive, what comes across avoids aligning the experience with even a specific kind of weather. Instead, it points to a phenomenon that occurs between subject and object, and depends as much on the narrator's state as it does on the state of the weather, each of which remain singular and impossible to anticipate. Might this be the distinguishing mark of a certain aesthetic experience? Might the narrator's "unique state" not be, in fact, the affective or positive dimension of disinterest, a state of heightened perception? To end this section, I will evoke Freed-Thall one final time. Here, she is writing on the hawthorn passage in *Du côté de chez Swann*, but it is just as fitting in this context: "In the instant of this perception, it is as if intentionality and cognition were suspended, eclipsed by the amplification of the senses. The perception, intense as it is, does not lead to epistemological riches."[49] Despite his taste for aesthetic objects and aesthetic experiences, Proust's narrator remains satisfied with mere perception, with its possibilities and impossibilities alike.

Insoucieux des vicissitudes de l'avenir

To conclude this chapter, I will turn briefly to the second of my "major" moments, which comes near the end of the work. The popularity of this moment rivals that of the madeleine scene in the scholarship, but it is a lengthier and somewhat more complex passage. Due to serving as a double culmination of the narrator's apprenticeship—both narratively and aesthetically—it shifts back and forth between narration and essayistic theorization several times, and is therefore of prime importance for the novel and the scholarship alike. It suggests some qualities that will be at work in the narrator's book to come, but more importantly it puts forth a general theory of experience which itself gestures toward said book. Because it states this aesthetic doctrine forcefully and at length, it poses a certain danger or difficulty for interpretation. Though many critics have cautioned against the temptation to equate the narrator with Proust himself, interpretations of the narrator's theory have not always taken this warning to heart—nor Proust's own warning about works of literature that contain their own theories. But this is ultimately beside the point for my purposes here. I hope to show that even if we could grant that Proust held the same ideas as stated in this portion of the text, this would leave open the possibility that some parts of the text simply fall outside of, and potentially undermine, this theory. These are precisely what I have been referring to as the text's quiet moments, as they generally go unannounced and even unrecognized within the narrative. For this reason, they deserve far more attention than they have heretofore been given. This passage comes in *Le Temps retrouvé*, and can be considered as doubly overdetermined. First, it contains several instances of involuntary memory in quick succession; and second, prompted by these instances, it is thereafter made up of a long essayistic digression that comments on involuntary memory and situates it within a larger aesthetic theory. Because of its length, I will mostly summarize it, giving select quotations only when relevant to my main point.

At the beginning of this passage, the now much older narrator is on his way to a party at the Guermantes mansion. Here we find him in a reflective mode, which leads, due to his inattention, to the first instance of involuntary memory that occurs in this portion of the text: the famous scene of the paving stones. He stumbles on the uneven stones on the street. The ensuing sensation recalls him to his earlier visit to St. Mark's Basilica in Venice, but not before he remains for a moment, standing awkwardly on the stones: "je restais, quitte à faire rire la foule innombrable des wattmen, à tituber comme j'avais fait tout à l'heure, un pied sur le pavé plus élevé, l'autre pied sur le pavé plus bas [I continued, ignoring the evident amusement of the great crowd of chauffeurs, to stagger as I had staggered a few seconds ago, with one foot on the higher paving-stone and the other on the lower]" (4: 445–446/3: 899). Alessia Ricciardi, focusing on mourning and what she calls Proust's "poetics of memory," reads this scene and the entire Proustian employment of the involuntary in a somewhat skeptical manner.[50] With reference to this passage, she writes:

> The narrator's emphasis on the "amusement" of his observers and his effort to stage the revelation anew by resuming the exact posture he was in when the recollection of Venice first struck him underlines the performative artifice of this most crucial instance of involuntary memory and belies the narrator's idealist claim to a "dazzling and indistinct," impressionist perception.[51]

I am more inclined—especially if we grant that the narrator at this stage is in possession of a greater degree of wisdom and ability to read his own experience compared, for instance, to the passage with Saint-Loup and Rachel—to understand this awkward gesture not as performative or cynical, as it might very well have been at an earlier stage in his apprenticeship, but instead as something along the lines of his repeated sips of tea in the madeleine scene. After all, he is trying to understand the sensation that is washing over him, with the difference that here, unlike in the madeleine scene, there are onlookers. He is forced into the performative role because of the passers-by, but not necessarily in any calculated way. This passage finds some interesting echoes in McCarthy's *Remainder*, whose narrator's odd attitude toward performance troubles the very idea of an audience from the very beginning.

Our hero's efforts lead him to a question that reaches to the depths of his theory, and which is of interest to me as a fundamental question of aesthetic experience:

> pourquoi les images de Combray et de Venise m'avaient-elles à l'un et à l'autre moment donné une joie pareille à une certitude et suffisante sans autres preuves à me rendre la mort indifférente? (4: 446)
> why had the images of Combray and of Venice, at these two different moments, given me a joy which was like a certainty and which sufficed, without any other proof, to make death a matter of indifference to me? (3: 900)

The question, which also haunts the madeleine passage and the quiet moment dealing with weather, is: what is it about aesthetic experience—whether in the form of involuntary memory or not—that leaves us indifferent to death or even willing to sacrifice everything to sustain it? The posing of this question, even before any answer is proffered, already has several implications. First of all, we see that the narrator is well aware of the effect that involuntary memory has on him. It is an ecstasy, a moment that, as I have noted, wishes only to sustain itself to the exclusion of all else, even at the price of death. He also wonders about the veracity of any connection between the present moment and any past place that is being evoked, which is also to say that he questions the very importance of memory in involuntary memory. It is helpful to again evoke Deleuze, who reminds us that Proust's novel is not ultimately about memory. The issue here then becomes the connection between moments separated in time as prompted by a material object, and what is revealed when that connection is experienced. In the previous section, I discussed this indifference to death in the context of the narrator's attunement to the atmosphere, where it also problematized the role, and even the very possibility, of narration in life. While the narrative aspect of this question will be explored more thoroughly in the final chapter by way of Cusk's *Outline* trilogy, here I will say that the very posing of this question already begins to undermine the theory that follows in this passage.

What happens next should be no surprise: the narrator undergoes a few more instances of involuntary memory while waiting to be admitted to the party, which are interspersed with the theoretical musings that they prompt. While there is not enough space to individually discuss all of these instances here, it is important that one of them involves him coming across a copy of George Sand's *François le champi*, which also figures in the crucial bedtime scene with his mother in the "Overture" section. This leads him to a digression about childhood reading which mirrors certain comments in the preface to his translation of Ruskin's *Sesame and Lilies* that I cited in the introduction. Of greatest importance for me here is the narrator's response to the above question about the indifference to death and its possibility within a narrative trajectory. While he goes on to assert the inadequacy of "l'impression factice que nous nous en donnons quand volontairement nous essayons de nous la représenter [the artificial impression of [a thing] which we form for ourselves when we attempt by an act of will to imagine it]" (4: 448/3: 902)—in other words, the vital importance of the involuntary over what is voluntary or engineered—he ends by articulating a theory that would resolve these disparate dimensions of experience. The accord between past and present in involuntary memory leads the narrator to conclude that there must be an extra-temporal self: "l'être que j'avais été était un être extra-temporel, par conséquent insoucieux des vicissitudes de l'avenir [the being which at that moment I had been was an extra-temporal being and therefore unalarmed by the vicissitudes of the future]" (4: 450/3: 904). Without wishing to delve too deeply into the metaphysical implications of this idea, I would contend that the narrator introduces this extra-temporal self to resolve any contradiction posed by the disjunction between past and present, which in a certain reading should give us pause when considering how to understand his aesthetic theory.

What I take issue with here has already been laid out in the previous section of this chapter. Do we need to be timeless beings for aesthetic experience to give us this sensation, and do we need the promise of transcendence for this sensation to have value? The passage I looked at in the previous section refers to memory, but only iteratively and in general. I argue that the quiet moments of *À la recherche du temps perdu* directly undermine the narrator's aesthetic theory as expressed in the final volume, as well as its critical reception. For one, these quiet moments do not theorize themselves, meaning that they demand a high degree of critical attention if their insights, which are not explicitly announced, are to even be perceived. In short, they urge us to read philosophically more than his quasi-philosophical theory would. But there is the further point that any experience of timelessness is situated in time. This is the whole question of the passage from *La Prisonnière*, and this is why *le temps* shows up so frequently. Weather in its various iterations does nothing if not thematize time. Finally, these quiet moments—whether a moment where the narrator recognizes the error of attempting to force an aesthetic experience, or a moment where he feels indifferent to death and even willing to sacrifice all else for the present sensation simply based on the atmosphere around him—are moments of paradox or impossibility.

Due to the paradoxical nature of these moments, they refuse to be situated in a stable system. As I have mentioned already, I think this hinges on the role of the involuntary *in general*. With Deleuze in mind, Proust's aesthetic experience is notable when its involuntary and accidental nature shines forth without being limited by any particular theory. This means that even where involuntary memory is concerned, memory—and, along with it, anything that can be considered originary, whether narratively or conceptually—is to a certain degree incidental. While the scholarship around the novel in many cases tends to prioritize Proust's evocation of memory, closer attention to the involuntary yields further insights about just what Proust is doing when he is describing aesthetic experience.

To end, I wish to emphasize one major irony of this final passage. It is situated in the context of a critique of theories of literature, a critique of works of literature that bear their theories within themselves. For one, the narrator bemoans realism, stating that nothing is less realistic than the flattened language that would purport to describe things "as they are," for, as we surely know by now—and here is perhaps one instance where we can safely collapse Proust and his narrator—literature is largely about impressions, experiences. Moving on, he is markedly critical of literature that contains theories: "Une oeuvre où il y a des théories est comme un objet sur lequel on laisse la marque du prix [A work in which there are theories is like an object which still has its price-tag on it]" (4: 461/3: 916). While we may agree with this point—after all, his logic is sound and follows from the progression of his apprenticeship throughout the novel—we would be remiss if we did not point out that this statement, which is itself theoretical, comes within a long theoretical digression *within* a work of literature. This, in miniature, is the problem that the quiet moments of the novel avoid, and this moment throws them into relief as theoretically instructive. And this is what ultimately calls the narrator's theory, and any wholesale acceptance of it, into question— without, of course, invalidating that theory full stop. His will to sacrifice in

La Prisonnière, since it is couched in poetic language and does not purport to theorize itself, is striking and believable. But here, the vitality of paradox is resolved by recourse to a pseudo-transcendental system. This tension will be further explored in Cusk's *Outline* trilogy, in a somewhat different form, namely, the feeling of a moment in time being disconnected from narrative. But first, I will proceed to a discussion of Tom McCarthy's *Remainder*, whose narrator obsessively stages re-enactments that resonate with both Huysmans and Proust, though perhaps with a darker tone and outcome, and in quite a different style.

End Notes

1 Thomas Baldwin, *Roland Barthes: The Proust Variations*, 1.
2 Leo Bersani, *A Future for Astyanax: Character and Desire in Literature*, 10.
3 Vincent Descombes, *Proust: Philosophy of the Novel*, 35.
4 Maurizio Ferraris, *Learning to Live: Six Essays on Marcel Proust*, vii.
5 James Dutton, *Proust Between Deleuze and Derrida: The Remains of Literature*, 1.
6 As Deleuze writes in *Proust and Signs*, with regard to the narrator's apprenticeship: "Learning is essentially concerned with *signs*. [...] Everything that teaches us something emits signs; every act of learning is an interpretation of signs or hieroglyphs. Proust's work is based not on the exposition of memory, but on the apprenticeship to signs" (4). It should be pointed out that these signs are particular to the encounters in which they arise—they are not signs that we can look for in any direct way. As such, any process of education or apprenticeship to signs does not proceed straightforwardly, whereby we learn what kinds of things to look for in signs. Instead, to learn how to interpret signs is first and foremost to learn how to recognize when we are having an encounter with a sign, and only then can we actually read that sign.
7 For a recent discussion of identification (and its subversion) in Proust, see Justine Balibar, "The Logic of Gomorrah: Proust and the Subversion of Identities," in *The Proustian Mind*, 325–334.
8 It is this tendency that Deleuze finds in common between Proust and Nietzsche. For a close comparison of the two thinkers and their many similarities, see Duncan Large's *Nietzsche and Proust*. Here, it should suffice to say that the logic of the *À la recherche du temps perdu*, even this early in the novel, offers a remarkable alternative to the logics of everyday life and philosophy alike, without simply opposing them.
9 Descombes, *Proust*, 267–268.
10 Joshua Landy, *Philosophy as Fiction: Self, Deception, and Knowledge in Proust*, 62–63.
11 Ibid., 63.
12 Gasché, *The Honor of Thinking: Critique, Theory, Philosophy*, 270.
13 Ibid., 266, emphasis added. Interestingly, this state of ill will bears similarity to the narrator's state before tasting the madeleine and tea: "machinalement, accablé par la morne journée et la perspective d'un triste lendemain, je portai à mes lèvres une cuillerée du thé où j'avais laissé s'amollir un morceau de madeleine [mechanically, dispirited after a dreary day with the prospect of a depressing morrow, I raised to my lips a spoonful of the tea in which I had soaked a morsel of the cake]" (1: 44/1: 48). The difference is that in the present passage from *Le Côté de Guermantes* the narrator's

bad mood is the catalyst for his attempt at making his experience an aesthetic one, whereas in the madeleine scene the experience truly comes as a surprise, without his mood seeming to intervene to any major positive degree. However, if we read slightly beyond the present scene, his eventual failure to "save his day" by conscious will does, in a strange twist of fate, result in what might be deemed an aesthetic experience. See my "Intoxication: Reading Between Proust and Barthes," for a discussion of the aftermath of the present passage. These passages, if the expression can be permitted, therefore foreshadow one another.

14 Insofar as he feels and views his state in this unfavorable light, his comments on his surroundings are fairly sarcastic. After being summoned by Robert to this back room, the narrator already expresses a degree of annoyance at what he finds:

> Je trouvai sa maîtresse étendue sur un sofa, riant sous les baisers, les caresses qu'il lui prodiguait. Ils buvaient du champagne. « Bonjour, vous! » lui dit-elle, car elle avait appris récemment cette formule qui lui paraissait le dernier mot de la tendresse et de l'esprit. (2: 468)
>
> I found his mistress stretched out on a sofa laughing under the kisses and caresses that he was showering on her. They were drinking champagne. 'Hallo, you!' she said to him from time to time, having recently picked up this expression which seemed to her the last word in affection and wit. (2: 173)

Though I will not develop the connection here, the re-narration in the quotation that follows could also be understood in the context of this sarcasm.

15 René Girard, *Deceit, Desire and the Novel: Self and Other in Literary Structure*, 7.
16 Ibid., 24.
17 As Girard writes: "The narrator experiences an intense desire to see Berma, the famous actress, perform. The spiritual benefits he hopes to gain from the performance are of a truly sacramental type. The imagination has done its work. The object is transfigured. But where is this object? What is the grain of sand which has violated the solitude of the oyster-consciousness? It is not the great Berma, for the narrator has never seen her. Nor is it the memory of previous performances; the child has had no direct contact with the dramatic art; he even conjures up a fantastic idea of the physical nature of a theater. We will find no object here because there is none" (*Deceit, Desire and the Novel*, 29–30). Interestingly, despite its ultimate disappointment for the narrator, the encounter with Berma's *Phèdre* is yet another example of a desire, and an experience, without origin.
18 Bryan Reddick, "Proust: The 'La Berma' Passages," 683.
19 Reddick, "Proust: The 'La Berma' Passages," 684. Reddick also points out the interplay between Rachel and la Berma with regard to performance, which is too complex to do justice to here. For now, it must suffice to say that Rachel, as a sort of counter-figure to la Berma, gives a recital near the end of the *Recherche* that, unlike la Berma's earlier performances, "calls attention to that which is *imposed upon* her material, her manner of conveying it" (691). With his emphasis here, Reddick highlights an artistic tension that fluctuates throughout the novel, which is also present in Legrandin's brief speech.
20 Kant, *Critique of the Power of Judgment*, 100.
21 Descombes, *Proust*, 267.
22 Ibid.
23 Miguel de Beistegui, *Proust as Philosopher: The Art of Metaphor*, 2.

24 Ibid., 54.
25 Gernot Böhme, *Atmospheric Architectures: The Aesthetics of Felt Spaces*, 14.
26 Ibid., 38.
27 Deleuze, *Proust and Signs*, 94.
28 Böhme, *Atmospheric Architectures*, 23.
29 Samuel Beckett, *Proust*, 22, emphasis added.
30 Richard Moran, "Proust and the Limits of the Will," *The Philosophical Imagination: Selected Essays*, 103.
31 Ibid.
32 Ibid., 105. He reiterates this, claiming also that "if the efficacy of involuntary memory requires the *exclusion* of any conscious effort, the meaning of its efficacy turns out to be the restoration of the will and the capacity to work themselves" (105).
33 Gérard Genette, *Narrative Discourse: An Essay in Method*, 139.
34 Freed-Thall, *Spoiled Distinctions*, 69.
35 Böhme, *Atmospheric Architectures*, 23.
36 Eve Kosofsky Sedgwick, *The Weather in Proust*, 14.
37 Ibid., 7.
38 Kant writes: "There is a certain lack of urbanity in music, in that, primarily because of the character of its instruments, it extends its influence further (into the neighborhood) than is required, and so as it were imposes itself, thus interfering with the freedom of others, outside of the musical circle, which the arts that speak to the eyes do not do, sine one need only turn one's eyes away if one would not admit their impression. [...] Someone who pulls his perfumed handkerchief out of his pocket treats everyone in the vicinity to it against their will, and forces them, if they wish to breathe, to enjoy it at the same time; hence it has also gone out of fashion" (*Critique of the Power of Judgment*, 207).
39 Pascal Quignard, *The Hatred of Music*, 71.
40 The full fragment reads: "The artist gradually comes to love for their own sake the means that reveal a condition of intoxication: extreme subtlety and splendor of color, definiteness of line, nuances of tone: the *distinct* where otherwise, under normal conditions, distinctness is lacking. All distinct things, all nuances, to the extent that they recall these extreme enhancements of strength that intoxication produces, awaken this feeling of intoxication by association: the effect of works of art is to excite the state that creates art—intoxication" (*The Will to Power*, 434).
41 Genette, *Figures III*, 153; *Narrative Discourse*, 123.
42 Roger Foster, *Adorno: The Recovery of Experience*, 140. However, besides this brief mention, he does not return to the passage or to the idea of the interior violin; the instrument is used mainly to illustrate Adorno's point about experience and concept.
43 Prendergast, *Living and Dying with Marcel Proust*, 121–122.
44 There is an echo of this dilemma in much of Maurice Blanchot's work, perhaps most notably in *La Folie du Jour* [*The Madness of the Day*]: "Et ce jour s'effaçant, je m'effacerai avec lui, pensée, certitude qui me transporte" (20). In Lydia Davis' translation, this reads: "And when this day fades, I will fade along with it—a thought, a certainty, that enraptures me" (6). But in his reading of this passage, Christopher Fynsk stresses the aspect of self-effacement that is not quite rendered in the translation: "He is envisioning the eclipse of the day and *with* it (perhaps in some con-sequence, but no causal relation is asserted) a self-effacement" (*Last Steps: Maurice Blanchot's Exilic Writing*, 61).

45 Freed-Thall, "*Zut, zut, zut, zut*: Aesthetic Disorientation in Proust," 897.
46 Ibid., 872.
47 Ibid., 889, 887.
48 Freed-Thall, *Spoiled Distinctions*, 15.
49 Ibid., 81.
50 Alessia Ricciardi, *The Ends of Mourning: Psychoanalysis, Literature, Film*, 69; see 74–75.
51 Ibid., 74–75.

Chapter 3

VIOLENT MOMENTS IN TOM MCCARTHY'S *REMAINDER*

The writings of British author Tom McCarthy, including his fiction and his essays, focus above all on violence. And while the novels are by no means short on acts of physical violence—for example, the many acts of political violence depicted in his 2007 novel *Men in Space*, or the violence of World War I in his 2010 novel *C*—McCarthy is also concerned with violence in an expanded sense that will take center stage in this chapter. In a 2010 essay on the fiction of Jean-Philippe Toussaint, McCarthy connects violence to another of his long-standing obsessions: the movements, positions, and relations of things in physical space. McCarthy names a moment in Toussaint's 1985 novel *La Salle de bain* [*The Bathroom*] where the narrator throws a dart into his lover's forehead as an example of "space being brought into its own, made present in the only true way possible: through acts of violence."[1] With several references throughout this essay to Alain Robbe-Grillet and the *nouveau roman*, McCarthy makes it clear that violence in its expanded sense can take the form of a kind of repetition and geometry of shifting viewpoints that often create an alienating reading experience, occasionally doubled by literal physical violence as if it were the culmination of the strange reading effect of spatial repetition. Indeed, in a short and incidental 2018 text, McCarthy begins by stating that "death is a question of geometry."[2] He goes on to discuss the forensic practice of drawing outlines not only around the body but also around any object in its immediate proximity, a practice that will show up in his 2005 novel *Remainder* to great effect. In doing so, he asks us to consider the possibility that the geometry of this procedure always already exists—that is, that the trace of violence is always there, so to speak, even before the occurrence of the act: "what if the forensic overlay, its lines, sectors, segments, angles, intervals, were there already, *prior* to the fatal event (not overlay but underlay)?"[3]

Just as often as actual violence is used, McCarthy gives shape to this principle by long, repetitive, complex descriptions of simple movements. In some cases—for example, an early passage from *C* in which the young boy Serge's movements throughout a garden are described in painstaking detail—these movements are largely incidental and do not serve to drive the plot in a direct way. Instead, the entire narrative seems to narrow down to encompass only the space being described or traversed with such detail. Not only are Serge's movements described extensively, but he quite literally exhausts the possibilities of movement along and across the garden's many forking paths.[4] This undoubtedly does have implications for the narrative of *C* (and potentially for understanding that narrative, or even narrative in general), but the passage in question is not directly relevant to the novel's plot.

Similar descriptions of motion are foregrounded and thematized so explicitly in *Remainder* as to create an overload of repetition that oscillates between monotony and extravagance. This strange effect stems from and seems to allegorize the narrator's obsession with recreating a certain unexplainable feeling by recourse to elaborate re-enactments of specific events. Due to the diminishing returns of such repetition, these re-enactments necessarily escalate, becoming more and more *actually* violent, even causing the loss of human life. Taken together, these two forms of violence are important factors in the very composition of space. For McCarthy, bodies *insert* themselves in space, rather than simply existing within it, and their movements (as well as the movements of narrative) *trace* or *describe* the spaces they inhabit.[5] As I just mentioned, this manifests as an extreme precision—not unlike that of Robbe-Grillet, though perhaps somewhat less exhaustive and exhausting—when movement in particular is being described. In one way, by referring to Toussaint and Robbe-Grillet, McCarthy is pointing to their descriptions of physical violence. But what he is really interested in is the doubling of this violence by the very fact of its deployment on the sentence level, which lends it its expanded sense. In both Toussaint and Robbe-Grillet, there is a violence of uncertainty, of repetition, that goes beyond the trope of the unreliable narrator to suggest the character's or even the narrative's amnesia. This kind of repetition can be seen in Robbe-Grillet's *La Jalousie* [*Jealousy*], for instance, which is a favorite reference for McCarthy, who has on multiple occasions decried Michel Houellebecq's dismissal of the *nouveau roman* icon.[6] While McCarthy's texts tend to feature both actual violence on the one hand and repetition that verges on boredom and absurdity on the other, a further violence emerges on the theoretical level.

What I am referring to is something that I would deem an *aesthetic* violence. While not the same thing as an aesthetics *of* violence, this is undoubtedly related to the charge (nowadays usually uttered disapprovingly) of "aestheticization." We can find examples of this aesthetic violence in the previous two chapters. First, there is des Esseintes's entire project of constructing Fontenay-aux-Roses as essentially a museum curated according to his own particular tastes. And second, there is Proust's narrator's attempt to re-narrate his day to himself in order to "endow [it] with an aesthetic character." Though these are instances take place on different levels—des Esseintes is doing something physically in the world, whereas Proust's narrator is engaging in the activity of narration—in both cases, there is violence being done with respect to the aesthetic, an attempt to bring about an aesthetic experience through force. These two forms of misunderstanding are two different forms of aestheticization. My aim in this chapter is to join them through a reading of McCarthy's *Remainder*.

These *violent moments* are closely related to Huysmans's curated moments, given that the attempt to control or force an aesthetic experience can result in disappointment, illness, bodily harm, and other forms of violence. And at the same time, they are closely related to the misunderstanding exhibited and subsequently corrected by Proust's narrator, since they instrumentalize the aesthetic object or scene in service of a desired sensation. More importantly for my overall argument, these moments betray an impatience, a misunderstanding of what aesthetic experience is and the subject's place in it. To develop these ideas further, I will examine *Remainder* along the lines of memory, repetition, and addiction, before ending with a brief look at his 2015 novel *Satin Island* to set up my consideration of Rachel Cusk's *Outline* trilogy in Chapter 4.

Though it does not explicitly thematize works of art or aesthetic experience as such, *Remainder* poses a number of problems that resonate with what I have been referring to throughout as an aesthetic paradox. Like des Esseintes in *À rebours*, or the narrator or Swann in *À la recherche du temps perdu*, the narrator of *Remainder* engages the problem of aesthetic taste as the taste for the aesthetic, and even for particular aesthetic experiences. That is, he engages with his particular aesthetic fantasy to such an extent that it has deleterious effects, though with the difference that these effects also concern those around him, rather than only himself and his ability to encounter the aesthetic.[7] This is because of the increasing physical violence of his project, which manifests as a by-product of its rising aesthetic violence, which will be my primary focus here.

Unlike either des Esseintes or Swann, McCarthy's unnamed narrator comes into the novel as something much closer to a question mark or a blank slate, having lost much of his memory (and, for a time, his motor functioning) as a result of an accident he can barely remember. Compared with des Esseintes in particular, McCarthy's narrator has a markedly ambiguous relationship to origins. Whereas des Esseintes seeks to distance himself from his ancestors, his peers, and the tastes of society in general, McCarthy's narrator poses the interwoven questions of memory and origin only to complicate them to an extreme degree, until any reader must be careful about making inferences about what precedes the first page of the novel and what exactly the narrator's "memories" consist of. The results of this are amplified by the fact that he is the narrator, and not merely a character in the novel.

In broad strokes, the novel's plot is as follows. After a mysterious accident resulting in a coma, and after the ensuing lawsuit, the unnamed narrator finds himself in possession of eight and a half million pounds. Living what is otherwise a relatively simple life, he has no need for this money and is at a loss as to what he should do with it. As des Esseintes does before embarking upon his project, McCarthy's narrator rejects the alternatives offered to him by his peers and society at large. Meeting at a pub after he has received his settlement, his friends Greg and Catherine offer their suggestions about how to spend his money. Greg's initial advice is to "start an account with a coke dealer" (33). Catherine, on the other hand, initially defers to the narrator, stating that it is ultimately up to him, but then offers her suggestion: "a resource fund. To help people" (33). These alternatives leave the narrator indifferent and even more lost. "Altruism and hedonism prove equally empty," as Zadie Smith argues in "Two Paths for the Novel."[8] The narrator finds himself unable to choose between a set of opposed positions that do not interest him in the slightest because they feel equally meaningless, because they are not derived from or connected in any way to his experience, as his eventual project will very much be.

The critical moment of *Remainder*, and the moment that incites the project that will occupy the bulk of the novel—according to the narrator, "the event that, the accident aside, was the most significant of my whole life" (64)—comes when, at a friend's party, the narrator sees a crack in the bathroom wall, which causes him to experience "a sudden sense of déjà vu" (64). This experience turns the narrator into what Smith calls a "re-enactor."[9] After this point, he has a project, meaning also some way to use his money: first to recreate this initial experience of déjà vu, but eventually to recreate any scenario that causes him to experience a certain feeling of authenticity that he associates with this initial moment. It is important to note, from the beginning, that the "remembered" space that emerges during this moment should not be taken as a true memory per se, a point that will be integral for my argument in what follows. It is rather the "tingling feeling" that comes along with these moments that drives the re-enactments.

Because of the fleeting nature of the feeling he is after, and because he is ultimately not satisfied with the initial re-enactment (because, as he learns but insists on ignoring, no re-enactment can be fully satisfying), he quickly moves on to a new one, again and again. Each successive re-enactment becomes not only more complex, wasteful, and difficult to execute, but also more potentially hazardous, and therefore more violent in multiple senses. The risk of physical harm is doubled by the violent attitude he has toward his project on a theoretical level: he will *force* this feeling, it seems, whatever it takes. If his is a hedonism—and I think the argument can be made—the distinction is that it is not derived from a model proffered by others, but is inherent in these experiences. In what follows, I will consider the narrator's trajectory in accordance with the themes of memory, repetition, and addiction. My purpose in doing so will be to highlight the ways in which *Remainder* represents an important entry in the philosophical conversation around aesthetic experience, particularly as it participates in a certain violent moment of the aesthetic that relates to, but deviates from, the curated moments found in Huysmans.

I can say very little

From the very beginning of *Remainder*, memory is a major theme insofar as it is constantly being called into question. Because of its uncertain status in the novel, memory is brought up primarily to prompt a reflection upon how memory takes shape and how it is accessed. Provocatively, the opening lines refer to the novel's inaugural event as such: "About the accident itself I can say very little" (1). While this statement on its face prepares the reader to assume forgetting or amnesia, we are told a few sentences later that what the narrator has said so far is in fact "all I can divulge" (1). Taken at its word, and given the legal ramifications of his accident that are clarified in the following pages, this opening section is absent of any concrete authority as far as memory is concerned; it simply poses memory as an open question. It may be the case that the narrator is not allowed, by the nature of his settlement, to *say* or *divulge* anything about the accident.[10] Of course, this is not to say definitively that the accident did not have deleterious effects for his memory, but whatever effects it may have had cannot be straightforwardly equated to any memory loss he may have suffered. Furthermore, any effects that the accident has had on his mind should not be confined, in a critical reading of the novel, only to the realm of memory.

In other words, despite this central role of memory, its complex, strange, and problematic status in the narrative means that it should be treated carefully, and we should avoid the temptation of taking as a solution the narrator's loss of—and therefore instances of recovering—certain memories, however much some of these moments in the text might read like instances of Proustian involuntary memory. Pieter Vermeulen reads memory primarily in terms of trauma's role in the novel's form, and in the novel form in general: "If *Remainder* officially wants to convey a tone of sturdy and affectless imperturbability in order to debunk the pieties of trauma fiction, such a reading is increasingly complicated as the narrator gets caught up in obsessively detailed reenactments of seemingly random scenes."[11] This reading should be granted with the caveat that the "randomness" of such scenes effectively stages the destabilization of the traumatic object, which stands in here for the object of aesthetic experience. This "randomness"—which, one might argue, actually *increases* cumulatively across the plot's trajectory—reflects what is in reality a lack of measure for what would be "random" (or not) in the first place, as we will later see when discussing the narrator's employment of the irrational as a methodological principle. By this, I mean to pose the question of what re-enactment could conceivably contain no randomness at all, either within the world of *Remainder* or beyond it—and, by extension, what aesthetic experience would likewise contain no randomness. Commenting on Freud's *Beyond the Pleasure Principle*, Cathy Caruth writes that the literary dimension of Freud's example (Torquato Tasso's *Jerusalem Liberated*) not only serves as a support for the articulation of Freud's theory, but also "exceeds, perhaps, the limits of Freud's conceptual or conscious theory of trauma" because it points to the unconscious element that is at play for the subject who repeats.[12] As Caruth argues, "trauma is not locatable in the simple violent or original event in an individual's past, but rather in the way that its very unassimilated nature—the way it was precisely *not known* in the first instance—returns to haunt the survivor later on."[13] Trauma is an effect of knowledge first and foremost, and indeed, any originary violence is not explicitly grappled with by McCarthy's narrator: he is unable or refuses to *know* it.

To return to Vermeulen's claim, I would add that it is the inability to guarantee a repetition of the initial affect being sought that drives the various re-enactments, both in their consciously repetitive nature and their serial succession. Wojciech Drag states in response to Vermeulen: "Accepting this interpretation would involve refraining from seeking to account for the baffling behavior of the protagonist-narrator and focusing on the challenges that *Remainder* poses to trauma literature and to the novel at large."[14] The novel's real contribution to the idea of trauma lies somewhere between the phenomenology of the narrator's world and any theory of trauma that would be operative in our reading, and the narrator's odd behavior—like his memory—must remain an open question. With this in mind, the complicated place of the object throughout the narrative further allows us to discuss aesthetic experience through a similar framework. It is not simply the randomness of the narrator's particular re-enactments that gets in the way of his project. Instead, the project is undermined by the critical difficulty of navigating the density of repetition that is operative on all levels throughout the novel. Vermeulen argues that "[t]he deployment of the narrative grammar of compulsive repetition without the motivation of a psychological trauma [...] is an obvious part of the novel's campaign against the psychological and ethical registers in which trauma is customarily rendered."[15] In a way, this deployment can also be considered as instrumental in breaking down the usual alignment of aesthetic experience to grandiose encounters with nature or works of art, a task that is accomplished through the narrator's refusal to verify the truth either of his accident or of the "memory" that gives rise to his first re-enactment, while at the same time prompting us to consider those very questions time and time again. The accident, and the question of memory along with it, are in effect red herrings.[16]

Sebastian Groes calls upon Proust's *À la recherche du temps perdu* in order to explore the phenomenon of memory in *Remainder* as it relates to contemporary understandings of subjectivity. Though, with Deleuze, I would question giving memory a primary role in Proust as well as in McCarthy, Groes's point about the relation between these two figures opens onto interesting terrain. Mainly preoccupied with the break between modernity and postmodernity, Groes claims that "beneath McCarthy's amnesiac there lies a deep engagement with, but also a correction of Proust."[17] He also writes that "whereas Proust aims to make sense of the archived past with a future perspective in mind, in McCarthy there is no past archive to decode."[18] The *Remainder* narrator is an apt counterpoint to Proust's hero, and his lack of "past archive"—or his refusal to share it with us—can be read as a nod to the difficulty inherent in deciding what exactly memory's role in aesthetic experience should be, especially if a certain understanding of Kantian aesthetic philosophy demands that beautiful objects surprise us. Groes writes that "the re-enactment is a constructive approach rather than a process of discovery, and can therefore never work; whereas Proust writes his way towards essence, the narrator's attempted literalisation of the scraps of memory by staging them in reality, in the hope of somehow merging them, aims to recreate the Ideal essence of the self in concrete reality."[19] Though I will disagree with the claim that the bathroom scene in *Remainder* "gives him [...] a glimpse of his childhood"[20]—a claim that, furthermore, seems to undermine Groes's main argument that the narrator possesses no "past archive"—I find the emphasis on the absent origins of the re-enactments fascinating and instructive for the present reading.

Sydney Miller focuses more closely on the novel's mobilization of the accidental, which is of key importance for the novel and for my understanding of aesthetic experience more broadly: "Steeped as it is in philosophical discourse and critical theory, the novel could potentially be read as a commentary on trauma, on authenticity, on the aesthetics of repetition, or on the status of the novel in the wake of postmodernism—that is, as a plea for fiction to continue its retreat from the brink of crippling self-consciousness."[21] In this one sentence, Miller surveys the major dimensions of the novel and its scholarship. What makes *Remainder* a lasting contribution to the question of aesthetic experience is what I consider to be its pinpointing not necessarily of "the aesthetics of repetition," but rather the place of repetition in the aesthetic—to be more precise, the repetition of difference that stems from the accidental nature of experience and renders each aesthetic encounter accidental, as well as the danger threatened by a *different* kind of repetition. Deleuze writes: "The interior of repetition is always affected by an order of difference: it is only to the extent that something is linked to a repetition of an order other than its own that the repetition appears external and bare, and the thing itself subject to the categories of generality."[22] Simply put, every repetition contains a core difference, which may be objectively imperceptible but nonetheless inheres in each instance of an act—for instance, affects or miniscule details that are noted only by a single observer. This can be seen in *Remainder* in the experiential and narrative fact of the re-enactments: it is precisely because they differ each time, and because they never offer complete satisfaction, that they must be repeated—a point that is not without its psychoanalytic resonances. This runs in parallel to the distinction that I noted in the previous chapter between the iterativity of aesthetic experience itself and the impulse to control or repeat aesthetic experience in a conscious way. In short, the novel's thematization of memory and repetition reaches far beyond the usual psychological or psychoanalytical understanding (while, of course, not completely departing from such understandings), and may be better understood as a vehicle for aesthetic theory, perhaps as contributing to a phenomenology of aesthetic experience.

Just as the accident is not confined to affecting his memory, any effects on or activations of his memory are not confined only to his accident. Indeed, memory haunts the entire text, significantly emerging as a provocation in what is perhaps its most iconic scene, the famous "bathroom scene," wherein a crack in the wall triggers in him "a sudden sense of déjà vu" (64). We might imagine this scene as occupying a space in the scholarship akin to that of the madeleine passage in Proust scholarship.[23] This is a feeling of having been in the same space—meaning, it eventually turns out, more precisely *in the same moment*—before. However, despite this feeling, the narrator admits: "I remembered it all, but I couldn't remember *where* I'd been in this place, this flat, this bathroom. Or when. [...] I couldn't place this memory at all" (65–66). The "memory" at the root of this feeling cannot be verified, but even this fact is dismissed as being beside the point, since the very experience has its own creative force: "And yet it was growing, minute by minute as I stood there in the bathroom, this remembered building, spreading outwards from the crack" (66).[24] Ultimately, the origin of this "memory" is second to the experience: it is an experience of the force of memory itself, rather than a memory *of* something, and the memory's "origin" embodies the figure of a crack in the wall, simply emerging of its own volition. And tellingly, the apartment complex that serves as the narrator's initial re-enactment site is called Madlyn Mansions, a near homophone for the madeleine that propels Proust's narrator back into his childhood and propels the whole of the *Recherche* forward.

After describing the scenarios and inhabitants in the apartment building that this déjà vu brings to light, he states: "I remembered how all this had *felt*" (66, emphasis added). He describes several sensory details—including the floors and how they felt to walk on, how it sounded to walk on them—so this mention of feeling is not merely a commonplace; he is truly referring to the senses. He calls this building, in the following paragraph, "this remembered building" (67). Clearly, the narrator's feeling of remembrance, which has "all the force of an epiphany, a revelation" (67), is not by any means negated by his inability to locate the original of this feeling in his memory. But the building is only nominally "remembered," which can be said merely because it is envisioned from within the intensity of his experience and his ability to be thrust back into the same affect. Memory must remain in quotation marks. As he remarks later to his lawyer: "Maybe it was various things all rolled together: memories, imaginings, films, I don't know. But that bit's not important. What's important is that I remembered it, and it was crystal-clear" (80).

Rather than being aimed at repeating an actual original experience, the narrator's project of re-enactment is spurred on by the event of remembering and what comes along with it, regardless of the truth or content of the "memory." Structurally, the force of this "memory"—that is, the force of this experience such that we might lend it even the provisional, in-quotes status of "memory" in the first place—resonates once again with Deleuze's new image of thought, just as Proust's novel does. In the present context, the point is that memory or remembering simply stands in for a kind of intensity that the narrator seeks, and exists only in a context that is coterminous with it. Furthermore, the destabilization of particular memories coincides with the activation in him of a creative impulse: "I sketched my whole remembered flat outward from the crack running down the bathroom wall" (73). But even this bathroom scene is secondary, in a narrative sense, to another striking instance of memory. Earlier in the novel, the narrator walks to a payphone after having been rendered with a "neutral" feeling upon receiving news of his settlement (8). As he walks home, he thinks of a minor car accident and a police raid on a nearby house ("They'd been looking for someone and had got a tip-off, I suppose" (9)), both of which had happened shortly before the novel's inciting accident. Suddenly he stops "right in the middle of the road," standing "in what had been the marksmen's sightlines" (9). As if his memory is jogged by recalling other events that came before it, and as if he is "targeted" by the force of memory, he seems to relive the instant right before the accident:

> I turned the palms of my hands outwards, closed my eyes and thought about that memory of just before the accident, being buffeted by wind. Remembering it sent a tingling from the top of my legs to my shoulders and right up into my neck. It lasted for just a moment—but while it did I felt not-neutral. I felt different, intense: both intense and serene at the same time. I remember feeling this way very well: standing there, passive, with my palms turned outwards, feeling intense and serene. (9)

Caught in the crosshairs of another memory event, these lines foreshadow the bathroom scene, but at this point, there is no view to a re-enactment. In terms of the scholarship, this is an obstacle to the primacy of the bathroom scene, since it can no longer be claimed as a true original, either in terms of the narrator's affective "tingling" feeling that is so crucial to his entire project, or in terms of holding the initial narrative place of memory-adjacent aesthetic experience.[25] Additionally, this passage forces us to consider the possibility that he both remembers and does not—cannot—remember his accident. He remembers "just before the accident," but is it possible for him to remember the exact moment of an accident that put him into a coma? This question may not receive an answer, but it at least complicates the narrator's alleged amnesia. Whether or not he can remember certain times, the point is that memory is an event undergone, rather than the retrieval of an archived image.[26] Recounting how the raid had failed since the suspect was not in the house, the narrator states that such events live on "even if just in the memories of the forty, fifty, sixty passers-by who'd stopped to watch. Everything must leave some kind of mark" (10). This final line reappears verbatim when the narrator realizes that he had likely seen the building he is looking for—the site of the first re-enactment—in the past, and that it would have left some kind of trace in his memory (99). This trace, if it does belong to memory, pushes the boundaries of memory beyond what we normally think of them. If he can find the building again by happenstance, then it would be a question of something bordering on involuntary memory.

 Both the tingling feeling noted by the narrator and the question of events leaving traces are tied in with his fixation on authenticity, which not only prompts but also complicates his re-enactments. An early mention of this idea of authenticity comes after the narrator's multiple calls with the lawyer about his settlement, and before he goes to retrieve Catherine, a visiting friend—who, significantly, marks the time in his life when he felt most "in-the-moment" (26)—from the airport. He has an internal debate about returning to his home once more before leaving to get her, since he does not have the flight details. This results in him walking back and forth over the same spot multiple times:

> I realized that I was jerking back and forth like paused video images do on low-quality machines. It must have looked strange. I felt self-conscious, embarrassed. I made a decision to go and pick up the flight details after all, but remained standing on the pavement for a few more seconds while I pretended to weigh up several options and then come to an informed decision. I even brought my finger into it, the index finger of my right hand. It was a performance for the two men watching me, to make my movements come across as more authentic. (14)

Self-conscious, de Manian irony—which McCarthy and his fellow necronaut Simon Critchley specifically refer to, and which I will return to later in this chapter—seems in this moment to complicate the fact that the narrator is in fact visible to those around him.[27] Besides foreshadowing the fantasy of his eventual re-enactments, this scene and the scene quoted above unmistakably echo the paving-stone passage in Proust. The language used is remarkably similar, and both narrators can be described as "jerking back and forth" in front of a crowd, "feeling intense and serene." However, the present scene specifically diverges from Proust's in its explicit reference to performance and the narrator's peculiar concern for what is authentic. In Proust, the narrator intentionally ignores the crowd of onlookers, focusing instead purely on his sensations, as at this late stage of the novel he is engaged in interrogating the phenomenon of involuntary memory. The focus on authenticity held by McCarthy's narrator originates in his accident. After coming out of his coma, the narrator "had to learn how to move" (19). The rerouting of the brain involved in this task involves the revelation that each action "turns out to be more complicated than you thought" (20), which for him means that each action must be rebuilt from the ground up, with a single action being relearned *in many pieces*. The subdivision of even the simplest action, "like lifting a carrot to your mouth" (20), plays a major role in the emergence of authenticity as a problem in the narrator's life, as it does in the meticulously staged re-enactments: "I still had to think about each movement I made, had to understand it. No Doing without Understanding: the accident bequeathed me that for ever, an eternal detour" (22–23).[28] In other words, the absolutely intentional and fragmentary nature of every conceivable physical action calls the authenticity of all actions into question, which is made all the more complex when an audience is involved.

Significantly, the description of the process of relearning basic motor skills is immediately followed by the narrator's viewing of the 1973 Martin Scorsese film *Mean Streets*, a film containing its fair share of violence. Before discussing the film, he states, significantly, that his

> memory had come back to me in moving images [...]. It could have been another history, another set of actions and events, like when there's been a mix-up and you get the wrong holiday photos back from the chemist's. I wouldn't have known or cared differently, and would have accepted them the same. (23)

Moving to the film, he then remarks on Robert De Niro's deftness: "Every move he made, each gesture was perfect, seamless. [...] [H]e seemed to execute the action perfectly, to live it, to merge with it until he was it and it was him and there was nothing in between" (23). De Niro becomes the narrator's touchstone for authenticity.[29] But just as with the arbitrariness of his recovered history, and just as with the "memory" brought up during the bathroom scene, De Niro only becomes a touchstone *during* the narrator's viewing of the film. He is not, in this sense, an origin for the idea of authenticity. Furthermore, as a noted method actor, De Niro's "seamless" movements are the result of intense research and preparation.[30]

The lack of origin—or, at least, the lack of *meaningful* or *final* origin, of an origin where we could stop the chain of associations—of the re-enactments both drives and problematizes the narrator's search for what he considers to be "authentic" experience. And, indeed, the "bathroom scene" and the "remembered building" are significant for him because "in these spaces, all my movements had been fluent and unforced. Not awkward, acquired, second-hand, but natural. Opening my fridge's door, lighting a cigarette, even lifting a carrot to my mouth: these gestures had been seamless, perfect" (67). Oddly, given that the entire basis for this "memory" is a crack in the wall (a kind of seam), what he seems to be seeking here is not really any particular kind of action—just as the aesthetic object in Proust, for instance, is not really any particular kind of object. Instead, it is a feeling, a state of being, that is not fractured by thought but rather is a form of thought itself.

According to Deleuze's formulation of the incidental nature of thought, "it is the fortuitousness or the contingency of the encounter which guarantees the necessity of that which it forces to be thought."[31] Extrapolating from this sentiment, thought can be taken seriously only if it occurs *necessarily*, from out of everyday life, as a result of variables that are ultimately *contingent*. This apparently counterintuitive idea can be placed into conversation with *Remainder* if the narrator's project is considered along its own lines, instead of being subject to realistic psychological scrutiny. His obsession with authenticity must be taken with a grain of salt in view of what, narratively, lies in store. In fact, this lack of origin strengthens the theoretical stakes of his feeling, which in turn drives his employment of repetition throughout the novel. The bathroom experience, for example, though (and also *because*) it markedly has no "true" original, therefore serves as the inaugural moment in the narrative economy of re-enactments. What matters in this analysis is the intensity of the narrator's sensation—and this is of prime importance to him as well, as we can trace through his own repeated invocation of the term "intense."

With the above in mind, memory is one fault line along which a violent paradox forms. On the one hand, if the experience sought out by the narrator is one that arises of its own accord and with a singular force, then it can be said to contain some degree of violence: it *forces* itself upon him. But on the other hand, once he becomes aware of this sensation, he begins to treat it as something to be *achieved*, something that he might bring about if he can recreate the appropriate conditions. This is another kind of violence, not unlike the Proustian gesture of re-narrating that we saw in the previous chapter. Even before the re-enactments are set into motion, aesthetic experience in *Remainder* is a site of danger.

It's not *unusual* features that I'm after

C. Namwali Serpell's reading of *Remainder* begins with some remarks about repetition's capacity to proliferate variations and readings of repetition itself: "Revolving around this central act of repetition"—that is, the narrator's re-enactments, though we might also take this to mean the bathroom scene in particular—"the novel seems to draw into its orbit nearly every extant theory, theme, and effect of repetition, too."[32] Responding in part to McCarthy's frequent evocations, in interviews, of various philosophers and theorists, Serpell points out: "Despite this interest in *ideas* about repetition, *Remainder* offers a philosophy of experience."[33] Taking up this juxtaposition between *ideas* and *experience*, along with Serpell's endorsement of the latter as the way toward philosophy, my hope in this section will be to suggest that this philosophy of experience is articulated precisely through repetition and its various aftermaths. If a philosophy of experience informed by repetition is to be differentiated from mere *ideas* about repetition, there must be something about *Remainder* that speaks directly to experience *through* its employment of repetition.

Over the course of the novel, repetition is increasingly revealed to have a double valence for the narrator. Repetition involves (or perhaps even *is*) both a possibility and an impossibility with regard to his experiences, and initially comes onto the scene as a real possibility during the bathroom episode, whose intensity and singularity awakens in him the intense desire to repeat it. Besides bringing to mind Kant's linking of the beautiful with "the determination of the mind *that sustains itself*,"[34] this recalls Julia Jordan's characterization of *Remainder* as

> a meditation on repetition and the possibility of a perfect reiteration, as the narrator attempts to recreate a single event or experience over and over: is it possible, the novel asks, not to swerve away from an original event in its reconstruction? Is it possible to keep on the straight and narrow of a singular experience?[35]

Taken in this light, repetition gives rise to two interrelated problems. First, it facilitates the narrator's taste for more of the same kind of experience, the dynamic that Schopenhauer points out in his discussion of the genius. Second, it forces a consideration of not only the possibility, in the first place, of recreating an experience physically, down to every last detail, but also the question of whether a material recreation will carry the same affective weight. Together, these are the problems that lead to the aesthetic violence that makes *Remainder* so compelling and so instructive for the thinking of aesthetic experience.

These issues follow the narrator throughout the novel, as he puts his money to work with the goal of being able to repeat these moments at will, first the bathroom scene and its "remembered building," and then a series of other experiences. He has an entire zone curated, down to his precise specifications: actors who are in fact also re-enactors, an apartment complex, the courtyard outside, and even a roof across the way with "black cats on the red roofs of the building facing the back of mine across the courtyard" (69–70). These specifications occur to him over a short span of time, as a memory fleshes itself out, a fact that the text is careful to convey. Looking at his sketch of the crack in the wall and gradually remembering the apartment, the narrator states: "Occasionally I'd look at the pattern I'd drawn across [the wallpaper]. Mostly I just sat there holding it, letting the world that I'd remembered grow. And grow it did" (71). This infection of the figurative by the literal, and vice versa, models the narrative's entire enterprise as far as the aesthetic is concerned. As he states: "I was going to recreate it: build it up again and live inside it" (69). "It" here refers not only to the crack in the wall or the entire remembered building, but indeed to the remembered moment itself.

Briefly, I wish to touch on a moment of narrative repetition that speaks to the theme of memory while also revealing an underlying thread in the narrator's project. In the third chapter, after meeting with his lawyer and signing his settlement documents, he is on his way to an appointment with a stockbroker to handle his newly awarded money. In a strange moment of disorientation, confused about the directions to the office, he pauses and recalls the instance "two days earlier"—noted above—where he stood "in the ex-siege zone between the perpendicular and parallel streets by my flat" (44). But he does not just remember this moment; he repeats it, with a peculiar difference, which is made all the more striking given his new wealth:

> I closed my eyes and turned the palms of my hands outwards again and felt the same tingling, the same mixture of serene and intense. I opened my eyes again but kept my palms turned outwards. It struck me that my posture was like the posture of a beggar, holding his hands out, asking passers-by for change. (44)

Immediately following this, and while he begins to feel a heightened intensity, he actually begins asking those passers-by for change, though of course he does not need it: "I just wanted to be in that particular space, right then, doing that particular action. It made me feel so serene and intense that I felt almost real" (44). The scene ends with these lines, and the following paragraph finds him in the office. However troubling his actions—his "acting"—here might be, this scene once again foreshadows the bizarre and arbitrary turns that his eventual re-enactments will take. It is undeniable that his attitude toward poverty here, and later toward race, is problematic, but the emphasis in his appropriative gestures seems to lay largely on his fantasy of authenticity, which has a deeper misunderstanding at its root.[36] This fantasy, increasingly, involves his abstraction from who he is in any moment within the narrative.

Once his created apartment is up and running, the narrator spends some time living within these re-enactments, immersing himself in the different scenes as he wishes. However, the impossibility of his project quickly begins to creep in, in the form of several discrete problems. First of all, if his intention is to recreate an "authentic" and natural experience, it is possible only through the work of a score of employees: architects, handlers, actors, and so on. This mirrors the issue inherent in his admiration for the method actor De Niro, and these employees frequently frustrate the narrator, especially when they allow him to see the seams in his project. Even apart from this, his initial ambitions about his project are already marred by an undue fidelity both to the scene as a particular object and to particular objects within the scene; as he states with reference to where he is living before the re-enactments begin: "I'd be able to recreate the crack back in my own flat—smear on the plaster and then add the colours; but my bathroom wasn't the right shape" (p. 69).

This statement, coming directly after the bathroom scene as the narrator is imagining the possibility of repetition while heading home for the night, sets the tone for his way of engaging with his own experience. To be sure, what he is seeking is undeniably a certain *feeling*, but he can seemingly only attain this feeling if the material circumstances all line up. As Seb Franklin has put it,

> this reenactment is centered on reconstructing a specific affective state, a vaguely recalled sense of "natural" being-in-the-world. But the reconstruction of this affective state relies not only on a particular sequence of movements but on the reproduction of an entire assemblage of specific spaces, objects, movements, smells, and sounds. [...] [I]t becomes clear that elements beyond the initially "triggering" set of objects and practices are of equal importance to the construction of the whole.[37]

If we look back at the nature of his initial experience with the crack in the bathroom, we see that impossibility is already at the heart of his initial impulse to repeat. The aftermath of this scene—which can be characterized as putting into motion the narrator's attempts to curate his experience, his wish to repeat the scene *at will*, and the indispensable economic underpinning—betrays this impossibility and forgets its surprise to a certain extent.

Serpell's reading of *Remainder* is the most relevant as far as this paradox is concerned. In particular, she asserts that the narrator turns his "déjà vu [...] into *a quasi-artistic experience.*"[38] If it is accurate to qualify this experience as "quasi-artistic," this should not be taken as indicating that it is any lesser than an "artistic" experience. Instead, the "quasi-" nature of this experience entails a shift, however limited, away from traditional understandings of how we are meant to, and how we habitually, encounter a work of art. According to Serpell, "the narrator is not just the first or the most exacting but, in effect, the sole audience member. The re-enactments, in this sense, are as much about the narrator as a reader as about his efforts as a creator."[39] As we might claim about Huysmans's des Esseintes, the narrator cares only for his own aesthetic experience, and if a work of art typically enjoys an audience, the narrator's re-enactments cannot deserve this designation. In fact, given the narrator's struggle with authenticity and with being a visible, tangible subject in the social space, we might claim that the re-enactments are private, rather than public, even as they increasingly encroach into the public and social space. At the same time, though, the re-enactments involve—or at least gesture toward—experiences that approximate those that we might associate with works of art (namely, his recurring "tingling" sensation). In this sense, what I have just called a shift away from normal encounters with art is at the same time a reevaluation of art, one that takes into account both the experience of its creation and the experience of its reception. For the narrator, of course, this entails a further complication—he does not simply create, and subsequently regard, an art work. Instead, both sides of the work approach one another in his re-enactments. We might also claim in response to Nietzsche that the narrator is a figure for the proximity of artist and spectator.

Instead of leading only to a self-conscious, interpretive paralysis, this doubleness affords us a view of something inherent in aesthetic experience. Serpell evokes Jungian synchronicity and Freud's uncanny, stating that they allow "the grounds of analysis [to] shift from causality to significance, from cognition to experience. That is, we move toward a phenomenology."[40] If there is a phenomenology at play in *Remainder*, it is due to this shift: significance (which, along with the narrator, I have earlier referred to as "intensity") and experience are privileged over causality and cognition, which would traditionally be considered the more "rational" options. In this context, such a phenomenology would undoubtedly be an aesthetic phenomenology, a phenomenology of aesthetic experience. But we can see this at work even before the first re-enactment "goes live," so to speak, in the narrator's method for finding its site, a moment I will discuss in the following section. Through both its stated goals and its unintended consequences, the narrator's project lays out, in sequence and from a subjective angle, several stages along a certain path of aesthetic experience. Far from being a hindrance, the novel's lack of explicit preoccupation with aesthetic experience (so named) lends all the more vitality and validity to its phenomenological insights. The narrative's unstudied approach and relative straightforwardness in this regard—including, for one, a descriptive style that can be called bare, almost minimally structural, in relation to the narrator's subjective experience of and association with things—allow for a reading that can take the narrative voice at more or less face value while avoiding the psychological. The transparency with which the narrative voice details the repeated re-enactments (and their attendant complications) is in stark contrast to the layered complexity of Huysmans or Proust, brought about by their aesthete narrators. This signals both a shift to our contemporary moment as well as a progression along the path of the aesthetic paradox where we are beginning to deviate more recognizably from the work of art proper.

What does this all have to do with repetition? If we return for a moment to Vermeulen's claim about how *Remainder* interacts with trauma theory, the stakes of repetition in the narrative become clearer. According to trauma theory, repeated experiences *are* traumatic, in the sense that the traumatic experience is what is repeated. The repetitions themselves are anything but random, given that they are particular moments seized upon by the narrator as material for re-enactments; however, within these carefully orchestrated re-enactments, there is an irresolvable element of chance or randomness in the particular details, as well as in the narrator's affective response. This is a fact that Matthew Younger, his stockbroker, is at no small pains to convince him in relation to market fluctuations: "there is a small degree of randomness—a capricious element that likes occasionally to buck expectations, throw a spanner in the works" (122). While the seeming randomness of these re-enactments problematizes the very structure of traumatic repetition, at the same time it displaces the trauma to a different level. What is repeated here is not simply the act in general, or each particular scene that the narrator happens upon and decides to restage, but rather repetition itself, insofar as it also depends upon a degree of randomness. Repetition is repeated in its very structure, and furthermore, its consequences are repeated, as the trajectory of each project ends with the narrator confronting the paradox of attempting to repeat an experience whose nature requires that it only ever be impossible to anticipate, thereby necessitating a shift into a new re-enactment. In short, he wants to repeat the experience of surprise in the face of the aesthetic.

Looking only to the apartment re-enactment, we can see several early effects of repetition within a discrete scenario. After the initial stages of the novel, and after the crucial bathroom scene, the apartment project is the main focus up until the midpoint of the novel, when the narrator happens by chance upon the scene that will become the next re-enactment. Until then, he is occupied by endless logistical matters: securing the proper building site for the apartment, hiring actors who are able to convincingly play the roles of his "neighbors," and preparing both the space and the actors for an initial launch of the re-enactment. That this re-enactment centers around an apartment building is no mistake, as the narrator both quite literally *lives in* the apartment, barely leaving it for a while once the system is in place, and *lives in*, or at least attempts to live in or sustain the moment—the atmosphere—that he takes such pains to recreate.

Before setting his first re-enactment into motion, the narrator is misunderstood by those he consults to carry out his vision. He ultimately hires Naz, who will stay with him throughout the novel, but he has bad luck with estate agents who misread his project because they are incapable of approaching it on purely material terms: "'It's not *unusual* features that I'm after,' I tried to explain. 'It's *particular* ones. [...] These are not preferences. [...] These are absolute requirements'" (78). As becomes clear throughout this process and the process of hiring the actors who will play his neighbors, the narrator does not want anybody involved who regards him as an eccentric who they must humor, and certainly not anybody who has ideas of their own.[41]

For him, this negative qualification is the only way to guarantee a minimum of authenticity. And since he is aiming at an experience that depends upon a certain ephemeral, enveloping atmosphere—involving sounds, smells, sights, etc.—it is moreover important that this atmosphere not only feels natural but also *is* natural. Unlike des Esseintes, he does not want artifice. The woman cooking liver must do so simply because it is what she does, as if covering the tracks of her training.[42] This is why he is disappointed when he finds out that the pianist has been playing back recordings of his practicing so that he could go out and perform a concert, or simply to take a break from playing to relax or do other tasks. Upon catching the pianist "red-handed one day, blatantly defrauding me" (156)—that is, after seeing the pianist coming up the stairs while his music is playing two floors above—the narrator is more upset than he is upon finding out that the cats he has placed on the neighboring roof keep falling to their deaths, as this once again is a seam in his project that he must contend with. Even the minor detail that he is hearing recorded music cuts into his experience because it reminds him that it is all a re-enactment. It reminds him that the pianist is simply playing a role, and can be replaced by a recording of his own playing when it is necessary for him to be elsewhere.

If the experience aimed at by the narrator—the experience that accompanies his initial déjà vu—can only be singular and unpredictable, this means first and foremost that it will resist engineering, at least if it is to have the desired effect. This, precisely, is the narrator's problem: he knows that he can materially re-enact a scene (after all, he has the money and other resources to do so). However, he seems to believe that he can in fact achieve the unpredictable feeling that drives the re-enactments by getting the entire scene exactly right, down to the last and most seemingly insignificant detail. For a time, he can; but this dynamic proves to be more complicated than it seems at first glance, and the argument can be made that the feeling that drives the series of re-enactments is eventually eclipsed by the re-enactments themselves. In a 2019 roundtable conversation, McCarthy notes:

> In *Remainder*, he's trying to have these sublime moments of just smelling the smell of liver wafting from another room like Proust and his madeleine [...]. But he can never quite get that moment because his staff are cooking so much liver that all this fat cunks up the vent [...]. Again, the interruption of the formless abject material [...].[43]

It is precisely in this dynamic between the repetitive impulse for aesthetic experience on the one hand and the material fact of the world on the other that we begin to see the aesthetic violence that I have already mentioned.

This violence, which manifests as a paradox faced by the narrator, is also implicated in the addictive nature of his entire endeavor.

Silently zinging with significance

After coming upon a particular "tingling" sensation, the narrator is compelled to recreate it at any cost, whether monetary or otherwise. As the narrative progresses, this feeling becomes increasingly difficult to achieve, which is at least partly why Smith calls it "addictive," and why she notes that "the enactments escalate, in a fascinating direction."[44] Indeed, they escalate exponentially: beginning with the relatively benign (though monumentally wasteful) apartment complex incited by the bathroom scene, the trajectory of re-enactments ends with a bank robbery and a plane hijacking which, though not necessarily part of the plan, the narrator makes happen in pursuit of his overall project. Because this hijacking leaves us quite literally "up in the air" at the end of the text, this escalation does not necessarily correspond to a progression as far as the narrator's relation to his experience is concerned—he is after the same feeling right up to the end, though his understanding of matter does eventually seem to change. This trajectory can be read in terms of addiction, not only because of the arguably addictive nature of the "tingling" that he experiences, which pushes him to further and further heights, but also because the discrete experiences along the course of this trajectory remain in contact with something that does not change. Addiction ties together the threads of memory and repetition in a way that is especially productive for thinking about aesthetic experience.

Of course, one cannot mention addiction in connection with *Remainder* without recalling the novel's many explicit references to drugs. From Greg's initial advice (quoted above) to the narrator to use his money for a cocaine binge; to the narrator's trip home after the bathroom scene, where he sees "younger black guys in big puffy jackets pushing cannabis and crack" (68); to Doctor Trevellain's mention of opioids and their effect on addicts (240), not to mention the setting—in 2003, Coldharbour Lane was named as the most dangerous street in London, notable for its violence and volume of crack cocaine sales—drugs are all over this novel. But, perhaps more problematically due to their social connotations, drugs function in a similar manner to memory in the novel: not quite as a red herring, but as only one site for addiction. Indeed, even the first mention of drugs by Greg is quickly called into question by the narrator, who states that neither he nor Greg "had ever taken cocaine" (38). Without wishing to ignore its social aspects, I will treat addiction in a more structural sense in this section, given the qualified status that it shares with memory in the novel.

Michael W. Clune begins *White Out: The Secret Life of Heroin* by calling addiction "a memory disease," a phrase that recurs time and time again throughout the book.[45] Even the very repetition of this phrase serves Clune's major insight about addiction, which, like *Remainder*, involves a decentering of memory and origin, and Clune's understanding of addiction substantiates my earlier hesitancy to trace the re-enactments back to some "original" memory or experience. As he clarifies:

> The secret is that the power of dope comes from the first time you do it. It's a deep memory disease. People know the first time is important, but mostly they're confused about why. Some think addiction is nostalgia for the first mind-blowing time. They think the addict's problem is wanting something that happened a long time ago to come back. That's not it at all. The addict's problem is that something that happened a long time ago never goes away.[46]

In other words, the addict does not use drugs in order to reclaim some originary experience. The popular narrative of the "first time" is taken to lay the ground for some kind of addict's nostalgia, but Clune argues that this is not the case. Instead, drug use brings the user to a time or place that is and always has been familiar, that always stays the same. Drug use opens up a space for the user to inhabit, while at the same time having no history. This state does not refer back to something else, not even its first emergence. It is a sort of other world that remains new every time, even in its familiarity, with even the first time having a kind of familiarity. In its encounter with addiction, what I have been referring to as an aesthetic paradox opens up onto another level of paradox. If one finds oneself *too* taken with the aesthetic, to a point resembling that of addiction, then one's ability to recognize the aesthetic may become impaired or otherwise endangered; and at the same time, the overload of aesthetic experience can be physically and emotionally hazardous, as we've also seen with des Esseintes.[47] I am not, of course, claiming that aesthetic experience is literally a drug; but if the addict might use in order to reach a certain experience, then there is something addictive about that experience that goes beyond the chemical effects of the drug.

With this minimal understanding of drug use and addiction in mind, it is worth touching on a moment before the apartment is even built, while he is still searching for the building that will become the site of this first re-enactment. This comes just a couple of pages after a dream wherein he has a vision of the building in even greater detail than before, after—crucially— winning at a kind of gambling scenario, again foregrounding chance.[48] Upon waking up, he realizes that he had thus far "been too rational about" finding the building (99). In one paragraph, he gives us a version of the paradox that will continue to occupy him for the rest of the novel.

> I hung up and went back to pondering methods of looking for my building in an irrational manner. I'd thought up so many by midday that I'd lost track of half of them. By early afternoon I'd realized that none of them would work in any case, for the good reason that implementing any one of them methodically would cancel its irrational value. I started to feel both dizzy and frustrated, and decided that the only thing to do was walk out of my flat with no plan at all in mind—just walk around and see what happened. (102)

By foregrounding the problem of the irrational, the text encounters the difficulty inherent in consciously setting out to do something in an irrational or uncalculated manner. The narrator's response to this question is to consider that the irrational will be neutralized by the rational the moment one decides to pursue one's goal too directly, as such directness would imply a kind of system, a formalized process that can be followed reliably and with a certain probability of success. It is only once he decides to seek out the building indirectly, rather than by conducting research with an entire team to find buildings that meet his specifications, that he finds his building.

Unfortunately for him, in what follows the narrator does not seem to heed this lesson. To illustrate this, I will turn to a passage in which he first engages with the apartment re-enactment. This is a much-anticipated moment, both for him and for the narrative, and it can only take place after prolonged and meticulous preparation. When the moment finally comes, the encounter is between the narrator and the "liver lady," an elderly woman whose place in his memory is to be cooking liver on a floor below his, and occasionally taking out her trash as he walks by. A crucial moment in the novel's plot, this experience is replayed more than once after it initially happens because of the narrator's affective response to the scene: it is successful, in that it achieves the feeling he is looking for. What actually happens is fairly simple. The narrator walks out of his apartment and down the stairs to the floor below his, where he finds the liver lady taking out her trash (the timing is orchestrated perfectly so that she comes out of her flat at the very moment that he arrives on her floor). As he walks down the stairs, he remarks upon the new status that is accorded to them in this moment: "I'd walked over this stretch a hundred times before, of course—but it had been different then, just a floor: now it was fired up, silently zinging with significance" (142).

Upon their encounter, the liver lady turns to look at the narrator. The action pauses for a moment, long enough for him to explain the context and history of what comes next:

> We'd spent ages practising this moment. I'd showed her exactly how to stoop: the inclination of the shoulders, the path slowly carved through the air by her right hand as it led the bag round her legs and down to the ground (I'd told her to picture the route supporting arms on old gramophone players take, first across and then down), the way her left hand rested on her lower back above the hip, the middle finger pointing straight at the ground. We'd got all this down to a *t*—but we hadn't succeeded in working out the words she'd say to me. [...] Rather than forcing it—or, worse, just making any old phrase up—I'd decided to let her come up with a phrase. I'd told her not to concoct a sentence in advance, but rather to wait till the moment when I passed her on the staircase in the actual re-enactment—the moment we were in right now—and to voice the words that sprung to mind just then. (143)

In this moment, we see the paradox again: the scene has been practiced for "ages," yet the narrator has enough concern for naturalness that he instructs the liver lady to improvise her line. Touching again on the de Manian irony of *Remainder*, this is where the aesthetic paradox is made most visibly psychological. For de Man, in the face of a doubling or "duplication" that he finds in Baudelaire, irony "is a relationship, within consciousness, between two selves, yet it is not an intersubjective relationship."[49] As becomes clear in his comments on Baudelaire, what is at issue is precisely a consciousness that is split between two aspects: "The ironic language splits the subject into an empirical self that exists in a state of inauthenticity and a self that exists only in the form of a language that asserts the knowledge of this inauthenticity. This does not, however, make it into an authentic language, for to know inauthenticity is not the same as to be authentic."[50] This irony is embodied in the narrator's entire project, where authenticity and surprise are met at every turn with planning, orchestration, re-enactment. This plays out in the present passage along the lines of his preparation for the scene, where rehearsal begets improvisation, and where the highest degree of control is underwritten by contingency. It becomes impossible to tell whether the improvisation afforded to the liver lady exists *within* the re-enactment or not.

Perhaps this inability to judge the status of the improvisation is partly the point. After his much anticipated and quasi-scripted encounter with the liver lady, the narrator has an experience that I would consider to be an aesthetic one:

> For a few seconds I felt weightless—or at least differently weighted: light but dense at the same time. My body seemed to glide fluently and effortlessly through the atmosphere around it—gracefully, slowly, like a dancer through water. It felt very good. (144)

His experience here, a sort of intoxication, is mirrored on the level of reception: it is caught between the importance of his project on the one hand, and its apparent insignificance for any outside viewer or bystander on the other hand. It must also be remembered that this same sort of experience has already repeated, recounted in similar language, a number of times so far in the novel.[51] Materially, the exchange is meaningless—it is simply a man exchanging pleasantries with his elderly neighbor who he meets by chance. For him, though, just like the crack in the bathroom wall, this encounter must be approached according to its own particular force, felt by him alone.

All of this underscores what happens next. As he continues on his way after speaking with the liver lady, his feeling diminishes. "As I reached the third or fourth step of this new flight, though, this feeling dwindled. By the fifth or sixth one it was gone" (144). His feeling of weightlessness is still bound to the workings of time. He immediately goes back and repeats this re-enactment, after which, as he comments: "Again I felt the sense of gliding, of light density. The moment I was in seemed to expand and become a pool—a still, clear pool that swallowed everything up in its calm contentedness. Again the feeling dwindled as I left the zone around her door" (147). Though he further elaborates on this feeling here, giving it a slightly different tone, it diminishes in the same way, and perhaps even more quickly. The gramophone line quoted above is curious in this regard: we might quickly grow tired of a favorite song after repeating it too many times in quick succession. Over time, additionally, the record will begin to wear out, a process that in its own right will diminish most listeners' pleasure in the music.

I evoke Clune's discussion of addiction in connection with *Remainder* in order to show that this feeling—seemingly timeless, or, as the narrator puts it, "weightless" or "differently weighted"—carries with it a disjunction between two realities. On the one hand, the feeling itself is incidental to the actual situation, which allows for a seemingly timeless reprieve from narrative progression; but on the other hand, it depends on this situation to occur in the first place, and therefore *takes time* to happen. In fact, it *takes time* in more than one sense: aesthetic experience occurs in time, but in the narrator's case, preparing for that experience takes time, much to his dismay. Upon being told, for example, that the floor near the liver lady's door will take an hour to prepare for the next run-through, he becomes disappointed: "I was quite upset. I wanted to slip back into it *now, right now*: the pool, the lightness and the gliding" (148, emphasis added).

The addict always remains in the present, even when touching on the timeless. This is the paradox that aesthetic experience, when pushed to its limits, holds in common with addiction. We see this in *Remainder* on a structural level: from the beginning, the narrator's project is a project of repetition aimed at achieving a certain experience. The trajectory of the novel escalates incessantly *while aiming at this very same feeling*. The narrator's recourse to his various re-enactments is driven by his taste for and concern with the lasting nature of his initial experience. The resonance with addiction does not end there, however, as he becomes aware of it himself:

> The realness I was after wasn't something you could just "do" once and then have "got": it was a state, a mode—one that I needed to return to again and again and again. Opioids, Trevellain had said: endogenous opioids. A drug addict doesn't stop to ask himself: *Did it work?* He just wants more—bigger doses, more often: more. (240)

If *White Out* is an account of coming to terms with the mechanism of addiction, *Remainder* is an account of following addiction (not to mention de Manian irony) to its endpoint—which, of course, only leads the narrator deeper into it—even though its workings are repeatedly made clear each time new obstacles are introduced.

What emerges in this reading is that the narrator's intense feeling gives rise to the desire for more of itself, not unlike free play in the Kantian beautiful, but with Schopenhauer's genius in mind. The narrator seeks out further such experiences, doggedly confined to the literal particulars of the moments in which he has this feeling, hence the re-enactments. Over time, each re-enactment loses its ability to surprise him, and there are diminished returns as far as his feeling is concerned. This does not, however, mean that something unanticipated cannot happen *during* a re-enactment, or that matter cannot intervene. McCarthy writes that J. G. Ballard's *Crash*, in the moment when Vaughan botches a planned crash, participates in "something close to this sudden intercession of the catastrophic real," "an *event* that would involve the violent rupture of the very form and procedure of the work itself."[52] A similar irruption occurs late in *Remainder*, during the bank heist "re-enactment," in quotations because they have decided to do the re-enactment in an actual bank, where only the robbers are actors—effectively meaning that it is a true bank robbery. At a point where one of the robbers is supposed to stumble on a kink in the carpet, he trips because the actual bank's carpet does not have a kink, as the rehearsal bank does. As he falls, he knocks over another robber, whose gun goes off, killing a third robber. It is significant, to say the least, that this "sudden intercession of the catastrophic real" occurs when a re-enactment (a performance) coincides, in so radical and literal a way, with the real (the authentic). By the end of the novel, memory is revealed as ever-present throughout, but not in the sense of discrete memories that are on the verge of being recaptured. Instead, what the narrator remembers—in fact, cannot stop remembering, to the detriment of everyone around him—is the feeling that makes him feel so alive.

After this bank robbery, the escape plan is executed: a flight away on a private jet. At this point, seemingly as a result of the robbery, it seems that the narrator finally realizes the importance of accident and remainders ("matter's what makes us alive" (304)), and he is in high spirits, experiencing a sort of aesthetically induced mania. He has gone through to the other side of his frustration with matter, and finds that matter is what surprised him in the first place. In this final stretch of the novel, the plane is turned around multiple times: back to the airport, then back out, then back again, until the narrator essentially hijacks it. In response to a question about his desired destination, he says: "Nowhere. Just keep doing this. […] Turning back, then turning out. Then turning back again. The way we're doing it right now" (307). The novel ends in suspension, dictated by the narrator in his serene state, circular not only in terms of the flight pattern but also narratively: eventually running out of fuel, we imagine that the plane will fall, perhaps on somebody just like him, perhaps inaugurating another narrative (or perhaps none at all).

In these last few pages, one line in particular serves as a callback to the beginning of the novel, as well as a charged symbolic gesture. After the plane turns back toward its departure point, and then back out again, the text reads: "Our trail would be visible from the ground: an eight, plus that first bit where we'd first set off—fainter, drifted to the side by now, discarded, recidual, a remainder" (306). This eight-plus-remainder brings to mind the narrator's question early in the novel about the sum of his settlement, though in that case, it was regarded more distastefully: "The eight was perfect, neat: a curved figure infinitely turning back into itself. But then the half. Why had they added the half? It seemed to me so messy, this half: a leftover fragment, a shard of detritus" (8). It is also the figure eight, the symbol for infinity, seeming to signal that the narrative has come full circle; he has gone back to matter. But perhaps it also tells us something about the unchangingness of the feeling he is after.

This spectacle of nature's defilement

To end this chapter, I will turn to McCarthy's 2015 novel *Satin Island*. My purpose for doing so is first to position it as a sort of response to *Remainder*, and second to provide a transition between McCarthy and Cusk's *Outline* trilogy. The concerns of *Satin Island* are similar to those of *Remainder*, though its narrator, its narrative style, and its relationship to irony are quite different. This time, the narrator U. is a corporate anthropologist:

> What do I do? I am an anthropologist. Structures of kinship; systems of exchange, barter and gift; symbolic operations lurking on the flipside of the habitual and the banal: identifying these, prising them out and holding them up, kicking and wriggling, to the light—that's my racket.[53]

Unlike the narrator of *Remainder*, U. is a writer, a fact that is not without its significance in the aesthetic tenor of the novel. Written in short numbered sections, *Satin Island* details U.'s endeavor to write a "Great Report," a sort of anthropology of the contemporary: "The Document [...] the Book. The First and Last Word on our age" (61). He is tasked with a project of research that, while not "creative" per se, at least nominally involves writing and the reflection required to produce a text.

In certain key ways, U. proves himself much more perceptive than our previous narrator. As such, the narrative involves more self-questioning than *Remainder*, and the paradigm has shifted, from one novel to the other, from experience to knowledge. In particular, U. thinks about how knowledge is created, recorded, and disseminated, though not without a degree of cynicism:

> What does an anthropologist working for a business actually *do*? We purvey cultural insight. What does that mean? It means that we unpick the fibre of a culture (ours), its weft and warp—the situations it throws up, the beliefs that underpin and nourish it—and let a client in on how they can best get traction on this fibre so that they can introduce into the weave their own fine, silken thread, strategically embroider or detail it with a mini-narrative (a convoluted way of saying: sell their product). (23)

Importantly, narrative is thematized in the novel quite explicitly as a problem. Narrative, U. points out, is always *shaped*, meaning that it always carries the mark of its author. His job as a corporate anthropologist is therefore to reveal the workings of narrative in order to better instruct his clients as to how they might narrativize and sell their products. This is simple enough, but he encounters a real problem—the problem that will become the novel's overall theme—when he is asked to write this Great Report. Who is an anthropology of the contemporary *for*? What should it include? What are its boundaries? How can it be used? How, in the first place, can it be written—that is, how would its author need to be positioned in order to write it? This shaping of narrative allows us to once again see how violence is operative in McCarthy's novels. To author a Great Report is also to shape (by force, if necessary) a massive narrative or set of narratives, to describe any number of spaces, patterns, and movements.

But most the relevant aspect of *Satin Island* is its Nietzschean undercurrent, which comes to fruition by the end of the novel, therefore highlighting its presence already at the beginning. The novel begins in Turin, where Nietzsche allegedly went mad. More precisely, as the narrator notes: "One evening, a few years ago, I found myself stuck in Turin. Not in the city, but the airport: Torino-Caselle" (4). The early fragments dealing with his time in this airport callback to *Remainder* (and, indeed, to an obsession of McCarthy's more generally): that of the replay. In fact, the beginning of the novel recalls the suspenseful ending of *Remainder* itself: "What was causing the delay was a rogue aeroplane, some kind of private jet, which, ignoring all instructions, was flying in idiosyncratic patterns over Southern England and the Channel" (4)—echoing the narrator's instructions to continue making figure eights up in the air at the end of *Remainder*. As U. sits in the airport waiting out this delay, he occupies himself by watching the television monitors near him. He becomes especially fascinated by footage of an oil spill that plays in a repeating loop:

> aerial shots of a stricken offshore platform around which a large, dark waterflower was blooming; white-feathered sea birds, filmed from both air and ground, milling around on pristine, snowy shorelines, unaware of the black tide inching its way towards them; and, villain of the piece, shot by an underwater robot, a broken pipe gushing its endless load into the ocean. (6–7)

His attention to the spill reveals a particular aesthetic attitude toward the world, one that is different from that of *Remainder*'s narrator, at least for most of the novel. This interest is aesthetic in the sense that his description highlights the oil spill with poetic language, in contrast to the bareness of the re-enactor, whose only concern is for eliciting an experience through mechanical or material reproduction. Even in this brief passage, U. seems alert to the actual aesthetic properties of matter, and the shift in descriptive method marks a major departure from *Remainder*.

U. has a brief exchange with a neighbor in the airport, who notices him watching the oil spill footage: "The man sitting beside me, noticing the rapt attention I was paying these pictures, tried at one point to spark up a conversation. Tutting disapprovingly in their direction, he opined that it was a tragedy. That was the word he used, of course: *tragedy*—like a TV pundit" (11). After U. responds by simply reciting the etymology of the word "tragedy" as deriving "from the ancient Greek custom of driving out a sheep, or *tragos*— usually a black one—in a bid to expiate a city's crimes" (11), this neighbor, not being met with the agreement that he so clearly expected, abruptly leaves. This brief moment reveals U.'s sensitivity to the misuse of and moralizing charge of the term, which again puts him on the side of Nietzsche. In the fifth section of *The Birth of Tragedy*, Nietzsche famously declares that "it is only as an *aesthetic phenomenon* that existence and the world are eternally *justified*."[54] Far from advocating for a light-hearted engagement with life, this must be understood in a strict sense as a rigorous endeavor that makes heavy demands of the subject. To take the world merely aesthetically means, first of all, to put oneself at risk of being shunned by one's fellow man, who may subscribe to a more "acceptable" or "proper" outlook. In a more direct sense, however, it could also entail putting oneself at risk of actual bodily harm, since at bottom it means accepting the ultimate indifference of the world, which offers no guarantees.

These two levels converge in a later passage in *Satin Island*. Having only received polite applause after presenting a paper about what he calls "Present-Tense Anthropology™" at a conference whose theme is "The Contemporary" (99–101), the narrator begins fantasizing about the talk that he *would have presented*, that he *would like to have presented*, instead. These fantasies increasingly occupy his time: "I spent most of the next week honing in my head the presentation that I *should* have given back in Frankfurt" (110). As it turns out, the oil spill returns in this hypothetical talk, becoming its main focus. Instead of decrying oil spills and denouncing the corporations responsible, he makes a subtle, Nietzschean, and (of course) controversial argument *in favor of* oil spills:

> It's an improvement. Oil has more consistency than water: it is denser, more substantial—and thus brings the latter into its own more fully, expressing the sea's splendour in a manner more articulate, more something. In a manner more poetic. No, more lyrical: the sea's splendour in a manner far more lyrical than that in which the original ever did. (113)

Again, we see his attention to matter in its own aesthetic being, and how a war of different matters might transform the world in a poetic way, rather than give us panic. For U., even "tar-drenched birds who float bewilderedly in blackened rock-pools" become "infused with all the pathos and nobility of tragic heroes. Living Pompeiians! Victims of the oil Gorgon! They, too, are improved [...] transformed into monumental versions of themselves, superior by the same token as statues are bigger, better versions of historic people" (114–115). Once more, the consequences of an oil spill are treated poetically here, against the grain of public opinion. U. imagines a heckler in the audience,

> bemoaning [...] this spectacle of nature's defilement; denouncing my aestheticizing of it. Me? I'd ask him, glancing exaggeratedly around and behind me for effect; *I'm* 'aestheticizing' it? Gentlemen, I'd reason, opening my arms up to my serried ranks of allies; was it not *he* who first used the term *tragedy*? (115)

This final remark about tragedy, of course, refers back to U.'s neighbor at the Turin airport. Besides touching on the unpopularity of his opinion, this allows U. to articulate the hypocrisy of his heckler. This hypocrisy hinges not on the employment of the term *tragedy*, but rather on its different valences for the respective speakers. When U.'s neighbor in the airport and his imagined heckler refer to the oil spill as a tragedy, it is an appeal to U. for moral agreement. What is asked of U. is to agree that this oil spill, because of the damage it causes, is *bad*, and that those held responsible should be condemned and held accountable. Furthermore, it is an injunction to not find anything beautiful, poetic, lyrical in the event—this would be heresy. But when U. states that the oil-slathered birds are "infused with all the pathos and nobility of tragic heroes," he is pointing out the creative thrust of the world that can be detected in even a destructive phenomenon such as an oil spill. As Robert R. Williams writes, for Nietzsche "tragedy means that in spite of its horrors and terrors, existence is nevertheless good. If tragedy reflects a certain pessimism, it is a pessimism of strength in which life rejoices at its own creativity."[55] In short, this scene is properly tragic for its beauty, for the fact that there can be beauty in the face of such horrors. It is a mistake, U. thinks, to employ ideas of tragedy only to sanitize the world of what is natural and proper to it.[56]

But how exactly does *Satin Island* respond to *Remainder*, if indeed it does? I would argue that on the aesthetic level—insofar as each novel concerns the problem of aesthetic experience—*Satin Island*, while not necessarily offering clear and definitive answers, does clarify or at least deepen some of the problems raised by *Remainder*. Since U., as a writer, is arguably one further degree removed, and since his take on the world is more reflective, he embraces the messiness of matter, which is where he finds its aesthetic dimension, whereas the narrator of *Remainder* is for the most part allergic to it, at least until the end of the novel. Relatedly, as Cynthia Quarrie writes, *Satin Island* is "full of increasingly recursive digressions about the impossibility of fully apprehending the present."[57] The narrator has some critical distance, but he is sufficiently involved in the world such that irony is still in play.

In short, the shift between the two novels reveals different dimensions of McCarthy's attunement to aesthetic experience as an issue that is always potentially hazardous, whether personally or on a larger ecological scale. As a gesture toward the next chapter, I will end by once again quoting Quarrie, who writes with reference to *Satin Island*: "The narrative arc, such as it is, follows U. as he tries to square one fantasy after another about the meaningfulness of his work and writing against his growing shameful consciousness that he is not, and never has been, the hero of his own narrative."[58] In the context of Quarrie's reading, we are meant to take U.'s not being a hero as a failure on his part, as something he is struggling against accepting. But in my mind, it is actually a gain—personally for him, narratively for the novel, and theoretically for us—rather than a point of shame. In contrast to the narrator of *Remainder* (who, recall, Serpell names as "the sole audience member" of his re-enactments), the mediating factor of writing affords U. the distance required to reflect upon his project in a way that destabilizes the usual boundary between subject and object. In a moral sense, he does not need to be a hero; he is content with being the antihero who stands up and declares an oil spill poetic. In a narrative sense, even if he is the novel's hero, he is constantly decentered—but this spurs him on to continue writing and reflecting about experience and the world around him. And through this writing we are afforded a different view on the way that aesthetic experience depends on a certain subjective decentering, at least as far as our will and intentions are concerned. A similar dynamic is at work in Rachel Cusk's *Outline* trilogy, where the elusive narrator is a writer who recounts several conversations where her interlocutors describe a similar distancing, a loss of faith in the authority of narrative, and therefore the possibility of there being no hero at all.

End Notes

1 McCarthy, *Typewriters, Bombs, Jellyfish: Essays*, 188.
2 McCarthy, "My Death in Eleven Postulations," 23.
3 Ibid., 24.
4 "Out in the warm March sunlight, Serge totters with his blocks towards a wooden trolley. It's a small trolley with a large handlebar at one end: it's been his for a year now, ever since he started walking. He stoops over it and, loosening the cradle of his left arm, lets the blocks fall into it. Grabbing the handle with both hands, he starts

pushing the trolley along the gravel footpath. To his right, women are moving among mulberry trees, climbing and descending ladders, carrying baskets to and from the spinning houses. One of them stops and waves at him but he ignores her, pushing on. To his left is the wall between the Mulberry Orchard and the Maze Garden; coming to the doorway in this, he steers his trolley through and pushes it into the corridor formed by the paving laid into the lawn. When the corridor forks, cutting at right angles in opposite directions, he chooses a branch and follows it until, after performing several more right-angled turns and forking twice more, it comes to a dead end. He doubles back to the last fork, advances down another branch and follows it until it, too, runs out—at which point he doubles two forks back and takes a new branch. There's no need to stick to the paved section—the maze is wall-less, two-dimensional as the figures on the blocks, and the grass is short and wouldn't slow his trolley down—but he continues working his way along the abruptly turning corridors, held by their pattern, until they deliver him back out, through the same doorway, to the footpath once more." McCarthy, *C*, 28.

5 Early in *Remainder*, the mirror relationship of the physical and theoretical or linguistic is announced, when the narrator refers to "my lawyer and the parties, institutions, organizations" as "*bodies*" (4, emphasis in original).

6 See McCarthy, *Typewriters, Bombs, Jellyfish*, 183, 188.

7 In terms of Proust, I am referring here in particular to the trajectory of Swann's engagement with the Vinteuil sonata. At first occasioning a rapturous experience, described by way of elaborate, almost excessive metaphor, this piece of music eventually becomes—as I have mentioned in the previous chapter—*domesticated*, with Odette learning and playing it for him in their home. It is reduced to "the passage in Vinteuil's sonata that contained the little phrase of which Swann *had been so fond*" (1: 570, emphasis added). James Grieve, in his more recent translation, has perhaps more strikingly rendered this phrase as "the part of the Vinteuil sonata with the little phrase that Swann *had once loved so much*" (*In the Shadow of Young Girls in Flower*, 103, emphasis added). Either way, what is at issue is the shift in Swann's relation to the sonata. It has become for him, over time, something of a museum piece in Adorno's sense, and therefore loses its ability to surprise him as it once did.

8 Zadie Smith, "Two Paths for the Novel."

9 Ibid.

10 A further and perhaps ironic or metatextual twist to all of this arises when we get the actual terms of the settlement, from his lawyer: "You can't discuss, in any public or recordable format, the nature and/or details of the incident" (12). A novel is, of course, a public format, so (if we can be permitted to collapse for a moment the distance between McCarthy and his narrator) the question that remains is whether or not the narrator really discloses "the nature and/or details of the incident."

11 Pieter Vermeulen, "The Critique of Trauma and the Afterlife of the Novel in Tom McCarthy's *Remainder*," 562.

12 Cathy Caruth, *Unclaimed Experience: Trauma, Narrative, and History*, 2–3.

13 Ibid., 4.

14 Wojciech Drag, "Compulsion to Re-enact: Trauma and Nostalgia in Tom McCarthy's *Remainder*," 378.

15 Vermeulen, "The Critique of Trauma," 562.

16 The second paragraph of the novel, following the statement that the narrator "can say very little" about the accident, reads: "It's not that I'm being shy. It's just that—well,

or one, I don't even remember the event. It's a blank: a white slate, a black hole. I have vague images, half-impressions: of being, or having been—or, more precisely, being *about* to be—hit; blue light; railings; lights of other colours; being held above some kind of tray or bed. But who's to say that these are genuine memories? Who's to say my traumatized mind didn't just make them up, or pull them out from somewhere else, some other slot, and stick them there to plug the gap—the crater—that the accident had blown? Minds are versatile and wily things. Real chancers" (3). It is worth quickly noting two things about this paragraph. First, the narrator's self-contradictory tendencies, which are announced here already: he isn't just being shy but in fact can't remember; but then he provides us with a series of impressions (which he then once more calls into question via the logic of trauma). Second, his use of the slang term "chancers" to describe minds, a term that denotes an opportunistic character operating manipulatively and in bad faith which, of course, stems from the term "chance." Chance becomes important for his eventual re-enactments, but it is also already a factor in the accident itself, in a moment whose mention of roulette recalls the opening of *La Peau de chagrin*: "I was hit because I was standing where I was and not somewhere else—standing on grass, exposed, just like a counter on a roulette table's green velvet grid, on a single number, waiting . . ." (63).

17 Sebastian Groes, "'An Eternal Detour': Reality Hunger, Post-Proustian Memory and the Late Modern Self in Tom McCarthy's Remainder," 150.
18 Ibid., 152.
19 Ibid., 156.
20 Ibid., 154.
21 Sydney Miller, "Intentional Fallacies: (Re)enacting the Accidental in Tom McCarthy's *Remainder*," 635.
22 Deleuze, *Difference and Repetition*, 25.
23 By this, I mean the overrepresentation of the madeleine passage and other instances of involuntary memory in the corpus of critical works on Proust, an overrepresentation that on the one hand is warranted, given the passage's novelty and narrative justification, but on the other hand obscures other salient moments of aesthetic experience that do not necessarily depend on involuntary memory, or on memory at all, but perhaps instead simply on the involuntary (e.g., on weather, atmosphere, etc.). Groes's comparison between *À la recherche du temps perdu* and *Remainder* is intriguing on this point, especially given the troubled status of memory in each text.
24 Returning again to a moment of resonance in *Difference and Repetition*, Deleuze, writing about art in its modern situation, states: "L'oeuvre se développe à partir, autour d'une fêlure qu'elle ne vient jamais combler" (*Différence et répétition*, 252). Paul Patton translates this as "Works are developed around or on the basis of a fracture that they never succeed in filling" (195), but we can also hear in *fêlure* "crack." In terms of *Remainder*, the crack that is the origin of the narrator's entire "work" cannot with any certainty be traced to another moment in the past. Its origin cannot be filled in, and it stands as a break, a fracture that sets into motion an entire irreversible enterprise.
25 As an aside, to highlight in advance what I will argue in what follows, just a few pages earlier the novel reads: "I remember feeling dizzy. Things I don't understand make me feel dizzy" (6). This, just the first of many instances in *Remainder* of becoming dizzy, is in reference to a call from the narrator's lawyer, Marc Daubenay, that ultimately brings the news that he has won his settlement. But the uncertainty is

much more basic and revolves around verbal communication: Daubenay's secretary says "Putting you through"—as in, patching one phone line in to another—and the narrator is unsure who is being patched in, whether it is him or Daubenay. Though the end result is the same, and the two men will be connected in either case, it is of note that this uncertainty, this "trivial distinction," causes a feeling of dizziness, the very feeling that is associated with wonder in Plato's *Theaetetus*. See Plato, *The Being of the Beautiful*, 155c9-11: "Yes indeed, by the gods, Socrates, I wonder exceedingly as to why (what) in the world these things are, and sometimes in looking at them I truly get dizzy."

26 Beyond the ambiguity surrounding the object of memory, and whether or not memory properly has an object, a third option might be considered. This is the possibility that what is being remembered is, in a way, *the passage itself*, in a sort of *mise en abyme*. Perhaps what is being remembered is the structure of the passage, and thus of memory.

27 This plays out when the narrator compares himself to Robert De Niro: "Even before the accident, if I'd been walking down the street just like De Niro, smoking a cigarette like him, and even if it had lit first try, I'd still be thinking: *Here I am, walking down the street, smoking a cigarette, like someone in a film.* See? Second-hand. The people in the films aren't thinking that. They're just doing their thing, real, not thinking anything" (24–25). The lesson, as I'll discuss further below, is deeper than a naïve belief in films as directly mirroring reality; it extends even to the actual experiences of the actors themselves, while filming. See also McCarthy and Simon Critchley, "Joint Statement on Inauthenticity," in *The Mattering of Matter*, 220–234.

28 The narrator's disdain for this process must be noted, as it directly reflects the novel's concern with matter, control, remainders: "then you take a carrot—they bring you a fucking carrot, gnarled, dirty and irregular in ways your imaginary carrot never was, and they stick it in your hands—and you know, you just know as soon as you see the bastard thing that it's not going to work" (20). On the next page, after detailing his saga with the carrot: "I hate carrots now. I still can't eat them to this day" (21). This portends his eventual disdain for another kind of undesirable matter, which might be deemed the social remainder, seen most explicitly in some of the narrator's comments about homeless people.

29 As he remarks to his friend Greg, who notes that De Niro's character is "a loser" and "messes everything up for all the other characters," "It's not about being cool [...]. It's about just being. De Niro was just being" (23–24). The narrator disregards the fact that De Niro is *acting*, that he has an *audience*—De Niro, in his mind, is just *being*. "Being" not even in the sense of *not acting*, but in the stronger sense of *being authentic*. But the context—De Niro's status as an actor in a film—raises a problem here. The narrator bases his vision of authenticity on an acted (and scripted) performance in a film. All of this will have important consequences for the narrator's development throughout the novel.

30 In *A Thousand Plateaus*, Deleuze and Guattari elaborate on De Niro's ability to *become* his role: "The actor Robert De Niro walks 'like' a crab in a certain film sequence; but, he says, it is not a question of his imitating a crab; it is a question of making something that has to do with the crab enter into composition with the image, with the speed of the image" (274). There is a certain passivity inherent in the process of becoming what one is not—say, a crab, or a gangster in a 1970s crime film—that involves untold hours of active preparation and effort. For an exemplary account of such preparation, see Constantin Stanislavski's *An Actor Prepares*.

31 Deleuze, *Difference and Repetition*, 145. It is worth noting that, though this remark does not explicitly evoke Proust, Deleuze says something similar in *Proust and Signs*: "What forces us to think is the sign. The sign is the object of an encounter, but it is precisely the contingency of the encounter that guarantees the necessity of what it leads us to think. The act of thinking does not proceed from a simple natural possibility; on the contrary, it is the only true creation" (97). Gasché, referring to both of these passages, writes that "[t]he chance encounter with a sign [...] forces thought upon us. Only because the thought thus provoked is the result of a violence or an encounter by which one is caught off guard is it a thought that, rather than being arbitrary, has genuine necessity" (*The Honor of Thinking*, 265).
32 C. Namwali Serpell, *Seven Modes of Uncertainty*, 230.
33 Ibid., 231.
34 Kant, *Critique of the Power of Judgment*, 115, emphasis added.
35 Julia Jordan, *Late Modernism and the Avant-Garde British Novel: Oblique Strategies*, 211.
36 An exhaustive discussion of these tendencies is beyond the scope of this chapter, but one other instance is worth noting: the narrator's encounter with a homeless man in chapter 3. The chapter ends with the revelation that the particular encounter was imagined, and that the (actual) homeless people on the street before him have nothing to teach him. It is curious that this insight is gained only after an imaginary dinner and conversation wherein the narrator attempts to discuss Robert De Niro; see 55–60.
37 Seb Franklin, "*Repetition*; *Reticulum*; Remainder," 164–165.
38 Serpell, *Seven Modes of Uncertainty*, 236, emphasis added.
39 Ibid., 238.
40 Ibid., 247.
41 In his initial conversation with Naz about the logistics of the apartment building, the narrator has trouble deciding how to consider those who will stand in for "neighbors": "All the ... performers—no, not performers: that's not the right word ... the participants, the ... staff ..." (88). This indicates an indecisiveness about whether they will actually be his neighbors, or will merely be standing in for them. A few pages later, he refers to them as follows: "Staff. Participants. Re-enactors" (90). Bemoaning difficulties with his employees some pages later, the narrator states: "The thickest groups by far were actors and interior designers. Morons, both" (114). A drama student approaches him, unaware that he is precisely the kind of "actor"—too studied, too eager to work—who turns the narrator off. A possible choice for the position of motorcycle enthusiast is prepared to perform "some piece of modern theatre by Samuel Beckett" (117). He does not get the job either.
42 She is crucial to the project mainly because he "remembers" smelling the liver emanating up to his floor. As a side note, once she begins cooking liver in the re-enactment apartment for the first time, the narrator reports that it smells off—"A bit like cordite" (132). This smell would be associated with the firing of a gun—another sign of violence—though it is somewhat anachronistic, as cordite would not have been used around the period of the narrative (and the narrator does not at this point have any history with guns, at least to the reader's knowledge).
43 McCarthy, *Tom McCarthy, Elvia Wilk: Just Fucking Weird*, YouTube, HKW—Haus der Kulturen der Welt, April 29, 2019, https://www.youtube.com/watch?v=7e0T8nclqQY&t=3203s, 50:52-51:25.

44 Smith, "Two Paths for the Novel." This "fascinating direction," for Smith, includes and is complicated by one particular re-enactment where "the Re-enactor himself assumes the role of the 'dead black man' (who is everywhere referred to like this). His tingling goes off the charts. It's so good, he begins to fall into trances. [...] Why is the closest thing to epiphany a dead black man? [...] If your project is to rid the self of its sacredness, to flatten selfhood out, it's simply philosophical hypocrisy to let any selves escape, whatever color they may be." Smith's point is well-taken, and certainly complicates any reading of the novel that attempts to deal with the overall vision of its narrator—not to mention his addictive personality.
45 Michael W. Clune, *White Out: The Secret Life of Heroin*, 1.
46 Ibid., 5.
47 For Schopenhauer, the genius is "constantly on the look-out for new objects that would be worth considering" (*The World as Will and Representation*, Vol. 1, 209)—that is, he is always seeking out new encounters with aesthetic objects and the realm of the aesthetic. Aesthetic contemplation is not only a state of pleasure, but at the same time a respite from suffering: "Whenever nature suddenly rises to meet our gaze, it almost always succeeds, if only for a few moments, in snatching us away from subjectivity, from our slavery to the will, and transporting us into the state of pure cognition. [...] [A]t the moment when, torn free from willing, we surrender ourselves to pure, will-less cognition, we enter into another world" (221). Schopenhauer's picture of the genius articulates the difficulty faced by any aesthetic subject, whereby aesthetic experience demands the absence of habit, yet also threatens a thirst for *more* of the aesthetic, a thirst that threatens to be folded into another order of habit altogether. This, I argue, is the problem faced by and articulated by the narrator of *Remainder*.
48 "My building was in there, being carried along somewhere in the complex interlacings. I caught glimpses of it as it slipped behind another building and was whisked away again to reappear somewhere else. It would show itself to me then slip away again. The belts were like magicians' fingers shuffling cards: they were shuffling the city, flashing my card, my building, at me and then burying it in the deck again. They were challenging me to shout 'Stop!' at the exact moment it was showing: if I could do that, I'd win. That was the deal" (98).
49 Paul de Man, *Blindness and Insight*, 212.
50 Ibid., 214.
51 For one example that resonates with the simplicity of Huysmans's language when describing des Esseintes's pleasure, we find these lines as McCarthy's narrator is going to canvas for the building he eventually uses for the apartment re-enactment: "I stopped for a moment in the street and felt a light breeze moving round my face. I turned the palms of my hands outwards and felt a tingling creeping up the right side of my body. It was good" (96). In the context of the tingling feeling, and the messianic or beggarly outstretched palms, this "good" feels almost too straightforward, as if he is selling the experience short, much like when we hear of des Esseintes feeling "perfectly happy" about his gilded and bejeweled tortoise.
52 McCarthy, *Typewriters, Bombs, Jellyfish*, 68.
53 McCarthy, *Satin Island*, 14. The rest of the parenthetical citations in this chapter will refer to this novel.
54 Nietzsche, *The Birth of Tragedy and The Case of Wagner*, 52. Joakim Wrethed also cites this passage in his reading of *Satin Island*, but his take ultimately hinges on a more or less eco-critical reading of the novel by way of phenomenology, and partly works

against its Nietzschean thrust. See Wrethed, "The Oil-Flower Unfurling its Petals: The Phenomenological Aesthetics of Tom McCarthy's *Satin Island*."
55 Robert R. Williams, *Tragedy, Recognition, and the Death of God: Studies in Hegel and Nietzsche*, 148.
56 Writing of tragedy's inevitability, its translation into philosophy, and our contemporary difficulty nonetheless in dealing with it theoretically, Kalliopi Nikolopoulou notes that "what is *tragic* in tragedy has nothing to do with justification or with reason's capacity for correction: the tragic flaw is ontological in its nature— not sociological or psychological—and it remains thus, regardless of our theoretical views of it" (*Tragically Speaking: On the Use and Abuse of Theory for Life*, xx). Some pages later, she has this to say about tragedy, which could very well help make a case for understanding McCarthy's narrators as tragic figures: "True enough, repetition is not only sameness but difference as well: nothing recurs exactly the same way. Time takes care of that, and we do not step in the same river twice. However, difference does not eliminate the persistence of that something that keeps reappearing, returning, piercing through" (xliii).
57 Cynthia Quarrie, "Sinking, Shrinking, *Satin Island*: Tom McCarthy, the British Novel, and the Materiality of Shame," 157.
58 Ibid.

Chapter 4

DISCONNECTED MOMENTS IN RACHEL CUSK'S *OUTLINE* TRILOGY

This chapter will examine the writing of Rachel Cusk to further develop the possibility that there does not have to be a hero in a narrative, and the corresponding idea that one might not even be the hero of one's own narrative. Narrative, beyond its necessary involvement in her work as a writer, is a large thematic preoccupation *within* Cusk's writing. Her novels and essays are strewn with various meditations on the relationship between narrative and life, oftentimes in connection with a specific feeling that will be my focus in this chapter: an experience of intensity that simultaneously seems disconnected from any larger sense of narrative, paired with an awareness of this disconnection. It is not only her novels themselves that are aware of this feeling, but also the characters, who tend to remark upon it, whether in speech or internal monologues. Narrative and narration are thus vital problems for Cusk, and this feeling of disconnection is at play in many passages that describe experiences that can be deemed aesthetic due to their affective valence and their resonance with such experiences in the novels discussed in previous chapters.

The problem of narrative surfaces in various ways throughout Cusk's entire body of work. Beginning on the more recent end with her 2021 novel *Second Place*, we find such phrases as "the telling comes after the fact," and "no story to life, no personal meaning beyond the meaning of any given moment."[1] *Second Place* is written as a series of letters addressed to "Jeffers"—the novel's stand-in for Robinson Jeffers, close friend of Mabel Dodge Luhan, whose letters regarding her relationship with D. H. Lawrence in *Lorenzo in Taos* provide a rich and complex backdrop of inspiration for Cusk here—and the above phrases reveal a narrative voice aware of its attempts to make sense of events at the same time as it narrates them. Moving to one of her earlier and more conventional novels, *The Temporary* (1995), a mundane workplace exchange about the previous weekend yields the following: "She would ask him questions with apparently no memory of repetition or rebuff, retaining nevertheless the few blunt details he was obliged to divulge about his activities outside the office and stringing together a little narrative from them of which it pained Ralph to be the subject."[2] In this case, as in certain others, narrative is a chore or even an embarrassment for Cusk's characters: not only do they often prefer not to be the heroes of their own stories, but they take pains to avoid it, to remain anonymous. And yet, they continue to speak, to write, to narrate.

Even her first-person essayistic writing is concerned with narrative and the possibility of telling a coherent story. About an experience she has had browsing for and trying on clothes in a shop, for instance, Cusk writes, "I have stood in such boxlike spaces before, alone with myself, and these moments seem connected to one another in a way I can't quite specify."[3] This 2017 essay, entitled "On Rudeness," focuses on the socially determined nature of storytelling and the unpredictability of the events that provide the basis for a story in the first place. While the point of this particular vignette lies in Cusk's retelling of it, later, to an acquaintance who misunderstands her point, what is interesting here is Cusk's sense of awareness of a peculiar feeling before any storytelling has occurred on her part: "It is as though life is a board game, and here is the starting point to which I keep finding myself unexpectedly returned."[4] Narrative is not only a chore; it is a repetitive necessity that we cannot seem to escape, no matter how much we may want to. Perhaps what is at stake across these cases is not necessarily an escape from narrative, but rather a certain relation to it.

All of these examples recall, in McCarthy's *Satin Island*, U.'s concern with the act of shaping narratives, and how the truth and status of a given narrative cannot be taken for granted at any stage of its formation. The potential connections, or disconnections, between different moments—both in a narrative and in life—will emerge as a major concern in Cusk's *Outline* trilogy, beginning with an echo of U.'s inability to assume the position of hero in his own narrative. My purpose in briefly citing these texts from various points in Cusk's career is to emphasize that narrative is a problem across Cusk's oeuvre, being usually treated with curiosity or even skepticism, whether this manifests as an acknowledgment of the arbitrary nature of any narrative that might emerge or an outright rejection of narrative. Furthermore, this concern with narrative is not incidental but indeed seems integral to her understanding of writing, whether in the form of fiction or non-fiction.

The pages that follow will mainly consist of close readings of passages selected from the three novels that make up Cusk's recent *Outline* trilogy: *Outline* (2014), *Transit* (2016), and *Kudos* (2018). While the context and subject matter differ from passage to passage, they are nevertheless united by virtue of placing narrative into question, especially insofar as it relates both to moments from everyday life and to the larger trajectory of life on the one hand, and of various characters' lives on the other. Keeping with the thematic designation of the previous chapters, I will discuss these passages under the sign of *disconnected moments* of the aesthetic. As will become clear, these moments are disconnected from a larger sense of narrative or plot, especially as the life of each respective speaker is concerned. They not only feel disconnected from a larger story, but also from other moments within any such story. Of course, they are moments in a written narrative. And given that much of the trilogy consists of stories *told* to the narrator Faye, they are portions of stories *within* the novels, which are oriented mainly around Faye's travels for work (in particular, for teaching writing, giving interviews, and speaking at author events). This tension only highlights the intensity of the sentiment of feeling disconnected or alienated from a narrative that would make sense of, or give value to, what is at bottom a discrete aesthetic experience. Finally, these moments gain significance by virtue of the fact that they all involve writers.

To further establish a major point of resonance between Cusk and McCarthy at the outset, I will turn briefly to a passage involving the issue of a curated repetition or re-enactment. At one moment in *Outline*, the writer Faye (who narrates the entire trilogy) is speaking with her friend and fellow writer Paniotis. After she asks about his writing, he explains that he has become inspired by the prospect of writing about his childhood, leading him to recount an anecdote he had read that concerns behavior resembling that of McCarthy's re-enactor:

> I read in the newspaper the other day, he said, about a boy with a curious mental disorder which compels him to seek physical risk and therefore injury whenever possible. This boy is forever putting his hand in the fire, and throwing himself off walls, and climbing trees in order to fall out of them; he has broken nearly every bone in his body, and of course is covered in cuts and bruises, and the newspaper asked his poor parents for their comment on the situation. The problem is, they said, he has no fear. But it seems to me that exactly the reverse is true: he has too much fear, so much that he is driven to enact the thing of which he is afraid, lest it should happen of its own accord.[5]

Though the terrain is different, the logic of this boy's actions bears similarity to that of the narrator of *Remainder*. Whereas the latter re-enacts an experience in order to feel a certain sensation of authenticity, the boy here preempts or pre-enacts his fears; in both cases, repetition is employed to empty out and instrumentalize a specific scenario. With his reversal of the parents' reading, Paniotis touches on an important possibility: the re-enactor's obsession with re-enacting accidental scenes might be aimed at controlling or eliminating chance, rather than amplifying chance or playing games with risk. Paniotis (and, by extension, Cusk) is therefore aware of the nonalignment of chance with any particular *kind* of behavior. While chance will not be explicitly foregrounded in my reading of the *Outline* trilogy, attention to detail, interpretive subtlety, and openness to the accidental nature of experience are borne out in Cusk's understanding of narrative.

Cusk comes in more on the side of *Satin Island* than *Remainder*—more questioning than accepting; more open to chance than willing to control it. If narrative is a concern for Cusk and her narrators, this entails a sensitivity to narrative's tendency to impose a shape on discrete and accidental experiences in order to create a larger plot. Of course, narrative is necessary and does not absolutely eliminate chance. However, by featuring accounts of characters who have experiences that *feel* disconnected from narrative—and furthermore, characters who are writers, and are therefore concerned with narrative in more than one sense—the *Outline* trilogy poses a question to narrative and the impulse to narrate. But her earlier novels, though they do not feature the same kind of direct problematization of narrative, nevertheless foreground the fact that what is being recounted is narrated and narrativized, and convey a similar feeling that is linked to this awareness. Therefore, before proceeding to a proper discussion of the *Outline* trilogy, it is fitting to touch more at length on three of Cusk's early novels: *Saving Agnes*, *The Temporary*, and *The Country Life*. In doing so, I hope to establish how her early writing already plays with narrative in a way that sets up her concern with narrative in her more recent writing, where it begins more legibly to affect the form of the writing itself.

Just fiction, really

Treating Cusk's early fiction serves two purposes. First, it straightforwardly demonstrates that Cusk has been preoccupied with the question of narrative, as well as the feeling that comes along with questioning narrative, from the very beginning. Second, it establishes a trajectory from the early to the late writings, as far as her attitude toward narrative and narration is concerned. Whereas the recent trilogy consists largely of a series of conversations, split between being reported and quoted, her early novels take on a more conventional style and narrative mode, and could more firmly be situated in a lineage of modernist literature.

In Cusk's first novel, *Saving Agnes* (1993), the story itself is fairly standard: the protagonist Agnes Day—named, of course, after Agnus Dei, the Lamb of God—struggles with her job, her relationships (romantic and otherwise), and her place within a larger narrative, which is constantly called into question. Rather than summarizing the novel's plot, I will cite some examples where the particular question of narrative shines forth. During a section recounting Agnes's identity crisis while coming of age, she is said to believe "that reality meant failure, ugliness and self-contempt" and also "that the good in her *was but fiction.*"[6] Of course, fiction and narrative cannot quite be collapsed together, but throughout the novel Agnes is concerned with arbitrarily shaping the value and meaning of things, whether in discrete qualities (i.e., "the good in her") or in the connections between events. Later, with reference to a time in her early childhood when she had gotten lost in a market while in Mexico for a family holiday, the text states that Agnes "had never been able to remember *the conclusion to that story,*" that is, how she had found her parents again.[7] In the present tense of the novel, and reading almost as a self-aware jab at the novel form itself, Agnes's roommate Nina says that "Westerns are *just fiction, really.*"[8] After briefly narrating a dream that she had about Agnes, Agnes's friend and coworker Greta "pause[s] as if to signal *the completion of her narrative.*"[9] At the end of a conversation where her mother discusses a miscarriage she had had before Agnes was born, "Agnes felt as if she had drifted off to sleep halfway through a film, and had jolted back to consciousness, bleary-eyed, *to find the plot had lurched forward* and the characters taken on an unsettling air of mystery."[10] These select quotations alone are enough to show that Cusk's first novel, even if in a different form, has narrative in mind, even to the extent that the protagonist oftentimes sees her life in terms of narrative fiction. Narrative is almost metaphorized to allow the characters to point out and problematize the implications of the novel's actual narrative. As Sonja Pyykkö points out, for example, "Agnes seems perched to discover that the apparently random events are not but *can be* linked and that this active process of plotting her life can counteract the disillusionment and despair that she has been feeling."[11] Not unlike Proust's narrator, Agnes is aware of the transformative potential of narrative for personal affect.

Underlying all of these signs of narrative reflexivity, furthermore, is Agnes's own particular mode of aesthetic experience, which carries with it a sense of disappearance. The first instance of this feeling accompanies a significant narrative event. Agnes, at thirteen years old, experiences a new and disorienting feeling, and says to her classmate "I don't feel as if I'm here," which seems, by the narrative's account, to have triggered a harsh round of bullying for Agnes.[12] Not unlike the *Remainder* narrator's tingling feeling, this sentiment returns several times throughout the novel, and oftentimes alienates, or signals an alienation from, those around Agnes. Once again more or less in the present tense, Agnes, out with her roommates, feels "as if she wasn't there at all" and has "a strange sense […] of being someone else."[13] Several pages later, she begins "to enjoy the sensation of encroaching invisibility."[14] There are other similar instances, but I point these out to show that the narrative, with all of its skepticism of plot, is punctuated by moments in which the protagonist feels as if she is either elsewhere or disappearing—which, in each case, carries with it the strange and unprecedented force of an aesthetic experience. Narrative reflexivity is thus not employed for its own sake, but has real stakes both for the characters and beyond the novel.

Saving Agnes also contains yet one further resonance between Cusk and McCarthy. The novel begins and ends with *a crack in the wall*: "a crack, a long narrow wound in the sitting-room wall,"[15] a crack that portends the downfall not only of the apartment but of Agnes's life (and her narrative) itself. This crack reemerges throughout the novel at several crucial points. It is a touchstone for the narrative's development, insofar as it appears at points of precarity. It does not occur once and prompt a series of re-enactments, but mainly serves as a reminder of Agnes's domestic situation. After the initial mention of this crack in the wall, there is, like in *Remainder*, an important scene that takes place in a bathroom. At the tail end of a party, Agnes gives the first glimpse of the odd feeling that haunts the novel: "In the bathroom, she peered into the mirror as if trying to see something beyond what was there."[16] This can be read according to her face, her sense of self, her experience, or the novel as a whole. Already, Cusk establishes the many dimensions of narrative, even when she is not writing about characters who are writers by trade.

Cusk's second novel, *The Temporary*, bears many similarities to *Saving Agnes*. Throughout the novel, Francine, a temporary secretary, also seems to be always on the verge of escape or disappearance, as well as possessing a relentless drive to narrate. Early in the novel, after giving her number to Ralph, who she meets at an art gallery, she feels "the satisfaction which customarily arose from the discovery of a personal advantage in the work of forces outside her control, and before long had gained the impression that the work had been her own."[17] In this moment, she is irritated because she has given Ralph her number rather than his friend Stephen whom she prefers; but then she realizes, to her satisfaction, that Stephen can contact her this way. But her words are prophetic in another way, as it is Ralph after all, and not Stephen, who she will have the brief relationship that occupies much of the novel. Whereas the peculiar attention to narrative in *Saving Agnes* serves to isolate her, in *The Temporary*, it seems at times to be shared between characters. For example, encountering Francine by chance at a cloth-seller's stall, Ralph bemoans the fact that he had called her already: "He cursed himself for yesterday's peremptory telephone message. If only he had known, how much better it would have been to have left things to chance!"[18] Chance is foregrounded here as a key component of experience—as well as romantic relationships—but it also exceeds the subject's knowledge in any particular moment: chance *here*, when the narrative makes this free indirect comment about it, is still over Ralph's head, as he cannot calculate the events that will play out throughout the rest of the novel. For, as the plot progresses, Francine becomes increasingly attached and even jealous of Ralph, despite her early preference for Stephen and concomitant coldness toward Ralph. At one point, she resents the fact "that she was not the star of his experiences" after he mentions a previous girlfriend.[19]

For her part, Francine's drive to narrate is also a will to unburden herself of narrative. In one passage, Francine resents the absence of her roommate Janice, who is thus unavailable to be her sounding board: "She never really assumed control over events until she had related them in some form: *untold*, their reality was too pressing, still sullied with *the awkwardness of the moment*."[20] Here, we get the sense of narration as a mediating act, whereby the difficult or uncertain lived experience of a moment is shunted into a telling, a plot. In this context, Francine feels the need to tell somebody about a particularly unsavory temporary job assignment with an inappropriate male boss, but the more general narratological takeaway is a kind of disjunction between experience and narrative: narration is cathartic, sublimating even, and transforms what it tells as it is told. Narrative is thereby characterized as a way to control and take ownership of experience through telling. Though they variously diverge and converge in *The Temporary*, experience and narrative are never too far apart.

Whereas Cusk's first two novels are similar, perhaps even counterparts in a sense, *The Country Life* is quite different in style. It is narrated in the first person and is a considerably longer novel. But it also feels decidedly *older* than both *Saving Agnes* and *The Temporary*, or maybe it can be placed in a much older tradition. Perhaps relatedly, it features less of an emphasis on the question of narration, being at the same time more keenly attuned to atmosphere and experience. In the novel, the narrator Stella has quit her job and her marriage and moved to the country to care for a handicapped teenage boy, Martin, partly in a quest to shake up her unfulfilling life. Upon arrival, however, she finds that things in the country are not what they seem. As the novel progresses, things become increasingly strange, and though it would be hasty to say that this novel features a definitively supernatural dimension, like Henry James's *Turn of the Screw* it walks the line of this possibility, heightening the eeriness of the entire situation.

Wandering around midway through the novel, Stella happens upon a new area within the Maddens' estate. Upon opening a gate and being met with "a boundless blast of heat and light," she feels a "sense of wonder" at this "gratuitous display of beauty."[21] The evocation of wonder, of course, should remind us of wonder's place at the origin of philosophy.[22] But, for Stella, "the feeling of insignificance was in itself a consolation," meaning that she "did not ascribe any more specific meaning to this feeling."[23] While it does in principle keep wonder alive, this statement opens onto a narratively significant scene, where Stella encounters the odd Mr. Trimmer. As the novel is at least partly a mystery, this scene is rife with *specific meaning*, insofar as it both foreshadows later developments and is referred to repeatedly later on in the novel. I cite this passage in particular because it shows how Cusk's preoccupation with the relationship between experience and narrative (as exemplified in her first two novels) remains even when she is writing in a very different mode. In this text at least, wonder is sustained as a kind of uncertainty, rather than something that would necessarily lead to knowledge or to a straightforward organization of a series of events. Even the scene of Stella's wonder, while narratively significant, itself contains much uncertainty and raises questions that do not find an answer by the novel's end.

These are only three examples, but all of Cusk's novels, including her recent *Second Place*, are concerned with this issue. Cusk, from the very beginning, is interested in the relationships between experience and narrative, life and literature, and especially in those moments of narrative interest where the question of narrative meaning arises for a character or narrator. In what follows, I will deal with each book of the *Outline* trilogy, with a focus on moments where this preoccupation is brought to bear on the stories of each respective speaker.

No particular story

In *Outline*, and in the trilogy's other two novels, reported speech is just as common as quoted speech, and the text weaves the two together, a narrative tactic that complicates our understanding of what might otherwise be simply a series of anecdotes. A single conversation in the novel may begin with Faye's interlocutor being quoted, move into Faye's paraphrasing of their speech—which itself oscillates between providing more and less detail—and eventually move back into quotation. Such frequent shifts between the two ways of reporting speech, I argue, not only reminds us of the fact that what we are reading is a carefully constructed narrative but manages to push that narrative to its limits by consistently forcing us to consider what it means in the first place to quote rather than paraphrase, and vice versa, especially in the context of conveying an actual experience. At times, when the paraphrased speech can only be distinguished from direct quotation by the lack of quotation marks, we become aware that the narrator Faye is telling somebody else's speech as she would tell a story. As we will see, this tactic deepens Cusk's already persistent concern with the relation between life and narration, particularly when we consider that it is not only speech and storytelling but also fiction writing that is the trilogy's key concern.

Outline begins with Faye en route to Athens to teach a course in creative writing, and her time in Athens takes up the rest of the novel. As Pieter Vermeulen succinctly characterizes *Outline*, it "consists of cool, factual observations of her surroundings and of the stories that other people tell and that end up taking over most of the space of the novel."[24] I would agree, adding only that "observations" is the operative term here, especially given the varying levels of self-awareness that we can sense in the other people she encounters. In particular, the narrative's seemingly indiscriminate switching between methods of conveying speech, with little to no explicit indication as to why such shifts would be necessary, may cause us to wonder whether there is really a difference between Faye's paraphrasing and her interlocutors' specific words. The fact that we never get Faye's direct, quoted speech, but only paraphrases of what she says back to her interlocutors, leaves us with the question of what that difference would be, in any given case. On the one hand, the missing explanation can be read alongside the narrative tendency toward anonymity and self-effacement, a tendency that we have already seen in Cusk's earlier novels; Faye herself says at one point that she "had come to believe more and more in the virtues of passivity, and of living a life as unmarked by self-will as possible" (170)—not unlike Raphaël's attempt to live passively, without will, in the later part of *La Peau de chagrin*. Accordingly, as Vermeulen comments, the narrative voice opens onto "an almost total elision of the first-person narrator herself."[25] These two functions—the narrator's style of "observation" and her near-disappearance—are related in a way that encompasses but is far from limited to a relation between form and content. In fact, the seemingly absent narrator can be felt most saliently through the unique stylistic tics of Cusk's prose, especially around certain characters' speech. For Vermeulen, "[t]he narrator [...] never comes into view as a centered object of empathetic identification and remains a dispersed presence between the lines of the novel."[26] By multiplying the ambiguity of its countless miniature narratives, this dispersed narrative voice heightens the stakes of aesthetic experience, especially since the novel is populated by writers and obsessed with interpretation. In seeming to be reserved, in seeming to be holding something back, Cusk's writing pinpoints the very fact of narration: what is being told is *narrated*, molded by the teller, even if he or she is striving for self-effacement. And whereas the narrator of *Remainder* was concerned with narrative only in the sense of re-enacting certain experiences, many of which were not, properly speaking, *his*, Cusk's trilogy employs narrative to pose a real question about experience itself. How much control do we have in our own experience, in our own story? How much of that story can really be conveyed, or told? What would be considered appropriate material for a writer's apprenticeship? When is it necessary, upon reflection, to make an intervention, a correction, about our previous narration—whether or not this correction is visible to the reader, as in *À la recherche du temps perdu*?

With these questions in mind, I turn to another passage from *Outline*, one which again concerns Paniotis—"an old friend of mine" (90)—the speaker of the lines quoted earlier in this chapter. Here, Faye is meeting him and his friend Angeliki, "someone else—a woman novelist I might have heard of" (90), for a meal. As the conversation progresses, Paniotis delves into his family life as a divorced father. As a result of what is functionally an interruption of Angeliki by the narrator, Paniotis launches into a tale of his first solo trip with his children after the divorce. Like many such tales in this trilogy, his story is split between quoted and reported speech. The conversation ranges from politics to the family, to the politics of the family, and the feeling of disconnection that Paniotis describes has, in part, to do with the disconnection from his wife. His trip with the children is at the same time a journey away from his relationship with his wife, both literally and figuratively. As Faye paraphrases, he "felt himself to be getting further and further away from everything trusted and known, everything familiar, and most of all from the whole security of the home he had made with his wife, which of course no longer even existed" (115). Touching first on the disparity between their lodgings on the trip, which rank unfavorably in comparison to earlier stays as an intact family unit ("he and his wife had only ever taken them to places of beauty and comfort" (117)), he then comments on the weather, which is appropriately dismal: "It was already raining very hard, and was so windy on the shore, where the hotel looked out, that the spume was lifted from the water and blew away in great desolate sweeps that looked like phantoms crossing the sky" (117). These conditions, with their evocation of the supernatural, lead Paniotis to leave the hotel with his children. Since they have left the hotel early, he checks them into an inn, where they wait out the storm.

Of course, this story is already eminently novelistic. Between the dissolution of a marriage, the mention of phantoms, and the stormy weather that seems to mirror his family situation, everything—even as it is falling apart—appears to come together narratively in this trip. In short, it is a notable, exemplary, significant story, just as it is important that Paniotis and his daughter remember different aspects of this trip (122), which makes the disconnection from narrative feel all the more real. Once the storm passes, Paniotis gives a poignant description which is mediated by memory. "'My daughter reminded me,' he said, 'on that last evening we spent here, of the walk we took later that day'" (122). The remembered instance that follows holds, in miniature, the entirety of what I consider to be the import of the trilogy, and of what I will be concerned with hereafter. What Paniotis recounts—in quoted speech—at the same time touches directly on a singular experience and a paradox that affects narrative itself. Describing a walk he took with his children to visit a monastery near the Lousios gorge, a walk that is beset with intense heat, Paniotis delivers the lines in question:

> 'On the way back up,' Paniotis said, 'the sun grew so hot, and our bites began to itch so unbearably, that the three of us tore off our clothes and leaped into one of the deep pools the waterfall had made, despite the fact that it was quite close to the path and that we could have been seen at any minute by passers-by. How cold the water was, and how incredibly deep and refreshing and clear—we drifted around and around, with the sun on our faces and our bodies hanging like three white roots beneath the water. I can see us there still,' he said, 'for those were moments so intense that in a way we will be living them always, while other things are completely forgotten. Yet there is no particular story attached to them,' he said, 'despite their place in the story I have just told you. That time spent swimming in the pool beneath the waterfall belongs nowhere: it is part of no sequence of events, it is only itself, in a way that nothing in our life before as a family was ever itself, because it was always leading to the next thing and the next, was always contributing to our story of who we were. Once Chrysta and I divorced, things did not join up in that way any more, although I tried for years to make it seem as though they did. But there was no sequel to that time in the pool, nor ever will be.' (123)

This quotation is taken from a paragraph spanning two pages, consisting of quoted speech from Paniotis, unbroken except for four instances of "he said" and one of "Paniotis said." While it is common to mark speech in this way, I mention it here because repeated attribution within one paragraph—especially repeated *bare* attribution, with only the most minimal variation between the third person and the proper name—is unusual. This passage exemplifies Cusk's concern with a certain disconnectedness that ties together both experience and narrative, as it emerges when experience is conveyed *through* narrative. Paniotis's words, with their reference to timelessness, recall a line from *Saving Agnes*, Cusk's very first novel, describing a bizarre moment in Agnes's childhood: "this moment—and it happened, literally, in a moment, nothing more—still retained *a clarity which allowed its details to be summoned up at any time.*"[27] This disconnection is also a sort of timelessness, it seems, as it allows the moment to stand apart from any events that come before or after.

In the present passage, Paniotis begins by first acknowledging a sense of risk, insofar as he and his children decide to swim in the nude even when they might be discovered. This element of chance, paired with the prevalence of the weather—first the wind and rain, and then the intense heat—lend a Proustian tinge to this passage, redolent especially of the passage from *La Prisonnière* that I have discussed already. And the atmospheric resonance remains throughout, as we are told how cold the water is while they drift around under the sun. Somehow, Paniotis's statement that "those were moments so intense that in a way we will be living them always" increases the resonance between this passage and Proust, insofar as it reminds us of Proust's narrator's wish to sacrifice all other times "for such a unique state of soul." With the timeless dimension of these moments comes the additional effect that "there is no particular story attached to them," a sentiment that could itself serve as a comment on the quiet moments in Proust. Paniotis goes on to state that their time swimming "belongs nowhere: it is part of no sequence of events, it is only itself, in a way that nothing in our life before as a family was ever itself." So, despite his crucial insight, Paniotis lapses here into a narrativizing tendency, and thus cannot be strictly taken at his word but must be read against himself. This is further emphasized in the final line I quote here, where he assures us that there will be no sequel, a curious line that echoes Proust's narrator's paradoxical wish to sacrifice everything to remain in his moment of atmospheric resonance.

Besides the resonance with Proust, I am interested in two major points here. First, there is Paniotis's experience of this moment as being timeless, disconnected, and singular. This moment stands out: it is not just a regular trip with his children, nor is it significant because it is a trip taken with his children alone, without his wife. There is something immanent to this moment that inheres despite its material particulars. Second is his zoomed-out comment about the narrative of his life: "there was no sequel to that time in the pool, nor ever will be." Together with the quiet moments in Proust, the disconnectedness of this passage is a complex response to the drive to control one's experience, a drive that can be seen in Huysmans's and McCarthy's novels. The moment described by Paniotis is disconnected in part because it is not engineered. This does not mean that he rolled dice or threw a dart at a map and made decisions based on pure randomness. He made a series of decisions in response to what was happening around him—his divorce, the storm—and accidentally arrived at a feeling that the present moment was timeless and not part of a larger narrative. If this is the case—if the moment indeed feels disconnected and timeless—then such a moment is truly remarkable and significant. But it does not gain its value from anything beyond itself, and even the moment seems mundane when recounted here, its novelistic qualities notwithstanding. The paradox deepens because Paniotis feels compelled to *narrate* this moment, to tell it aloud as a story that in turn winds up in a novel, as part of a narrative. But perhaps there is something ultimately unnarratable in Paniotis's experience that drives him to share this story. The paradox here—which Proust and Cusk each give shape to so carefully in their respective texts—is that, despite this seeming dissolution of narrative, or a feeling that seems to resist narration, there is nevertheless an *injunction* to continue, to narrate. Cusk's characters, when feeling disconnected from a larger plot, are able to relate a sense of unnarratability within a narrative.

It should be noted that, once we hit on the passage quoted above, Paniotis has already been speaking uninterrupted for nearly ten pages. Again, why this seemingly excessive recourse to attribution in punctuating Paniotis's speech, when it has been so extensively established that he is the speaker? The distance that we are afforded from Paniotis (whether he is paraphrased or directly quoted) arguably further indicates a neutral position that could be associated with his feeling of disconnection from narrative. Tom Eyers refers to the narrator in the *Outline* trilogy as "Cusk's ambient subject," and also remarks upon the "neutrality" of Cusk's inversion of free indirect style.[28] Creating distance in this way is not simply an experiment in narrative or style; it draws attention to the length of the speech and the identity of the speaker, giving the trilogy something of an epic quality. Moreover, since Paniotis's speech occurs as part of his spoken narrative that is itself an entry in a larger written narrative, he and his experience are at least doubly narrativized, despite his intentions and the content of his speech. He tells a story that features a disconnected moment, meaning that this moment is *notable* for not seeming to be part of any story. Then, this narrative about a non-narrative is included in *Outline*, a novel. I will set aside any implications that this might have for the novel (i.e., what this says about the novel's relation to story, plot, or narrative), since what is most immediately striking is that Paniotis cannot avoid folding his account of this experience into a narrative: "'Yet there is no particular story attached to them,' he said, *'despite their place in the story I have just told you.'*" Like in Proust, there is a self-effacing gesture here. But Paniotis's speech exercises some restraint: it does not hyperbolically imagine what amounts to his own death, which would be properly unnarratable, but instead in more precise terms asks a searching question about the relationship between experience and narrative.

Despite Paniotis's ultimate conclusion about narrative, his speech reads as plotted in an unmistakable way because it is precisely a narrative of family life and divorce. Initially, responding to a question from the narrator, he launches into a highly dramatized account of a particular trip with his children. He delivers this speech in conversation with two women, the narrator and Angeliki, another Greek novelist with whom Paniotis is already acquainted. I take some issue with Vermeulen's claim that "the recurrent shifts between different reporting modes serve to make visible the narrator's affective labor as she negotiates her distance from the stories that are dumped onto her."[29] Instead, I argue that his story is granted subtlety precisely through the narrative interruption of the "he said," and this subtlety is in line with Faye's striving toward passivity, which I noted earlier. If Faye is performing affective labor, it is in service of Cusk, not necessarily some other character in the novel. The narrative style is how attention is brought to the implications of Paniotis's story, including his investment in a moment that he feels to be disconnected from any narrative, but it also plays out across the entire trilogy: these implications are the mark of the narrator and of the narrative itself.

Among critics of Cusk, I come down closest to Tom Eyers's reading, in which he "assess[es] free indirect style for its ability to produce narrative voices beyond the confines of the subject/object dichotomy" and finds that Cusk innovates this style to her own unique ends.[30] Such a reading opens out toward an attunement to what might be deemed the atmospheric, to recall Böhme's discussion of that same dichotomy and how atmosphere complicates it. Eyers also writes that "the putative shutting down of narrative possibility and choice, and the modeling of a practice of close reading that is severe rather than expansive, gives us access to narrative-subjective worlds otherwise hidden from view."[31] In short, we can find already operative in *Outline*, and therefore as a key to the trilogy as a whole, a self-awareness about the bind in which a storyteller within a narrative is placed. As one of Faye's students says during a class session, "all I could think of was a line describing the exact moment I was living in: *a woman stood in her kitchen and thought about trying to write a story*. The problem was that the line didn't connect to any other line. It hadn't come from anywhere and it wasn't going anywhere either, any more than I was going anywhere by just standing in my kitchen" (209). As "severe" as this self-interpretation might be in Eyers's mind, the trilogy's dogged literalness and struggle against the narrative impulse is expansive despite itself.

The randomness and cruelty of reality

In the second novel of the trilogy, *Transit*, Faye has moved to a new flat in London and is dealing with numerous renovations. These renovations, as well as her divorce, set the backdrop for the novel, and indeed serve as its plot, at least in the eyes of many reviewers. Helen Dunmore, in her review, mentions early on that the "renovation is a tale in itself."[32] Dwight Garner opines that *Transit* "is a calm novel about chaos."[33] Heller McAlpin acknowledges that both *Outline* and *Transit* "offer little in the way of plot thrills."[34] Daniel Aureliano Newman, who is more attuned to the stakes of the always-receding narratorial style, nonetheless cannot avoid drawing attention to the novel's plot in terms of the reader's expectations.[35] All of this is to say that critics are aware that plot itself is a theme in the trilogy, even if this means that plot is allegorically displaced onto something as mundane as a renovation project.

Nevertheless, *Transit* begins by once again thematizing the very question of plot, narrative, and meaning. The opening pages describe an (automated) email Faye receives from an astrologer, but as Faye says, "I did not have the blind belief in reality that made others ask for concrete explanations."[36] Interestingly, and despite reviewers' insistence on discussing the plot of *Transit*, this second novel in the trilogy is arguably more narratively disjunctive than *Outline*. Other than the renovations to Faye's new home, she encounters her ex Gerard, visits the hairdresser, meets with one of her writing students, and goes to visit her cousin Lawrence, all the while engaging in conversations with various characters, much like in *Outline*. But my concern in discussing *Transit* is the literary festival that Faye speaks at alongside fellow writers Julian and Louis. I would consider this *Transit*'s major event in the sense that it engages with and describes a disconnected moment of the aesthetic that poses a singular question to narrative, and furthermore from the perspective of a literary writer.

This passage is notable for the tension between the two other writers, which apparent upon their introduction. Julian, who speaks first, is gregarious—especially relative to Louis—and has the audience laughing on more than one occasion during his talk. It quickly becomes clear that the rift between the two, besides the fact that they have already oftentimes found themselves speaking alongside each other at similar such events and are therefore rivals of sorts, has to do with how they understand their place or task as writers, especially as far as narrative is concerned. At first glance, Julian's talk places him in the position of entertainer, and the narrative maneuvers of his story only deepen the implications of this designation. After sitting down on the stage, he opens his talk with a joke:

> 'Have we come to the right place?' Julian said, speaking into the darkness and looking around himself with pantomimed confusion. 'We're looking for the wet T-shirt competition. We were told it was here.' The audience immediately laughed. Julian shook out his jacket and made a face as he gingerly put it back on. (91)

For context, the group has had to trudge through the rain immediately before the event, and at this point they are all soaking wet. While there is no reason to assign bad faith to Julian at this point, it quickly becomes apparent—though, of course, the narrator does not say so and we must read between the lines—that he operates with a kind of opportunism. Especially if examined with Louis's talk in mind, Julian can be said to capitalize on the flashy aspects of his story and his identity. Over the course of his talk, we should note, his mentions of writing mostly have to do with the position or status of being a writer—that is, the appearance of being a writer, instead of the work it requires—rather than writing as a vocation, which he despises.

Early in his talk, Julian states: "Me, I hate writing. I have to sit there with someone massaging my shoulders and a hot-water bottle in my lap. I only do it for the attention I'll get afterwards—I'm like a dog waiting for a treat" (92). He makes these comments in order, in part, to distinguish himself from Louis, "who," he says, "actually claims to enjoy the writing process" (92). Drawing more laughter from the crowd, and even from Louis (though Louis's laughter is certainly forced, since, "watching Julian with his brown teeth slightly bared" (92), he "[bares] his teeth even more, his pale blue eyes with their yellowed whites fixed on Julian's face" (93)), this comment is also a self-aware gesture of non-committal. If he feigns suspicion at Louis's claim to enjoy writing, we can also be suspicious of the "honesty" of Julian's talk. And the "studied nonchalance" of the event's Chair, in the following line, finally names what Julian seems to be doing (94). In light of the trajectory of this section of the novel, Julian is worth mentioning because he represents a stylistic and ethical position that is negated by that of Louis, who speaks next, after displaying quiet hostility during Julian's speech.

Louis's talk is comparatively difficult, as his story is more a figure for his writing process than a reflection on his biography and his life as a writer. His tone is much different, and he is not concerned with pleasing or entertaining the audience. His talk demands more of the audience than Julian's, and in a way models literarity itself through the injunction—and difficulty—of interpretation. It is harder to "read" Louis, though it is tempting to understand him as straightforwardly sincere in comparison to Julian's feigned, but ultimately egotistical, self-effacement. This is not to say that Louis is entirely sincere and unaware of the implications of his style. Before embarking on this story in earnest, Louis responds to Julian and their seemingly shared terrain.

> There was another reason, he said, that he was put on a platform next to Julian so often, and that was that both their books were categorized as autobiographical. That made things easy for the people who had to organize events like this one. But in fact his and Julian's books had nothing in common at all. They might almost be described as functioning through mutually oppositional principles. (102)

Louis is talking about genre conventions here, but his comments could also be applied to the difference between their respective ideas about writing in general. It is not insignificant that, while this paragraph is reported, when he actually launches into his story, it is initially delivered in quotations, perhaps framing this initial (paraphrased) assessment of his difference from Julian as a sort of preface. Louis's comments touch on the pensive quality of the trilogy in general, and not only the difficulty of categorizing these novels but the inability, within them, to definitively identify even something as fundamental as tone. This becomes increasingly important when Louis describes his own writing process, and when he returns to assessing the differences between his and Julian's writing.

Louis begins reflecting on the task of writing by way of an anecdote about his cat, Mino.[37] In the typical narrative fashion of the trilogy, his story alternates between being quoted and being reported. In his story, Louis (unlike Julian) is engaged in the act of writing. He is in his study, and has suddenly noticed that his cat Mino has trapped a bird out in the yard, only to allow it to escape when distracted by "a sudden noise, some sort of bang or report from the road" (103). What would otherwise seem like an everyday occurrence is, for Louis, a productive moment, because it prompts reflection about experience and about storytelling:

> Nobody, he realized, was controlling that story: either he [Louis] needed to act and intervene, or he would be hurt by the sight of Mino killing the bird, because it was of course with the bird that he identified, despite the fact that he knew Mino and that Mino was his cat. As it was, the incident was quickly resolved: the narrative had somehow taken care of itself. (104–105)

These words, which recall the interplay between control and chance in *The Temporary*, are spoken in the context of Louis's struggle with his fame as a writer, but they can also be understood alongside his difference from Julian. As he states at the beginning of his talk, "I don't want to be known [...] I don't want anyone to know me" (102)—a line that cannot necessarily be taken at face value, but nevertheless marks a clear distinction from Julian's way of presenting himself. Louis's wish for anonymity could be understood as a writerly posture; indeed, when he is first introduced, the narrator notes that the apparent indifference of his presentation and attire "made so obvious a contrast with Julian's luxurious navy suit and mauve silk cravat that his appearance seemed, despite his attitude of slouching indifference, premeditated and deliberate" (88–89), a suggestion that we cannot dismiss. However, Louis can be read not only as coming out favorably in contrast to Julian—who seems in every respect to be much more calculating—but also as asking an actual question about writing, narrative, and his place as a writer. Furthermore, his concern with anonymity is not alone among the trilogy: it mirrors Faye's own concern with anonymity, as well as that of other characters throughout, and furthermore shares something in common with the preoccupation with moments disconnected from narrative.

Whereas Julian's speech reads as flashier and more rehearsed, the narrator's account of Louis's speech indicates his vulnerability, and he seems to be much less concerned with pleasing the crowd. Instead, it is as if we can hear him thinking, as if he is trying to work out a problem in real time. Still speaking about the encounter between Mino and the bird, his tale continues:

> there had been something far more profound and disturbing in his witnessing of these events, which in themselves meant nothing, but to which his feelings of responsibility and knowledge gave an entirely different cast. His public identification with his cat Mino was in conflict with his private identification with the bird: the sense of responsibility, he realized, came from the active realization that those two things were about to collide. Part of him must hate Mino, yet Mino was part of himself. Watching the bird get away, he was reminded of the randomness and cruelty of reality, for which the belief in narrative could only ever provide the most absurd and artificial screen; but greater still was his sense of the bird as symbolising something about truth. (105)

The tale of Mino and the bird occasions, or is occasioned by, Louis's meditation on his status as a writer. Louis's reluctance to be seen—as a public figure, as a writer, or even at all—finds its basis here in his understanding of the arbitrary nature of narration, which mirrors and is "the most absurd and artificial screen" for "the randomness and cruelty of reality." Counterintuitively, he is reminded of this cruelty not by a vision of animal violence, but instead by the escape of the prey, the bird. This cruelty is perhaps more aligned with true randomness, indifference to meaning, than it is to objective violence—after all, Louis could have achieved the same result, the bird's escape, by intervening. Besides serving as a counterpoint to U.'s hypothetical speech about the oil-soaked birds in McCarthy's *Satin Island*, Louis is also talking about an awareness of the arbitrary nature of narratives and a sense of alienation from the position of narrator or, as a writer, the position of one who produces narratives.

Louis's contribution to the panel is of interest here for two reasons. First, because he is in part responding to Julian's highly narrativized speech, Louis—however "premeditated and deliberate" we might judge the way he presents himself—is protesting the merit of a neat, legible plot. Somehow, he shows how such a plot would actually run counter to a real consideration of writing, as it would enjoy "the screen of fiction" (107). Second, by choosing to begin with—and thus, paradoxically, to place *within a narrative*—an account of bare animal life, he thematizes what is meaningless, innate, and unpremeditated from the very beginning. As was the case with Paniotis's tale in *Outline*, Louis's problematization of narrative is only possible within the doubled boundaries of narrative—his narrative and the narrator's summary of it. Louis heightens the stakes of this question by appealing explicitly to the animal kingdom and to reality itself; it is not only narrative that is arbitrary, but also nature. Narrative attempts to rectify or repair the "randomness and cruelty of reality," but in a way that is also random and cruel.

It is worth lingering for a moment on Louis's sense that the bird might symbolize something about truth. In the struggle between Mino and the bird, Mino is the aggressor, with control of the situation—at least, this seems to be the case. The bird is trapped, pinned down, and is physically unable to overpower the cat and defend itself. The bird's death, in other words, seems like a done deal. But at the very moment that this seems to become clear, something intervenes from outside, distracting Mino, and offering the bird its escape without, however, being designed to do so. If Louis understands the bird to be symbolizing truth, then this scene is saying that truth does not lie in the hands of the one in control, Mino, or even the one telling the story, Louis. Instead, truth is on the side of what flies in the face—or more accurately here, what flies *away from* the face—of the one seemingly in control. Truth is what shows us that no single being is in fact in control. Blanchot theorizes this fact about artistic creation with recourse to the myth of Orpheus and Eurydice. To put it briefly, Blanchot writes that Orpheus, who is prohibited from glancing back at Eurydice as they are leaving the underworld, "can descend toward [his work]; he can [...] draw it to him and lead it with him upward, but only by turning away from it."[38] We know that Orpheus does look back, once he stops hearing Eurydice's footsteps, and they are both condemned to death as a result. As far as this relates to the role of the artist, Blanchot writes that "impatience must be the core of profound patience, the pure flash which an infinite waiting, which the silence and reserve of this attention cause to spring from its center not only as the spark which extreme tension ignites, but as the brilliant point which has escaped this mindful wait—the glad accident, insouciance."[39] I take this to mean that there is a contradictory element whereby the writer can only articulate the work by turning away from it, with the result that our engagement with a work (whether reader or writer) will always have something secret about it, something that cannot be engineered or anticipated. This makes good on the paradox presented by Louis's story and the fact that the randomness of narrative and nature is identified precisely when the bird escapes, rather than in a moment of animal violence whereby we could more easily identify cruelty. The same can be said of the oil spill in *Satin Island*, which is both tragic and true, though not for the commonplace reasons that U.'s airport neighbor implies.

In its relative obscurity, Louis's story asks a serious question about the relationship between life and narrative. This question cuts across both the position and the vocation of a writer, as it concerns how readers engage with the work. Moving to a comparison of his work with Julian's, the account of his speech continues:

> People believed that Julian didn't need to make things up because the extremity of his experiences was such that it released him from that obligation. Reality, on this occasion, could serve in the place of fantasy as a means of distracting people from the facts of their own lives. [...] A lot of writers seemed to think that the higher a truth—or to be more accurate, since truth was something altogether different, a fact—was pitched from the earth, the less of a supporting structure it required: so long as something could be proved to have actually occurred it could be left to stand on its own, and if that thing happened to be so bizarre or grotesque that it caught people's attention, the need to explain it was diminished even further. (107)

While not a takedown of Julian's book exactly, which Louis claims to have "quite liked" (107), these lines reveal the difference between the two writers. Julian's book, which details his difficult upbringing and, if his talk is any indication, is written in a very catchy or showy style, seems controversial or difficult in an immediately legible way. And actually, it is in the mixture of Julian's speech and the narrator's account of it that the particular tone of his writing comes through. See, for example, these lines: "Coming to himself was like opening a Christmas present and finding that what was inside was already broken. 'Which in our house,' Julian said, 'it usually was'" (95). The shift from reported to quoted speech, as well as the pause for attribution in place of the usual comma or temporal pause that would be there in usual speech, reinforces, through performance, the idea that Julian is a calculating speaker and writer—a writer who pauses for effect. This is further evidence that the affective labor Faye performs is, at least in some cases, to the detriment of those whose speech she is reporting.

On the other hand, from the account we are given here, Louis's book is controversial due to its treatment of mundane, everyday matters, namely through "his accounts of eating and drinking and shitting and pissing and fucking—or more often masturbating," which readers claimed to find "monotonous, disgusting or even offensive," though "they continued to buy his book all the same" (107–108). Instead of narratively shocking content,

Louis's book features content that is more basely shocking or lacking in decorum, which he himself finds ironic: "It was amusing, if faintly sad, to see people call disgusting the things they themselves did on a daily basis," things which, he continues, were not the point of the book (108). This implies that the shocking parts of his book were not written with shock value in mind. But it also suggests that Louis is more concerned with presenting reality or experience in a way that challenges readers to do the interpretive work required to make sense of it, as he does with his talk. If these basic bodily functions are not the point, they serve as a sort of Barthesian reality effect that not only serves a mimetic function, but in fact furthers the critique of narrative that Louis has been speaking about this entire time.[40]

The story about Mino and the bird is therefore not typical of his writing, a fact that Louis is careful to highlight, though it is perhaps lurking in the background as a relevant touchstone for what he does write. Faye paraphrases him as follows:

> For all the hours spent shitting and pissing and staring out of the window, the moments when life could be observed in a meaningful arrangement were rare: his attempt to represent this fact had cost him most of the five years it took for the book to be written, yet it was always one of the other parts, the rare, choice extracts, that he selected. [...] Things could look very different while remaining the same: time could seem to have altered everything, without changing the thing that needed to change. (108–109)

The story of Mino and the bird, which so deeply exemplifies his outlook on the position of the writer, is "rare" among the pages of his writing. This contrast between repetitive mundanity and insight—that is, between experience and the narrative that grows out from it, even when that particular narrative is one that critiques the narrativizing tendency in general—is reminiscent of the *Recherche*, where we find crucial, nearly imperceptible truths interspersed among hundreds of otherwise arguably boring pages. Boring, that is, unless we do the interpretive work that Louis urges us to do, and read between the lines (which also means reading otherwise). Louis's comments about writing also shed light on the *Outline* trilogy as a whole, as well as on what happens when it is Faye's turn to speak at the event.

As the final speaker, Faye closes out the event. Interestingly, she is the only writer of the three who has brought something to read; the others only comment on their own work. Her entire contribution to the panel is narrated thus:

> I said that I had brought something to read aloud, and out of the corner of my eye saw the Chair make a gesture of encouragement. I took the

papers out of my bag and unfolded them. My hands shook with cold holding them. There was the sound of the audience settling into its seats. I read aloud what I had written. When I had finished I folded the papers and put them back in my bag, while the audience applauded. The Chair uncrossed his legs and sat up straight. I felt his brown eyes, opaque as two brown buttons, glancing frequently at me. (113)

The brevity of this account is most immediately striking. But there is also the complete omission of Faye's entire talk, an omission committed, in a way, by Faye herself. Of her actual reading, all we get is the single sentence: "I read aloud what I had written." Recently, Mary K. Holland has suggested that this entire scene—Julian's and Louis's apparent monopolization of the event compared to Faye's brief reading, not to mention the Chair's odd behavior after the event—"gives us abundant information for reading what this scene teaches about the intersection of reality, writing, and gender," namely, that Faye is written out of the event by the misogyny of the male writers and even the Chair.[41] Without wishing to downplay Holland's careful reading of this passage, two facts remain. First, Faye *is* the narrator. She has narrated her own short reading, however foreshortened it is. Second, she is a narrator who, just a single page after the event concludes, remarks that "I wasn't sure it mattered whether the audience knew who we were. It was good, in a way, to be reminded of the fundamental anonymity of the writing process, the fact that each reader came to your book a stranger who had to be persuaded to stay" (114). And just a page after that, she delivers criticisms of the other two speakers, Julian for his enjoyment of "the physical exposure such events entailed" and Louis for "his cowardice and deceptiveness" (115). In other words, Faye still has a voice, even if it is one that, to recall Vermeulen, "remains a dispersed presence between the lines of the novel."[42] Whatever this scene tells us about writing, Faye remains an invested participant who, at the same time, turns a keen critical eye on the proceedings.

Arguably, this skipping over of the talk (by Faye herself) does not indicate, or at least does not only indicate, an inherent misogyny in the event. Instead, it substantiates Eyers's assessment of the narrator as a reader: "Cusk's narrator's intensity of sensory reception is […] a kind of reading."[43] Can we write, or speak, while we read? Must we not read in order to write? In this case, Faye's reading comes at the expense of her speaking, but not of her writing. After all, much (narrative) ink is spilled in recounting, shaping the tone of, and ultimately criticizing the speakers that precede her at this literary event. Even if her talk never truly comes, the narrator, as a writer, has essentially written the accounts of the two previous talks, even repeatedly delivering them *in her own words*; perhaps, having done so, she feels that she has done enough.

If nothing else, we at least have Julian's boyfriend Oliver's reaction to her reading after the fact: "it was me you were describing, that woman was me, her pain was my pain, and I just had to come and tell you in person how much it meant to me" (121). Besides giving us a vague hint as to what Faye did read, which we can imagine responded at least indirectly to the male-centric space of the event, Oliver also gives us a response: "Enormous, shining tears were dripping from his eyes and rolling down his cheeks. He didn't wipe them away" (121).

Bound neither to the future nor the past

Finally, we come to the third novel of the trilogy, *Kudos*. One reviewer of this particular installment calls the trilogy as "an attempt to remake the novel, to establish a blueprint for a form of negative literature" and claims that "Cusk [...] is pursuing the impossible."[44] For another reviewer writing about *Kudos*, Faye "meets and talks only with people who have been through the thorough fictionalizing that is required to make them breathe on the page."[45] This reviewer finds a shift that differentiates *Kudos* from the previous two novels in the trilogy: "Almost all Faye's conversations are with people who are also interested in writing down stories, or indeed are in the act of writing Faye down for an interview, and there is a self-consciousness to all this, a riddling, hall-of-mirrors element that is the reverse of the radical humility of the first two books."[46] The back and forth between writers in *Kudos* finds oddly appropriate expression in something like an actual hall of mirrors in the passage I will turn to here.

In the early part of the novel, we find Faye waiting for her publisher at the bar of a hotel, where she is scheduled to participate in an event as part of a literary festival. The context is somewhat mundane and in a way demystifies the vocation of the writer; it concerns schedules, her duties as a writer interacting with the public, and the fact of having to speak with her publisher, who she seems to not have meet before. Unlike Louis's talk, the actual task of writing does not seem important here. And yet, Faye turns her writerly eye and mind toward the scene at hand. The main part of what I am concerned with in this passage involves her description of the hotel bar and its inhabitants:

> Part of the hotel bar had been cordoned off for a wedding reception. People stood in the dark, low-ceilinged space holding glasses of champagne. The windows along the rounded wall let in a strong, cold light from one side and the contrast of light and dark gave the guests' clothes and faces a slightly garish appearance. A photographer was

leading people in pairs or small groups out on to the terrace where they stood in the cool, breezy day, holding their expressions for the camera. The bride and groom were talking and laughing in a circle of guests, side by side but turned away from one another. Their faces wore an expression of self-consciousness, almost of culpability. I noticed that everyone there was around the same age as the married couple, and the absence of anyone older or younger made it seem as though these events were bound neither to the future nor the past, and that no one was entirely certain whether it was freedom or irresponsibility that had untethered them.[47]

Like much of the trilogy, this passage can be read as a comment on Cusk's usual themes of gender, family, marriage, and freedom, but the scene is of interest here for a different reason. Immediately remarkable is the fact that, of the main three passages I have cited, this is the first instance that is spoken entirely by Faye herself, in the narrative voice—or, at least, it is the first one that does not include the reported or summarized speech of others. With that in mind, it is a particularly "writerly" or novelistic paragraph, with special attention accorded to the space ("dark, low-ceilinged") and its atmosphere ("strong, cold light"), which give us an uncharacteristically vivid image of what is occurring. Accordingly, the people involved are more vividly described as well, and there is a vague sense of judgment: the space lends "the guests' clothes and faces a slightly garish appearance." This, and what follows, quite literally casts the others *in a bad light*, or at least a less-than-flattering one. This tension deepens and gains complexity when we realize that these wedding-goers are "holding their expressions for the camera." The "self-consciousness, almost [...] culpability" of the bride and groom betray the paradox of the photographer's task: the photographs are meant to seem casual, candid, all the while being thoroughly staged and performed. Faye's awareness and implied judgment of this posturing once again draws attention to the strange narrative paradox that Cusk so often highlights.

Already, the concern for writing is mirrored from the very beginning of this passage, and is operative on several levels. First, there is the bare plot: a writer, waiting for her publisher to arrive before an event she is to speak at, in the meantime observing her surroundings. Then there is the literary bent of her descriptions, the pondering nature of her writing: she does not just describe her surroundings and those around her, she asks a question about their relation, about how the scene is to be understood. The third level comes with the final line, where we once again get the sense of disconnection: "as though these events were bound neither to the future nor the past." By now, and as I've argued so far in this chapter, Cusk has established this as a specifically literary feeling—with its previous instances voiced by other characters who are also writers—and in this passage it is described beautifully in a literary text by a narrator who is a writer. Unlike the passages from *Outline* and *Transit*, however, this feeling is observed from without, since Faye is not involved in the ongoings of the wedding party, but simply watches on as an observer as she is waiting for her meeting with the publisher. As a moment of waiting, perhaps even of boredom, in which Faye is observing her surroundings, this description also perhaps gives us a window onto what happens in the apprenticeship of a writer.

At this moment, Faye finds that she is being observed by the only other person in the bar, her publisher, who furthermore identifies her by her photograph on one of her books. He then explains his difficulty in recognizing her by that photograph, since it is "more than fifteen years old": "You are nothing like your photograph!" (33). We do not get anything else about Faye's photograph; the publisher instead begins to describe the author's photographs of others in his roster. His exclamation to Faye, as well as his ensuing digression, is situated all too closely to Faye's own ruminations on the photoshoot taking place near her. Before concluding this chapter, it is worth looking at the next few pages of this passage, as they thematize the relationship between writing and life in a more explicit, albeit practical, way.

Continuing along this line of questioning involving the author's likeness to their back cover or dust-jacket photo, the publisher begins talking "about another of his authors, whose book photograph showed a slim and lovely woman with a long, fair waterfall of shining hair":

> In the flesh she was grey-haired and somewhat overweight and unfortunately suffered from an eye condition that obliged her to wear glasses with thick bottle-like lenses. [...] [H]e had occasionally raised the delicate question of using a more recent photograph, but she wouldn't hear of it. Why should her photograph be accurate? [...] The whole point of her profession, she said, was that it represented an escape from reality. (34)

In contrast to Faye, who is not noted as having gained weight or actually looking different in any other particular manner, but who is still "nothing like [her] photograph," this feels at first like the publisher presenting an extreme case to prove his point. However, the other writer's words are surprisingly poignant, and perhaps reflect something of Faye's wish to remain anonymous, though she does not comment on it here. The following lines provide an oblique counterpoint to the publisher's musings. After the publisher asks how she likes the hotel, Faye describes her confused impressions of it, and the difficulties she has faced in navigating within it. It is here that Clanchy's "hall-of-mirrors" comment takes literal shape:

> Several times already I had tried to go somewhere and found myself back where I started. I hadn't realized, I said, how much of navigation is the belief in progress, and the assumption of fixity in what you have left behind. I had walked around the entire circumference of the building in search of things I had been right next to in the first place, an error that was virtually guaranteed by the fact that all the building's sources of natural light had been concealed by angled partitions, so that the routes around it were almost completely dark. You found the light, in other words, not by following it but by stumbling on it randomly and at greater or lesser length; or to put it another way, you knew where you were only once you had arrived. (34–35)

With a dizzying number of shifts between the literal and the figurative, Faye's description of her actual experience trying to find her way around the confusing hotel implies, and morphs into, a set of observations about storytelling. Trying to "go somewhere" is both physical and narrative, as is finding oneself "back where one started." The same can be said about Faye's comment on the belief of progress: if one does not at least minimally and generally believe in narrative, one can never believe in any particular narrative—though, as we have seen with Louis's talk, a particular narrative can question our beliefs in all narratives. Daniel Lea has recently drawn attention to the uncertainty of Faye's progression across the trilogy, suggesting that "[t]here is no strong sense […] in which her evolution across the trilogy amounts to a journey of authentic self-realization, but then that is not really the point."[48] Faye at this moment in *Kudos* remains the same in certain manners, arguably including her personal life, but more importantly, she continues to question the validity of narratives and the process of narration in every situation—thus destabilizing the (narrative) question of "self-realization" in the first place.

Cusk's evocation of light here is also striking, read alongside the long critical tradition of privileging light as the exemplary object of literary description.[49] Taking up the already doubled nature of this passage, the thematization of light as both something by which to find one's way and also something to be found in the first place further heightens the literary stakes of this passage. I note these aspects of the passage because they involve literarity in what can perhaps be deemed a more formal or critical nature than the previously cited passages. Faye is very much a writer, and this is asserted in a much more self-conscious way here, especially considering that it occurs in a conversation with her publisher. In a passage so overdetermined with respect to literariness, something else about literature shines through: the moment that cannot properly be narrated, that cannot properly be placed within a narrative, and yet drives the impulse to narrate.

The fact of Faye's status as a writer is not ignored within the text—far from it, despite the scholarly tendency to forget this and allow Faye to be excised from her own accounts of events. In fact, it is highlighted when Faye remarks upon the metaphorical stakes of her speech thus far:

> I don't doubt that it was for such metaphors that the architect had won his numerous prizes, but it rested on the assumption that people lacked problems of their own, or at the very least had nothing better to do with their time. My publisher widened his eyes. 'For that matter,' he said, 'you could say the same thing about novels.' (35)

There is a bit of ambiguity here, since the publisher could be referring to Faye's statement about the architect and the problems of the general public, or he could be realizing, somewhat belatedly, the metaphorical nature of Faye's preceding comments. I would argue that, like the man's silence in response to Faye in *Outline*, of which Alissa G. Karl writes that "[h]e's either not listening to her, or he doesn't care about what she's just said—or both,"[50] the meaning of the publisher's words cannot be definitively decided, as the narrative voice immediately truncates any further conversation by launching into a physical description of the publisher, in a way that mirrors, in reverse, the opening of the chapter in *Outline* that featured the man's silence. Even keeping his next comments about the uncertain profitability of Faye's novel in mind, he could be referring either to the difficulty of narration itself or to the comparative "difficulty" of certain novels.[51] In either case, it is clear that Faye's difficult narration has, indirectly, raised a question about the difficulty of narration.

As Ella Ophir has written, "*The Outline Trilogy* pays tribute to ordinary storytelling while matter-of-factly acknowledging the distance between actual talk and writing. The monologues quite brilliantly capture the rhythms and shifts of conversational speech while their undisguised writtenness—their fluency and cohesion, as well as their regular punctuation by speech tags— keeps the mediating writer [...] firmly in view."[52] Succinctly and accurately, these lines clarify the stylistic stakes of the trilogy. If Cusk is understood here to be exhibiting an "undisguised writtenness," it is precisely insofar as writtenness can no longer be anything but undisguised. And this is not something to be lamented; far from it. The understanding of writing put forth in this trilogy is one that not only understands the arbitrariness of narrative, but also understands the origin of narrative in something unnarratable. Thus, what is told is "written," in the sense of being constructed, originated at some moment in time by an author.

In a short essay on Proust, Blanchot writes of Proust's particular, ambiguous, and seemingly inscrutable experience, the experience that was the fuel for his eventual writing. Much of Blanchot's essay is concerned with what he considers to be the mystical nature of Proust's experience, which also means its nature of "a nonrational revelation."[53] Whereas Blanchot ends up placing this experience in the context not only of life, but also of death, the resonance with Cusk comes in the following lines: "Despite all the studies, doubt about the character of this experience remains, and Proust's own explanations, so extensive, complete, and clear, have not sufficed to pinpoint its quality. Such an ambiguity undoubtedly stems from the nature of the experience; it also stems from the need that Marcel Proust had not only to interpret it but also to reduce it to an interpretation that was serviceable for literary knowledge."[54] In other words, Proust's "experience" was something not only unnarratable, but unknown even to Proust himself; nevertheless, it gave him an injunction to write, and he was thereby forced to make something of it, to understand something by it, to somehow learn to narrate it. It is this paradox precisely that I have tried to highlight in Cusk's trilogy. The characters, and even the narrator, are constantly remarking upon—that is, *narrating*—experiences or moments that seem unnarratable or irrelevant to narrative insofar as they are disconnected from a sense of a larger plot. These moments are indicative of a kind of aesthetic experience undergone by these speakers and narrators. There is an intensity and an immanence to these moments that seem to separate them off from everything else.

I wish to end by emphasizing the proximity of Cusk's writing to Proust's in a different way, therefore making a further connection between the two respective aesthetic moments they present. In her 2006 novel *Arlington Park*, we get a scene where protagonist Amanda Clapp is waiting for her friends to arrive for coffee—a scene of waiting not unlike Faye's waiting for her publisher, and for Amanda, it is also a break from her usually hectic daily schedule. Within this scene, the narrative launches (almost as a *mise en abyme*) into a description, seemingly taking place within her thoughts in that moment of waiting, of a certain "moment" that reemerges from time to time in her life after some renovations (and here we can think of Faye's renovations in *Transit*) were done to her home:

> But there was a moment, like a new soul, that had flickered into life when Amanda's kitchen was created. It had occurred on a winter's day when heat surged in the radiators like blood in clean, vigorous veins and the warm air blazed with electric light, and the appliances thrummed

steadily like the engine room of a majestic ship around which the grey, cluttered world outside churned like a roiling sea; and in summer, when the French doors were open and the light lay in golden, quiescent panels on the oak floors. These moments came and they were beautiful, fragile pauses, like bubbles, in which Amanda experienced a feeling of summation, almost of symbolism.[55]

Whether we take the mention of various moments—divided seasonally according to winter and summer—as either iterations of the same moment (like Paniotis's statement about "moments so intense that in a way we will be living them always"), or as two "moments" within the moment that is mentioned in the initial phrase, the fact remains that, like many passages in *À la recherche du temps perdu*, this passage engages the iterative. But more importantly, it ties together Cusk's disconnected moments and Proust's quiet ones. As moments within the everyday narrative of routine and repetition, these are also outside of routine and repetition, as quiet, solitary moments, moments with no audience—even if Amanda wishes for one: "It irked her that more people were not there to witness them."[56]

End Notes

1 Rachel Cusk, *Second Place*, 36, 119.
2 Cusk, *The Temporary*, 105.
3 Cusk, *Coventry*, 63.
4 Ibid.
5 Cusk, *Outline*, 101. All references to *Outline* hereafter will be given parenthetically.
6 Cusk, *Saving Agnes*, 16, emphasis added.
7 Ibid., 110, emphasis added.
8 Ibid., 120, emphasis added.
9 Ibid., 146, emphasis added.
10 Ibid., 189, emphasis added.
11 Sonja Pyykkö, "Perceptions of Failure in Rachel Cusk's *Saving Agnes* and *Second Place*," 81.
12 Cusk, *Saving Agnes*, 89.
13 Ibid., 102.
14 Ibid., 129.
15 Ibid., 1.
16 Ibid., 2.
17 Cusk, *The Temporary*, 17.
18 Ibid., 32.
19 Ibid., 124.
20 Ibid., 88, emphasis added.
21 Cusk, *The Country Life*, 203–204.
22 To cite the young Theaetetus once more: "Yes indeed, by the gods, Socrates, I wonder exceedingly as to why (what) in the world these things are, and sometimes in looking

at them I truly get dizzy" (155c9-11). Socrates replies that "this experience is very much a philosopher's, that of wondering. For nothing else is the beginning (principle) of philosophy than this" (155d2-4). As the originating principle of philosophy, wonder (*thaumazein*) is a thought about thought, but also has the ability to act on the body itself, making us dizzy. In the context of my larger project here, it is worth noting that, as Gasché suggests with about Deleuze's idea of thinking, "one could perhaps conjecture that Deleuze wishes to hold on to the *thaumazein*, preventing it from developing into a 'genuine science,' the latter being precisely that in which, dominated by the image of thought, the *thaumazein*, and thus the difference that thinking makes, becomes domesticated" (*The Honor of Thinking*, 268).
23 Cusk, *The Country Life*, 204.
24 Vermeulen, "Against Premature Articulation: Empathy, Gender, and Austerity in Rachel Cusk and Katie Kitamura," 88.
25 Ibid.
26 Ibid.
27 Cusk, *Saving Agnes*, 88, emphasis added.
28 Tom Eyers, "Criticism and the Non-I, or, Rachel Cusk's Sentences," 257, 255.
29 Vermeulen, "Against Premature Articulation," 89.
30 Eyers, "Criticism and the Non-I," 244.
31 Ibid., 251.
32 Helen Dunmore, "Transit by Rachel Cusk review—a woman's struggle to rebuild her life," *The Guardian*, August 28, 2016.
33 Dwight Garner, "Review: Rachel Cusk's 'Transit' Offers Transcendent Reflections," *The New York Times*, January 17, 2017.
34 Heller McAlpin, "'Transit' Is A Journey You Won't Want To End," *NPR*, January 17, 2017.
35 Daniel Aureliano Newman, "Portrait of an Invisible Artist: *Transit* by Rachel Cusk," *The Toronto Review of Books*, May 9, 2018.
36 Cusk, *Transit*, 2. All references to *Transit* hereafter will be given parenthetically.
37 Mino is also the name of a cat in *Women in Love* by D. H. Lawrence, a favorite of Cusk's. In the eponymous chapter, Mino strikes a wild female cat with his paw, inciting Ursula and Birkin to discuss (and disagree about) gender relations:

> "Mino," said Ursula, "I don't like you. You are a bully like all males."
> "No," said Birkin, "he is justified. He is not a bully. He is only insisting to the poor stray that she shall acknowledge him as a sort of fate, her own fate: because you can see she is fluffy and promiscuous as the wind. I am with him entirely. He wants superfine stability." (*Women in Love*, 141)

Similar exchanges—especially using as examples stories that revolve around animals—can be found all throughout Cusk's trilogy.
38 Blanchot, The Space of Literature, 171.
39 Ibid., 175–176.
40 Barthes writes that "if analysis seeks to be exhaustive […], if it seeks to encompass the absolute detail, the indivisible unit, the fugitive transition, in order to assign them a place in the structure, it inevitably encounters notations which no function (not even the most indirect) can justify; such notations are scandalous (from the point of view of structure), or, what is even more disturbing, they seem to correspond to a kind of narrative *luxury*, lavish to the point of offering many 'futile' details and

thereby increasing the cost of narrative information" (*The Rustle of Language*, 141). The takeaway is that such moments, narratively insignificant in themselves, form "the basis of that unavowed verisimilitude which forms the aesthetic of all the standard works of modernity" (148). Louis's instances of the reality effect are thus doubly scandalous and disturbing (though perhaps not luxurious). It is worth pointing out that Barthes also writes that such notations are "apparently detached from the narrative's semiotic structure" (142), an idea that complements Cusk's disconnected moments.

41 Mary K. Holland, "Rachel Cusk's New Realism: Gender, Power, Voice, and Genre in the *Outline* Trilogy," 67–68. More damning, in my mind, are the interviews in *Kudos* that seem to end without Faye having said anything; in the final part of the novel, she is interviewed by a man, and then a woman, and doesn't say (or at least doesn't report having said) anything. It is only in the third interview, with a young man who is "hardly more than a boy" (*Kudos*, 198), that Faye speaks—and in fact, she dominates the conversation this time around.

42 Vermeulen, "Against Premature Articulation," 88.

43 Eyers, "Criticism and the Non-I," 260.

44 Katy Waldman, "'Kudos,' the Final Volume of Rachel Cusk's 'Faye' Trilogy, Completes an Ambitious Act of Refusal," *The New Yorker*, May 22, 2018.

45 Kate Clanchy, "Kudos by Rachel Cusk—a daringly truthful trilogy concludes," *The Guardian*, May 4, 2018.

46 Ibid.

47 Cusk, *Kudos*, 32–33. All references to *Kudos* hereafter will be given parenthetically.

48 Daniel Lea, "'Some things are artificial and some are authentic': Rachel Cusk's Depth Perception," 104.

49 Light, seemingly everywhere in literature, plays a key role in descriptions of weather and atmosphere, as well as factoring into countless passages where a character's mood or mental state is metaphorized. Light is also what allows us to see, thereby being closely aligned with the optical paradigm of both literature and philosophy. Even in literary criticism, light is exemplary: critics and reviewers often single out descriptions of light in their writing. And yet, light in itself means nothing, making its proliferation throughout literature paradoxical. See Bryan Counter and Nathan Wainstein, "Mere Light."

50 Alissa G. Karl, "Rachel Cusk's Empathy Work," 133. The moment in question comes when Faye is on a boat with a man she met during her flight to Athens, which opens the novel. As with much of the novel, the chapter is composed of the two sharing various anecdotes from their lives. There is only one instance of direct quotation in the 30-page chapter: the man asks Faye if she had slept well (*Outline*, 30). It is the first instance of speech in the chapter; before this, we get only Faye's description of the man, her difficulty in recognizing him on solid ground, and their awkward greeting. Later in the chapter, Faye shares a story about her children, which Karl characterizes as a rare instance of Faye "becom[ing] quite thoughtful and even lyrical" when sharing about her own life" (133). Following the conclusion of Faye's story, however, the text reads: "My neighbour was silent for a while. Presently he said that in his case his children had been his mainstay, through all the ups and downs of his marital career" (83). Karl's reading of this passage finds issue with the man's response: "The neighbor does not take up the thread that the narrator has unwound. Instead, he shifts the conversational focus to how he feels about his own children" (133). But is there not a further possibility, even if it only adds to the ambiguity around his silence?

He is silent at first, to be sure, but when he resumes speaking it is not a complete non sequitur—he does talk about his own children, just as Faye did, and for that matter *her* speech began after his previous speech about his marriage had ended. Given the rambling nature of many of the conversations throughout the trilogy, which intersect and overlap with one another in often oblique ways, perhaps the man's silence is a sign that he does not know what to say, wants to keep his opinions to himself, is considering Faye's words carefully, or is simply out of his depth. His silence could in fact signal a number of things at the same time. If we consider that Cusk herself is doing work in writing this novel, we should also consider that the flatness of the text may, at the same time, be flatly refusing to show us certain things.

51 Regarding the current state of publishing, he says: "What all publishers were looking for [...] were those writers who performed well in the market while maintaining a connection to the values of literature; in other words, who wrote books that people could actually enjoy without feeling in the least demeaned by being seen reading them" (37). From "the values of literature," the two go on to discuss difficult literature (Robert Musil and T. S. Eliot are offered as examples) as well as the value of defending literature. On the latter point, Faye and the publisher disagree; the publisher thinks that "Dante [...] could look after himself" in the face of negative online book reviews, whereas Faye, calling him "cynical," believes that "[j]ustice [...] was something you had to honour for its own sake, and whether or not he believed that Dante could look after himself, it seemed to me he ought to defend him at every opportunity" (41–42). Regardless of whether this indicates a growing outspokenness on Faye's part, this principled stand is intriguing, especially in the way that it draws together literature and a value like justice.

52 Ella Ophir, "Neomodernism and the Social Novel: Rachel Cusk's *Outline Trilogy*," 4.
53 Blanchot, *Faux Pas*, 42.
54 Ibid.
55 Cusk, *Arlington Park*, 59.
56 Ibid.

Conclusion

NEARLY IMPOSSIBLE TO REPRESENT

The paintings [...] possessed a great eeriness that was partly the result of their manufacture by an unknown hand and partly that of the strangeness of what they saw. They were often scenes in which apparently nothing was happening [...]. In one, for instance, a middle-aged woman was sitting alone in an empty room reading a book. The room was full of a bare light but the windows behind her were dark: it was nighttime. [...] This woman was alone in a way that was nearly impossible to represent [...]. Immersed in being herself, she was indifferent to how she was seen. [...] How had someone observed her in that way, alone?[1]

Describing the contours of aesthetic experience is no easy matter. In itself, it is a fairly simple phenomenon: we experience the world around us without reference to the cognitive, the moral, and the practical, at least in Kant's version. But actually detaching ourselves from these concerns and entering a disinterested state is where the difficulty comes in. A certain strain of thinking imagines that we can achieve disinterest, or at least be more prepared for it, through cultivation and various forms of aesthetic education. And this may be true—contemplating nature and reflecting on works of art surely have benefits for our ability to recognize the various modalities of experience. But as I've argued throughout this book, the dimension of chance goes unnoticed when we conceive of aesthetic experience as a voluntary, intentional situation. And, as it turns out, chance is one of the most difficult forces to recognize, articulate, and grapple with, whether experientially or analytically.

The four moments of aesthetic experience as I've laid them out here are an attempt to foreground the importance of chance in this conversation. Both positive and negative moments are necessary due to the complexity of chance, which demands to be interpreted in a dialectical fashion. It is not enough to thematize chance—as we see with Balzac's *La Peau de chagrin*—for chance to really be understood and made present, whether in a narrative or in life. A negative view of chance, such as des Esseintes's moments of curation in *À rebours*, helps bring into relief the ways that chance undermines our attempts to control it. Des Esseintes has virtually all the aesthetic objects he could possibly need at his fingertips, and it is not enough; he overuses the aesthetic and becomes ill. And we see another failure of this attempt to control, namely, the occasional moments of beauty that shine through despite him. In *Remainder*, this impulse is heightened, as are its violent effects. For one, the narrator not only harms himself (as is the case with des Esseintes), but also takes part in, and seemingly relishes, accidental deaths, not to mention hijacking a plane at gunpoint. The novel might be considered an extreme case of aesthetic experience: the narrator is absolutely unconcerned with any categories or morals that we might recognize, and strives to chisel away the world around him until it becomes a purely aesthetic realm. This, I think, is why he ignores the many setbacks and contradictions inherent in his project.

Moving on to the positive moments, *À la recherche du temps perdu*—a text that could easily be used to illustrate all four moments—is instructive on multiple levels for evoking instances of quietness. First, these moments do not get theorized or overanalyzed by the narrator—they simply occur, ephemerally, and pass by. And second, perhaps because of this nontheorization, not much (if anything at all) has been said about them in this context in the scholarship. To be sure, this is interesting for Proust studies, but it also helps address the question that I raised in the introduction: why literature, rather than philosophy or even some other art form? In other words, what is it about the discursive and often indirect quality of literary writing that makes it such fertile ground for investigating aesthetic experience in particular? In keeping with the opposition that I set up in Proust between the major, theorized moments and the minor, quiet, untheorized moments, I would argue that the readerly activity of interpretation lends something vital—something that is otherwise only present in relief—to the text at hand. When we make sense of a literary text, we extend ourselves beyond our usual boundaries. "Examples" from literature are not merely examples, no matter how schematically they might be arranged and dealt with in a theoretical text. Instead, because literature is also experienced aesthetically, it participates in a complex interweaving of what we normally think of as opposites: fiction and fact, story and life. In doing so, it forces us to negotiate between competing impulses, theories, and biases in evaluating what exactly is happening in a given moment. In this sense, we do not simply go to literature to recognize instances of this or that concept or phenomenon. Literature and our reading of it shape those concepts and those phenomena.

The final moment that I discuss, disconnection, bears on something in common among all of the passages I've chosen: solitude. In each instance, whether literally (like des Esseintes, or Proust's narrator in *La Prisonnière*) or figuratively (like McCarthy's narrator, or the various characters from Cusk's

Outline trilogy), the moments of aesthetic experience are solitary ones. This does not mean that one must be alone to undergo aesthetic experience. Far from it; for would somebody truly alone endeavor to write, to create art, to share that experience with others? I would instead argue that this solitude can be considered virtual, that the event of aesthetic experience, while not premised on aloneness, conveys a quiet solitude on us and our surroundings. This accounts, for example, for the poetry of McCarthy's narrator when he says that the floor in his recreated apartment building is "silently zinging with significance," though this significance is for him only. This explains why Paniotis, in Cusk's *Outline*, says about his trip with his children that "there was no sequel to that time in the pool, nor ever will be." This is why, in *À rebours*, des Esseintes's solipsistic reveries take place on a night when "[a]bsolute silence enveloped the little house as it slumbered in the shadows." And this, I think, helps us make sense of Proust's narrator's indifference to death in the face of intense aesthetic experience, why he would sacrifice everything "for such a unique state of soul." Translated into a systematic philosophical text, the import of this risks being hollowed out, dangerous, or even ridiculous. But when we are struck with moments like these in the scene of reading, we feel and understand how this solitude opens us up to the world.

End Note

1 Cusk, *Parade*, 196.

REFERENCES

Acquisto, Joseph. *Thought as Experience in Bataille, Cioran, and Rosset*. New York: Bloomsbury, 2024.
Adorno, Theodor. *Prisms*. Translated by Samuel Weber and Shierry Weber. Cambridge, MA: MIT Press, 1981.
Agamben, Giorgio. *The Man Without Content*. Translated by Georgia Albert. Stanford: Stanford University Press, 1999.
Antosh, Ruth. *J.-K. Huysmans*. London: Reaktion Books, 2024.
Baldick, Robert. "Introduction." In *Against Nature*. London: Penguin, 1956.
Baldwin, Thomas. *Roland Barthes: The Proust Variations*. Oxford: Oxford University Press, 2019.
Balibar, Justine. "The Logic of Gomorrah: Proust and the Subversion of Identities." In *The Proustian Mind*. Edited by Anna Elsner and Thomas Stern. London: Routledge, 2023.
Balzac, Honoré de. *La Peau de chagrin*. Paris: Gallimard, 1974.
———. *The Wild Ass's Skin*. Translated by Herbert J. Hunt. Middlesex: Penguin, 1977.
Barthes, Roland. *Image, Music, Text*. Translated by Stephen Heath. New York: Hill and Wang, 1977.
———. *The Rustle of Language*. Translated by Richard Howard. Berkeley: University of California Press, 1989.
Baudelaire, Charles. *The Painter of Modern Life and Other Essays*. Translated by Jonathan Mayne. London: Phaidon Press, 1964.
Bauer, Dominique. *Beyond the Frame: Case Studies*. Brussels: Academic & Scientific Publishers, 2016.
Beckett, Samuel. *Proust*. New York: Grove, 1931.
Bell, David F. *Circumstances: Chance in the Literary Text*. Lincoln: University of Nebraska Press, 1993.
Bersani, Leo. *A Future for Astyanax: Character and Desire in Literature*. New York: Columbia University Press, 1984.
Blanchot, Maurice. *Faux Pas*. Translated by Charlotte Mandell. Stanford: Stanford University Press, 2001.
———. *The Madness of the Day*. Translated by Lydia Davis. Barrytown: Station Hill Press, 1981.
———. *The Space of Literature*. Translated by Ann Smock. Lincoln: University of Nebraska Press, 1982.
Böhme, Gernot. *Atmospheric Architectures: The Aesthetics of Felt Spaces*. Translated and edited by Tina Engels-Schwarzpaul. New York: Bloomsbury, 2017.
Bray, Patrick. "Balzac and the Chagrin of Theory." *L'Esprit Créateur*, vol. 54, no 3 (fall 2014): 66–77.

Brooks, Peter. *Reading for the Plot: Design and Intention in Narrative*. Cambridge, MA: Harvard University Press, 1984.
Caruth, Cathy. *Unclaimed Experience: Trauma, Narrative, and History*. Baltimore: Johns Hopkins University Press, 1996.
Cevasco, George A. "J.-K. Huysmans and the Impressionists." *Romance Notes*, vol. 16, no. 2 (1975): 278–282.
Clanchy, Kate. "Kudos by Rachel Cusk—a daringly truthful trilogy concludes." *The Guardian*, May 4, 2018.
Clune, Michael. *White Out: The Secret Life of Heroin*. Center City, MN: Hazelden, 2013.
Counter, Bryan. "Intoxication: Reading Between Proust and Barthes." *Barthes Studies*, 7 (2021): 85–109.
Counter, Bryan and Nathan Wainstein. "Mere Light." *Textual Practice*, vol. 38, no. 9 (2024): 1357–1379.
Cusk, Rachel. *Arlington Park*. New York: Picador, 2006.
———. *The Country Life*. New York: Picador, 1997.
———. *Coventry*. New York: Picador, 2019.
———. *Kudos*. New York: Picador, 2018.
———. *Outline*. New York: Picador, 2014.
———. *Parade*. New York: Farrar, Straus and Giroux, 2024.
———. *Saving Agnes*. New York: Picador, 1993.
———. *Second Place*. New York: Farrar, Straus and Giroux, 2021.
———. *The Temporary*. New York: Picador, 1995.
———. *Transit*. New York: Picador, 2016.
De Beistegui, Miguel. *Proust as Philosopher: The Art of Metaphor*. London: Routledge, 2012.
De Man, Paul. *Blindness and Insight*. Minneapolis: University of Minnesota Press, 1983.
Deleuze, Gilles. *Difference and Repetition*. Translated by Paul Patton. New York: Columbia University Press, 1994.
———. *Différence et répétition*. Paris: Presses Universitaires de France, 1968.
———. *Proust and Signs*. Translated by Richard Howard. Minneapolis: University of Minnesota Press, 2000.
Deleuze, Gilles and Félix Guattari. *A Thousand Plateaus: Capitalism and Schizophrenia*. Translated by Brian Massumi. Minneapolis: University of Minnesota Press, 1987.
Descombes, Vincent. *Proust: Philosophy of the Novel*. Translated by Catherine Chance Macksey. Stanford: Stanford University Press, 1992.
Drag, Wojciech. "Compulsion to Re-enact: Trauma and Nostalgia in Tom McCarthy's *Remainder*." *Hungarian Journal of English and American Studies*, vol. 21, no. 2 (2015): 377–392.
Dunmore, Helen. "Transit by Rachel Cusk review – a woman's struggle to rebuild her life." *The Guardian*, August 28, 2016.
Dutton, James. *Proust Between Deleuze and Derrida: The Remains of Literature*. Edinburgh: Edinburgh University Press, 2022.
Eyers, Tom. "Criticism and the Non-I, or, Rachel Cusk's Sentences." In *The Work of Reading: Literary Criticism in the 21st Century*. Edited by Anirudh Sridhar, Mir Ali Hosseini, and Derek Attridge, 243–260. London: Palgrave Macmillan, 2022.
Ferraris, Maurizio. *Learning to Live: Six Essays on Marcel Proust*. Leiden: Brill | Rodopi, 2020.
Finney, Gail. "In the Naturalist Grain: Huysmans' 'A Rebours' Viewed through the Lens of Zola's 'Germinal.'" *Modern Language Studies*, vol. 16, no. 2 (1986): 71–77.

Foster, Roger. *Adorno: The Recovery of Experience*. Albany: State University of New York Press, 2007.

Fox, Paul. "Dickens À La Carte: Aesthetic Victualism and the Invigoration of the Artist in Huysmans's *Against Nature*." In *Art and Life in Aestheticism: De-Humanizing and Re-Humanizing Art, the Artist, and the Artistic Receptor*. Edited by Kelly Comfort, 62–75. London: Palgrave Macmillan, 2008.

Franklin, Seb. "*Repetition*; *Reticulum*; Remainder." *Novel*, vol. 50, no. 2 (2017): 157–175.

Freed-Thall, Hannah. *Spoiled Distinctions: Aesthetics and the Ordinary in French Modernism*. Oxford: Oxford University Press, 2015.

———. "*Zut, zut, zut, zut*: Aesthetic Disorientation in Proust." *MLN*, vol. 124, no. 4 (2009): 868–900.

Fynsk, Christopher. *Last Steps: Maurice Blanchot's Exilic Writing*. New York: Fordham University Press, 2013.

Garner, Dwight. "Review: Rachel Cusk's 'Transit' Offers Transcendent Reflections." *The New York Times*, January 17, 2017.

Gasché, Rodolphe. *The Honor of Thinking: Critique, Theory, Philosophy*. Stanford: Stanford University Press, 2007.

———. *The Stelliferous Fold: Toward a Virtual Law of Literature's Self-Formation*. New York: Fordham University Press, 2011.

Genette, Gérard. *Figures III*. Paris: Seuil, 1972.

———. *Narrative Discourse: An Essay in Method*. Translated by Jane E. Lewin. Ithaca: Cornell University Press, 1980.

Girard, René. *Deceit, Desire and the Novel: Self and Other in Literary Structure*. Translated by Yvonne Freccero. Baltimore: Johns Hopkins University Press: 1965.

Goodstein, Elizabeth S. *Experience Without Qualities: Boredom and Modernity*. Stanford: Stanford University Press, 2005.

Groes, Sebastian. "'An Eternal Detour': Reality Hunger, Post-Proustian Memory and the Late Modern Self in Tom McCarthy's Remainder." In *Tom McCarthy: Critical Essays*. Edited by Dennis Duncan, 137–160. Exeter: Glyphi, 2016.

Hanson, Ellis. *Decadence and Catholicism*. Cambridge, MA: Harvard University Press, 1998.

Holland, Mary K. "Rachel Cusk's New Realism: Gender, Power, Voice, and Genre in the *Outline* Trilogy." *Contemporary Women's Writing*, vol. 17, no. 1 (March 2023): 57–75.

Huysmans, Joris-Karl. *À rebours*. Edited by Marc Fumaroli. Paris: Gallimard, 1977.

———. *Against Nature*. Translated by Margaret Mauldon. Oxford: Oxford University Press, 1998.

Johnson, Warren. "That Sudden Shrinking Feeling: Exchange in *La Peau de chagrin*." *The French Review*, vol. 70, no. 4 (1997): 543–553.

Jordan, Julia. *Late Modernism and the Avant-Garde British Novel: Oblique Strategies*. Oxford: Oxford University Press, 2020.

Kant, Immanuel. *Critique of the Power of Judgment*. Translated by Paul Guyer and Eric Matthews. Edited by Paul Guyer. Cambridge: Cambridge University Press, 2000.

Karl, Alissa G. "Rachel Cusk's Empathy Work." In *Rereading Empathy*. Edited by Emily Johansen and Alissa G. Karl, 123–138. New York: Bloomsbury, 2022.

Landy, Joshua. *Philosophy as Fiction: Self, Deception, and Knowledge in Proust*. Oxford: Oxford University Press, 2004.

Large, Duncan. *Nietzsche and Proust*. Oxford: Oxford University Press, 2001.

Lawrence, D. H. *Women in Love*. New York: Penguin, 1976.

Lea, Daniel. "'Some things are artificial and some are authentic': Rachel Cusk's Depth Perception." In *Rachel Cusk: Contemporary Critical Perspectives*. Edited by Roberta Garrett and Liam Harrison. London: Bloomsbury, 2024.

Lucey, Michael. "Conceptualizing Trajectories of Readability." *Nineteenth-Century French Studies*, vol. 52, nos. 1–2 (Fall-Winter 2023–2024): 1–35.

McAlpin, Heller. "'Transit' Is A Journey You Won't Want To End." *NPR*, January 17, 2017.

McCarthy, Tom. *C*. New York: Vintage Books, 2010.

———. *Men in Space*. New York: Vintage Books, 2007.

———. "My Death in Eleven Postulations." In *The Death of the Artist*. New York, Cabinet Books, 2018.

———. *Remainder*. New York: Vintage Books, 2007.

———. *Satin Island*. New York: Knopf, 2015.

———. *Tom McCarthy, Elvia Wilk: Just Fucking Weird*, YouTube, HKW—Haus der Kulturen der Welt, April 29, 2019, https://www.youtube.com/watch?v=7e0T8nclqQY&t=3203s.

———. *Typewriters, Bombs, Jellyfish: Essays*. New York: New York Review of Books, 2017.

McCarthy, Tom and Simon Critchey. *The Mattering of Matter: Documents from the Archive of the International Necronautical Society*. London: Sternberg Press, 2012.

Mickelsen, David. "*À Rebours*: Spatial Form." *French Forum*, vol. 3, no. 1 (1978): 48–55.

Miller, Sydney. "Intentional Fallacies: (Re)enacting the Accidental in Tom McCarthy's *Remainder*." *Contemporary Literature*, vol. 56, no. 4 (2015): 634–659.

Moran, Richard. "Proust and the Limits of the Will." In *The Philosophical Imagination: Selected Essays*. Oxford: Oxford University Press, 2017.

Newman, Daniel Aureliano. "Portrait of an Invisible Artist: *Transit* by Rachel Cusk." *The Toronto Review of Books*, May 9, 2018.

Nietzsche, Friedrich. *The Birth of Tragedy and the Case of Wagner*. Translated by Walter Kaufmann. New York: Vintage Books, 1967.

———. *On the Genealogy of Morals and Ecce Homo*. Translated by Walter Kaufmann and R. J. Hollingdale. Edited by Walter Kaufmann. New York: Vintage Books, 1967.

———. *The Will to Power*. Translated by Walter Kaufmann and R. J. Hollingdale. Edited by Walter Kaufmann. New York: Vintage Books: 1968.

Nikolopoulou, Kalliopi. *Tragically Speaking: On the Use and Abuse of Theory for Life*. Lincoln, NE: University of Nebraska Press, 2012.

Ophir, Ella. "Neomodernism and the Social Novel: Rachel Cusk's *Outline Trilogy*," *Critique: Studies in Contemporary Fiction*, vol. 64, no. 2 (2023): 353–364.

Ovid. *Metamorphoses*. Translated by Rolfe Humphries. Bloomington, IN: Indiana University Press, 1955.

Plato. *The Being of the Beautiful: Plato's Theaetetus, Sophist, and Statesman*. Translated by Seth Benardete. Chicago: University of Chicago Press, 1984.

Prendergast, Christopher. *Living and Dying with Marcel Proust*. New York: Europa Editions, 2022.

Proust, Marcel. *À la recherche du temps perdu*. 4 vols. Edited by Jean-Yves Tadié. Paris: Gallimard, 1954.

———. *La Bible d'Amiens, Sésame et les Lys et autres textes*. Edited by Jérôme Bastianelli. Paris: Éditions Robert Laffont, 2015.

———. *In the Shadow of Young Girls in Flower*. Translated by James Grieve. Edited by Christopher Prendergast. New York: Penguin, 2002.

———. *On Reading Ruskin*. Translated and edited by Jean Autret, William Burford, and Phillip J. Wolfe. New Haven: Yale University Press, 1987.

———. *Remembrance of Things Past*. 3 vols. Translated by C. K. Scott Moncrieff and Terence Kilmartin. New York: Vintage Books, 1981.

Pyykkö, Sonja. "Perceptions of Failure in Rachel Cusk's *Saving Agnes* and *Second Place*." In *Rachel Cusk: Contemporary Critical Perspectives*. Edited by Roberta Garrett and Liam Harrison. London: Bloomsbury, 2024.

Quarrie, Cynthia. "Sinking, Shrinking, *Satin Island*: Tom McCarthy, the British Novel, and the Materiality of Shame." *Journal of Modern Literature*, vol. 41, no. 2 (2018): 147–164.

Quignard, Pascal. *The Hatred of Music*. Translated by Matthew Amos and Frederik Rönnbäck. New Haven: Yale University Press, 2016.

Reddick, Bryan. "Proust: The 'La Berma' Passages." *The French Review*, vol. 24, no. 4 (1969): 683–692.

Ricciardi, Alessia. *The Ends of Mourning: Psychoanalysis, Literature, Film*. Stanford: Stanford University Press, 2003.

Schopenhauer, Arthur. *The World as Will and Representation*, Volume 1. Translated and edited by Judith Norman, Alistair Welchman, and Christopher Janaway. Cambridge: Cambridge University Press, 2010.

Schwenger, Peter. "Reading's Residue." *SubStance*, vol. 51, no. 2 (2022): 61–72.

Sedgwick, Eve Kosofsky. *The Weather in Proust*. Edited by Jonathan Goldberg. Durham: Duke University Press, 2011.

Serpell, C. Namwali. *Seven Modes of Uncertainty*. Cambridge, MA: Harvard University Press, 2014.

Smith, Zadie. "Two Paths for the Novel." New York Review, November 20, 2008.

Stanislavski, Constantin. *An Actor Prepares*. Translated by Elizabeth Reynolds Hapgood. London: Routledge, 1989.

Tanke, Joseph. "Communicability Without Communication: Kant and Proust on Aesthetic Pleasure." *Diacritics*, vol. 45, no. 1 (2017): 76–92.

Vermeulen, Pieter. "Against Premature Articulation: Empathy, Gender, and Austerity in Rachel Cusk and Katie Kitamura." *Cultural Critique*, no. 111 (2021): 81–103.

———. "The Critique of Trauma and the Afterlife of the Novel in Tom McCarthy's *Remainder*." *Modern Fiction Studies*, vol. 58, no. 3 (2012): 549–568.

Waldman, Katy. "'Kudos,' the Final Volume of Rachel Cusk's 'Faye' Trilogy, Completes an Ambitious Act of Refusal." *The New Yorker*, May 22, 2018.

Weinreb, Ruth Plaut. "Structural Techniques in *A rebours*." *The French Review*, vol. 49, no. 2 (1975): 222–233.

Williams, Robert R. *Tragedy, Recognition, and the Death of God: Studies in Hegel and Nietzsche*. Oxford: Oxford University Press, 2012.

Wrethed, Joakim. "The Oil-Flower Unfurling its Petals: The Phenomenological Aesthetics of Tom McCarthy's *Satin Island*." *C21 Literature: Journal of 21st-century Writings*, vol. 9, no. 1 (2021): 1–26.

INDEX

accident 4, 14, 17, 35, 36, 41, 46, 74, 76, 80, 92, 99–101, 103–7, 122, 128n16, 130n26, 137, 138, 153, 168
Acquisto, Joseph 14, 21n29
acting 5, 111, 130n29
action 16, 23, 32, 74, 107, 108, 111, 119
addiction 59, 80, 99, 101, 116, 117, 120, 121, 132n44
Adorno, Theodor 49, 51n37, 95n42, 128n7
aesthete 19, 25, 65, 69, 113
aesthetics 1–3, 6, 9, 10, 12–14, 16–20, 23–29, 31–33, 36, 38–40, 42–49, 51n16, 53–56, 58–63, 65–69, 71–76, 78–80, 83–88, 90–92, 94n13, 98, 99, 101–4, 106, 108–10, 112–17, 119–21, 123–27, 129n23, 132n47, 135, 137, 139, 143, 149, 162, 165n40, 167–69
aesthetic experience 1–3, 6, 9, 10, 12–14, 17–20, 23–26, 36, 39, 42, 44–49, 53–56, 58, 60–62, 66, 68, 69, 71–76, 78–80, 83, 84, 86–92, 94n13, 94n17, 99–103, 106, 109, 110, 112, 113, 115–17, 120, 121, 126, 127, 129n23, 132n47, 137, 139, 143, 162, 167–69
aesthetic judgment 1, 2, 3, 9, 17, 25, 68, 72
affect 7, 14, 58, 88, 101, 104, 106, 110, 112, 114, 118, 135, 148, 154
aficionado 11, 12
Agamben, Giorgio 10, 11, 21n21
An Actor Prepares 130n30
anonymity 136, 143, 151, 152, 156, 159
Antosh, Ruth 51n21

apprenticeship 13, 57, 67, 69, 85, 88, 90, 92, 93n6, 143, 159
art 1, 2, 10–13, 15, 17–19, 25–27, 31, 36–39, 45, 47–50, 60, 66–68, 78, 79, 85–87, 94n19, 95n40, 99, 103, 112, 113, 129n24, 140, 153, 167–69
artifice 18, 23, 26, 27, 33–38, 42–44, 47, 51n16, 89, 91, 115, 152, 165n48
artist 9, 10, 36, 38
atmosphere 8, 16–18, 34, 35, 37, 46, 55, 64, 72, 73, 75–82, 84, 85, 91, 92, 114, 115, 120, 129n23, 141, 146, 148, 158, 165n49
attribution 145, 147, 154
attunement 1, 6, 12, 18, 26, 46, 55, 75, 77, 91, 127, 148
audience 10, 64, 90, 107, 112, 126, 127, 130n29, 149, 150, 156, 163
authenticity 9, 27, 100, 103, 106–9, 111, 112, 115, 119, 122, 130n29, 137, 160, 165n48

Baldick, Robert 26, 50n9
Baldwin, Thomas 53, 56, 93n1
Balibar, Justine 93n7
Ballard, J. G. 121
Balzac, Honoré de 2, 4, 6, 21n3, 21n8, 27, 167
  La Peau de chagrin 2, 4, 6, 21n3, 21n7, 31, 38, 129n16, 143, 167
Barthes, Roland 21n6, 56, 93n1, 94n13, 155, 164n38
Baudelaire, Charles 36, 38, 51n19, 51n22, 119
Bauer, Dominique 50n13

beautiful 1, 2, 4, 7–11, 16, 18, 36–38, 45, 46, 49, 62, 66, 68, 69, 84, 103, 110, 121, 126, 141, 144, 163, 168
Beckett, Samuel 74, 95n29, 131n41
Bell, David F. 6, 21n9, 40, 51n23
Bersani, Leo 56, 93n2
Beyond the Pleasure Principle 102
Blanchot, Maurice 95n44, 153, 162, 164n38, 166n53
Böhme, Gernot 72, 76, 95n25, 95n28, 95n35, 148
boredom 29, 37, 44, 66, 69, 98, 155, 159
Bray, Patrick 5, 21n8
Brooks, Peter 4, 21n4

canon 1, 15, 16, 45, 86, 87
Caruth, Cathy 102, 128n12
Cevasco, George A. 50n11
chance 2–6, 14, 20, 21n6, 23, 25, 27, 31, 34, 37, 38, 40, 44, 58, 77, 78, 82, 114, 117, 120, 129n16, 131n31, 138, 140, 145, 151, 167
Clanchy, Kate 160, 165n45
Clune, Michael W. 117, 120, 132n44, 132n45
connoisseur 60
contingency 4, 6, 14, 17, 55, 73–75, 80, 82, 83, 108, 119, 131n31
control 5, 19, 23, 34, 36, 38, 49, 55, 72, 74, 76, 78–80, 99, 104, 119, 130n28, 138, 140, 141, 143, 146, 151, 153, 168
Crash 121
Critchley, Simon 107, 130n26
curation 18, 19, 20, 23, 25, 46, 55, 70, 71, 79, 98, 99, 101, 110, 112, 137, 167
Cusk, Rachel 18, 20, 24, 84, 91, 93, 99, 123, 127, 135–38, 140–43, 145, 147, 148, 156–58, 160–66, 163n1, 163n2, 163n3, 163n5, 163n6, 163n11, 163n12, 163n17, 163n21, 163n22, 164n23, 164n24, 164n27, 164n28, 164n32, 164n33, 164n35, 164n36, 164n37, 165n40, 165n41, 165n44, 165n45, 165n47, 165n48, 165n50, 166n52, 166n55, 168, 169n1
  Arlington Park 162, 166n55
  Country Life, The 138, 141, 163n21, 164n23

Faye 20, 137, 142–44, 148, 149, 152, 154–62, 165n41, 165n44, 165n50, 166n50, 166n51
Kudos 136, 157, 160, 165n41, 165n44, 165n45, 165n47
"On Rudeness", 136
Outline 20, 24, 91, 93, 99, 123, 127, 136–38, 142–44, 147–49, 153, 155, 159, 161, 163n5, 165n41, 165n50, 166n52, 169
Saving Agnes 138, 140, 141, 145, 163n11, 163n12, 164n27
Second Place 135, 142, 163n1, 163n11
Temporary, The 135, 138, 140, 141, 151, 163n2, 163n17
Transit 136, 148, 149, 159, 162, 164n32, 164n33, 164n34, 164n35, 164n36

Davis, Lydia 95n44
de Beistegui, Miguel 70, 94n23
de Man, Paul 107, 119, 121, 132n49
De Niro, Robert 108, 111, 130n26, 130n29, 130n30, 130n36, 131
death 3, 11, 14, 19, 48, 90–92, 97, 147, 153, 162, 169
decadence 23, 26–28, 33, 49
déjà vu 100, 104, 105, 112, 115
Deleuze, Gilles 13, 14, 16, 21n25, 21n28, 21n33, 35, 51n17, 57–59, 62, 63, 71, 72, 90, 92, 93n5, 93n6, 93n8, 95n27, 103–5, 108, 129–31, 129n22, 129n24, 129n30, 131n31, 164n22
Descombes, Vincent 57, 63, 70, 93n3, 93n9, 94n20
disconnection 17, 18, 20, 24, 74, 93, 135–38, 144–49, 152, 158, 162, 163, 165n40, 168
disinterest 1, 7, 9, 10, 11, 12, 69, 79, 84, 88, 167
disposition 8, 28, 59
Drag, Wojciech 102, 128n14
drug(s) 100, 116, 117, 121
Dunmore, Helen 148, 164n32
Dutton, James 57, 93n5

education 28–32, 66–69, 93n6, 167
error 55, 60, 67, 69–72, 92, 160
Eurydice 153

INDEX

experience 1–4, 8, 9, 11–14, 16–20, 24–26, 32, 34, 35, 39, 42, 44, 46–49, 51n17, 53–56, 60–64, 66, 67, 69–77, 79–88, 90–92, 94n13, 94n17, 95, 97, 99–105, 108–13, 115–18, 120, 121, 123, 124, 127, 128n7, 130n26, 132n51, 135–47, 151, 154, 155, 160, 162, 164n22, 167–69
Eyers, Tom 147, 148, 156, 164n28, 164n30, 165n43

Ferraris, Maurizio 57, 93n4
fiction 24, 97, 101, 103, 136, 138, 139, 142, 152, 168
Finney, Gail 23, 49–51, 50n4, 51n38
flower 11, 12, 18, 38, 45
force 5, 13, 15, 28, 36, 38, 54, 55, 58, 59, 61, 65, 74, 92, 99, 101, 104, 105, 109, 120, 124, 140
Foster, Roger 81, 95n42
Fox, Paul 47, 51n34
François le champi 16, 91
Franklin, Seb 112, 131n37
Freed-Thall, Hannah 43, 51n25, 76, 85, 86, 88, 95n34, 96n45, 96n48
Freud, Sigmund 102, 113
Fynsk, Christopher 95n44

gambling 2–6, 117
Garner, Dwight 148, 164n33
Gasché, Rodolphe 23, 27, 50n5, 63, 93n12, 131n31, 164n22
Genette, Gérard 75, 79, 95n33, 95n41
genius 12, 14, 35–37, 110, 121, 132n47
Girard, René 65, 67, 94n15, 94n17
Goodstein, Elizabeth 44, 51n27
Grieve, James 128n7
Groes, Sebastian 103, 129n17, 129n23
Guattari, Félix 130n30

habit 14, 26, 28, 29, 32, 45, 46, 49, 61, 74, 76, 79–85, 87, 123, 132n47
Hanson, Ellis 23, 25, 26, 48, 50n1, 50n5, 50n6, 50n8, 50n10, 51n36
hasard 6, 14, 39–41, 56, 58
hawthorn 45, 88
Holland, Mary K. 156, 165n41
Houellebecq, Michel 98

Huysmans, Joris-Karl 18–20, 23–26, 33, 43, 50n1, 50n4, 50n9, 50n12, 51n21, 51n24, 51n34, 71, 74, 93, 99, 101, 112, 113, 132n51, 146
À rebours 18, 19, 23–27, 35, 37, 39, 40, 42, 43, 49, 50n12, 65, 99, 167, 169
des Esseintes 18, 19, 23–51n24, 55, 67, 70, 79, 87, 98–100, 112, 115, 117, 132n51, 167–69

idolatry 44, 45, 65, 67, 86
impression 6, 13, 51n35, 54, 69, 91, 95n38, 140
indeterminacy 37
indifference 5, 28, 59, 76, 87, 90, 91, 92, 100, 125, 151, 152, 167, 169
instrument 47, 78, 79–82, 95n42
intensity 12, 14, 20, 29, 31, 34, 38, 43, 48, 50, 58, 73, 85, 88, 94n17, 105–11, 113, 121, 135, 137, 145, 146, 156, 162, 163, 169
interest 1, 7–12, 18, 25, 47, 65, 71, 80, 83, 85, 90, 100, 109, 124, 142, 152, 158
interpretation 2, 6, 16, 69, 71, 89, 93n6, 102, 113, 138, 143, 148, 150, 155, 162, 168
intoxication 43, 79, 80, 95n40, 120
involuntary memory 13, 14, 17, 47, 53–57, 74, 89–91, 101, 106, 129n23
involuntary, the 14, 54, 55, 58, 74, 82, 89, 91, 92, 129n23
irony 26, 49, 92, 107, 119, 121, 123, 127
irrationality 41, 79, 102, 118
iterative aspect 42, 62, 75–77, 79–81, 83, 91, 104, 163

James, Henry 141
Jerusalem Liberated 102
Johnson, Warren 5, 21n7
Jordan, Julia 110
judgment 1–3, 7, 8, 9, 11, 16, 17, 25, 60, 63, 64, 67–69, 72, 82, 86, 88, 158

Kant, Immanuel 2, 6–9, 11, 12, 17, 20n2, 21n10, 25, 36, 37, 45, 51n18, 51n20, 68, 69, 78, 79, 84, 88, 94n20, 95n38, 103, 110, 121, 131n34, 167
Karl, Alissa G. 18, 23, 50, 161, 165n50

Kilmartin, Terence 57
knowledge 7, 12, 14, 66, 68, 74, 102, 119, 123, 131n42, 140, 142, 152, 162

La Jalousie 98
La Salle de bain 97
Landy, Joshua 63, 93n10
Large, Duncan 93n8
Lawrence, D. H. 135, 149, 164n37
Lea, Daniel 160, 165n48
life 2–4, 6, 10–12, 14, 16, 23–25, 29, 32, 33, 41, 43, 48, 49, 53, 55, 59, 62, 65, 66, 67, 70–72, 74, 83–85, 87, 91, 93n8, 98, 100, 106–8, 125, 126, 135, 136, 139–47, 150, 153–55, 159, 160, 162, 164n32, 165n50, 167, 168
literature 1, 2, 6, 17, 22n34, 23, 25, 26, 50n5, 55–57, 62, 65, 70, 88, 89, 92, 93n2, 93n5, 96n50, 102, 138, 142, 157, 161, 164–66, 164n38, 164n49, 166n51, 168
Lorenzo in Taos 135
Lucey, Michael 22n34
Luhan, Mabel Dodge 135

madeleine 53, 54, 56–58, 60–62, 71, 72, 82, 83, 86, 88, 90, 93n13, 104, 115, 129n22s
Mallarmé, Stéphane 6
McAlpin, Heller 148, 164n34
McCarthy, Tom 18–20, 27, 33, 43, 51n26, 80, 90, 93, 97–100, 102, 103, 107, 109, 115, 121, 123, 124, 127–33, 127n21, 127n2, 128n4, 128n6, 128n10, 128n11, 128n14, 129n17, 129n21, 130n26, 131n43, 132n51, 132n52, 132n53, 133n54, 133n56, 133n57, 136, 137, 140, 146, 152, 168
  C, 3, 5, 13, 30, 47, 58, 97, 98, 109, 128n4, 131n32
  Men in Space 97
  Remainder 19, 27, 33, 34, 41, 43, 51n26, 65, 80, 90, 93, 97–4, 108–13, 115–17, 119–21, 123, 124, 126–29, 128n5, 128n11, 128n14, 129n17, 129n21, 129n23, 129n25, 131n37, 132n47, 137–40, 143, 168

  Satin Island 99, 123–27, 132n53, 132n54, 133n54, 133n57, 136, 138, 152, 154
Mean Streets (1973) 108
memory 12–14, 16, 19, 35, 47, 48, 51n17, 51n35, 53–61, 71, 74, 82, 83, 85, 87, 89–95, 94n17, 95n32, 99–9, 110, 116–18, 122, 129n23, 130n26, 135, 144
metaphor 7, 39, 41, 47, 48, 61, 77, 82–84, 128n7, 161
Mickelsen, David 23, 35, 50n2
Miller, Sydney 103, 129n21
misunderstanding 99, 111
moment 3, 7, 11, 13, 17–20, 23–25, 39, 49, 54–56, 58, 62, 71, 74, 79, 81, 86–92, 99–101, 110, 113, 115, 121, 129n23, 132n47, 136, 137, 140, 142, 145, 146, 152, 155, 162, 163, 165n40, 167–69
Moncrieff, C. K. Scott 57
Monet, Claude 81
mood 8, 94n13, 165n49
Moran, Richard 74, 95n30
Moreau, Gustave 37
movement 37, 83, 97, 98, 107, 108, 112, 124
museum 10, 36, 49, 98, 128n7
music 17, 25, 47, 78, 81, 95, 115, 120, 128n7

narration 20, 68, 69, 71, 72, 75, 84–88, 91, 94n14, 99, 135, 138, 141–43, 147, 152, 160, 161
narrative 4, 6, 13, 18, 20, 21n6, 24, 27, 42, 46–48, 54–57, 62, 69, 70, 75, 79, 83–85, 88, 89, 91–93, 98, 101–6, 109, 110, 111, 113, 116–18, 120, 122, 123, 127, 129n23, 131n42, 135, 136, 138–46, 147–49, 151–56, 158, 160–65, 164n38, 165n40, 167
nature 2, 4–6, 8–12, 14, 17, 18, 23, 27, 28, 31, 33–38, 42–44, 46, 50n9, 50n12, 51n16, 51n34, 58, 61, 63, 68, 70, 73, 74, 77, 80–83, 86, 92, 94, 100–2, 104, 107, 108, 111, 112, 114–16, 121, 123, 126, 128n10, 131–33, 131n31, 132n47, 133n56, 136, 138, 152, 153, 158, 160–62, 166n50, 166, 167

INDEX

Newman, Daniel Aureliano 148, 164n35
Nietzsche, Friedrich 6, 9, 10–12, 17,
    21n18, 69, 79, 93n8, 113, 124–26,
    132n54, 133n55
  Birth of Tragedy, The 125, 132n54
  On the Genealogy of Morals 9, 21n18
  Will to Power, The 95n40
Nikolopoulou, Kalliopi 133n56
nouveau roman 97, 98

object 1, 2, 4, 6–9, 11, 12, 14–16, 18,
    19, 24, 25, 28, 37, 39, 45–49, 54,
    58–60, 65–68, 70, 72, 73, 75–77,
    79, 82, 84–88, 90, 92, 94n17, 97, 99,
    102, 103, 108, 111, 112, 127, 130–32,
    130n26, 131n31, 132n47, 143, 148,
    160, 168
Ophir, Ella 161, 166n52
origin 19, 27, 33, 38, 41, 54, 55, 59, 61,
    69, 72, 94n17, 99, 102, 104–6, 108,
    109, 110, 117, 125, 128n5, 129n24,
    141, 161
Orpheus 153
Ovid 21n20

paradox 1, 12–14, 18, 26, 60, 85, 92, 93,
    99, 109, 112–14, 116–19, 121, 144,
    146, 153, 158, 162
passivity 5, 6, 55, 73, 78, 81, 84, 87,
    130n30, 106, 143, 148
paving stones 83, 86, 89, 107
perception 7, 26, 63, 79, 88, 89
performance 66, 78, 82, 90, 94n17, 94n19,
    107, 122, 130n29, 154
Phèdre 66, 94n17
phenomenology 15, 57, 102, 104, 113,
    132n54
phenomenon 13, 14, 17, 24, 53, 54, 63, 88,
    103, 107, 125, 126, 167, 168
philosophy 1, 2, 6, 13, 14, 17, 21n33, 24, 25,
    54, 55, 57, 61, 70, 72, 73, 92, 93n8,
    101, 103, 109, 132n44, 133n56, 141,
    164n22, 165n49, 168, 169
Plato 70, 130n25
  Theaetetus 130n25, 163n22
pleasure 8, 12, 15, 16, 29–31, 34, 35, 43,
    49, 59, 65, 75, 76, 85, 120, 132n47,
    132n51

plot 15–17, 20, 23–25, 42, 98, 100, 102,
    118, 137, 138, 140, 141, 147–49, 152,
    158, 162
plotlessness 23, 24
Prendergast, Christopher 1, 20n1, 81,
    95n43
Proust, Marcel 6, 13–22, 20n1, 20n2,
    21n25, 21n26, 21n27, 21n30, 21n31,
    22n34, 29, 34, 35, 37, 39, 42, 44–47,
    49, 51n17, 51n30, 51n32, 51n33,
    51n35, 53–57, 61–63, 65, 67, 70–75,
    77–81, 84–90, 92–96, 93n1, 93n3,
    93n4, 93n5, 93n6, 93n7, 93n8,
    93n9, 93n10, 94n13, 94n18, 94n19,
    94n20, 94n23, 95n27, 95n29,
    95n30, 95n36, 95n43, 96n45, 98,
    99, 101, 103–5, 107–9, 113, 115,
    128n7, 129n17, 129n23, 131, 139,
    146, 147, 162, 163, 168, 169
  À la recherche du temps perdu 13, 16, 19,
    51n17, 51n35, 53, 54, 56, 57, 62, 68,
    70, 85, 91, 93n8, 94n19, 99, 103,
    105, 129n23, 144, 155, 163, 168
  Du côté de chez Swann 57, 88
  La Prisonnière 72, 73, 92, 93, 146, 168
  Le Côté de Guermantes 62
  Le Temps retrouvé 86, 89
  Swann 82, 87, 99, 128n7
Pygmalion 9, 10
Pyykkö, Sonja 139, 163n11

Quarrie, Cynthia 127, 133n57
quietness 18–20, 54–56, 62, 72–74, 76, 79,
    89–92, 146, 150, 163, 168, 169
Quignard, Pascal 78, 95n39

randomness 4, 41, 102, 114, 146, 148,
    152, 153
reading 9, 13, 15–17, 22n34, 24, 26, 28,
    32, 50, 54, 57, 61–63, 67, 69, 71, 80,
    91, 95n44, 97, 99, 101–3, 109, 112,
    113, 121, 127, 132n44, 132n54, 137,
    139, 142, 148, 155, 156, 165–69,
    165n50, 166n51
Reddick, Bryan 66, 67, 94n18, 94n19
re-enactment 19, 33, 44, 80, 93, 98, 100,
    102–9, 111–21, 127, 129n16, 131n42,
    132n44, 132n51, 137, 140

re-enactor 100, 124, 137
repetition 29, 77, 80, 83, 88, 97–99, 101–3, 109, 110, 112–17, 121, 133n56, 135–37, 155, 163
resonance 46, 77, 82, 84, 85, 87, 121, 129n24, 135, 137, 140, 146, 162
Ricciardi, Alessia 89, 96n50
risk 100, 125, 137, 138, 145
Robbe-Grillet, Alain 97, 98
rose 1, 45, 48, 65, 66, 68, 69
Ruskin, John 15, 21n31, 44, 51n30, 51n33, 67, 86, 91

sacrifice 83, 84, 87, 90, 92, 146, 169
Salomé 37
Sand, George 16, 22n34, 91
Schopenhauer, Arthur 6, 12, 14, 17, 21n22, 25, 36, 110, 121, 132n47
Schwenger, Peter 16, 21n32
Scorsese, Martin 108
Sedgwick, Eve Kosofsky 77, 78, 95n36
sensation 7, 13, 14, 23, 44, 47, 54, 56, 58, 60, 61, 69, 77, 82, 89–91, 99, 109, 112, 116, 137, 139
senses 7, 26, 47, 59, 61, 72, 84, 88, 100, 105
Serpell, C. Namwali 109, 112, 113, 127, 131n32, 131n37
Sesame and Lilies 15, 91
sign 13, 14, 31, 57–60, 68, 70, 71, 93n6, 131n31, 131n42, 137, 139, 166n50
silence 29, 33, 46, 49, 81, 82, 118, 153, 161, 165n50, 166n50, 169
singularity 6, 17, 55, 60, 62, 68, 75–77, 80, 83, 84, 88, 109, 110, 115, 144, 146, 149
Smith, Zadie 100, 116, 128n8, 132n44
Socrates 130n25, 163n22
solitude 28, 29, 46, 49, 66, 67, 73, 81, 82, 94n17, 168
song 78, 81–83, 120
sound 47, 61, 76–82, 84, 85, 92, 112, 115, 156
St. Mark's Basilica 89
Stanislavski, Constantin 130n30
story 4, 24, 54, 70, 74, 135–38, 142–51, 153–55, 165n50, 168

subject 1–4, 7–9, 11–14, 18–21, 21n33, 37, 44, 46, 53, 55, 60–62, 67, 70, 72, 73, 75, 76, 78, 80, 81, 84–88, 99, 102, 104, 109, 112, 113, 119, 125, 127, 132n47, 136, 140, 147, 148
sublime 8, 16, 38, 115

Tanke, Joseph 20n2
Tasso, Torquato 102
taste 7, 12, 14, 15, 17, 19, 25, 27, 28, 31, 33, 35–37, 41, 42, 44–47, 49, 51n35, 60, 61, 65, 67, 68, 80, 86–88, 98, 99, 110, 121
temporality 42, 71
temps 13, 16, 19, 21n26, 26, 35, 40, 51n17, 51n35, 53, 54, 59, 68, 70, 72, 74–76, 81, 84, 85, 87, 91, 93n8, 99, 103, 129n23, 144, 163, 168
theory 1, 5, 17, 19, 27, 34, 53–59, 62, 63, 71, 85–88, 90–93, 98, 101–3, 109, 113, 128n5, 133n56, 168
thinking 1, 9, 13, 14, 36, 41, 42, 45, 60–64, 66, 71, 92, 101, 106, 107, 110, 116, 117, 130n26, 130n31, 131n31, 148, 152, 154, 162, 164n22, 167–69
thought 13–15, 38, 40, 57, 58, 63, 71, 72, 95n44, 105–8, 118, 131n31, 148, 164n22
time 4, 7, 9–11, 16–18, 20, 23, 26, 27, 29, 35–37, 42–44, 46–51, 51n17, 53, 58, 59, 61–67, 69, 71, 72, 74, 75, 79, 81–85, 87, 88, 90, 92–95, 94n14, 95n38, 99, 103, 104, 106, 107, 110–12, 114, 115, 117, 118, 120–25, 128n7, 131n42, 132n47, 135, 139–46, 152, 155, 156, 160–62, 165–67, 165n41, 166n50, 169
timelessness 91, 92, 120, 121, 145, 146
Toussaint, Jean-Philippe 97, 98
tragedy 125, 126, 133n56, 133n57, 154
trauma 101–3, 113, 114, 129n16
tune 81–83
Turn of the Screw, The 141

uncertainty 14, 98, 129n25, 142, 160
unnarratable, the 84, 147, 161, 162

Venice 89, 90
Venus 10
Vermeulen, Pieter 101, 102, 113,
    128n11, 128n15, 143, 147,
    156, 164n24, 164n29,
    165n42
violence 8, 13, 18–20, 97–99, 102, 108–10,
    115, 116, 124, 131n31, 131n42,
    152, 153
violin 78–81, 83, 85, 95n42

Wainstein, Nathan 165n49
Waldman, Katy 165n44
weather 5, 33–35, 46, 72, 73, 75–78,
    80–87, 90, 129n23, 144, 146,
    165n49
Weinreb, Ruth Plaut 24, 50n7

will 1, 4, 5, 6, 9, 11, 12–14, 30, 37, 38, 47,
    55, 63, 68, 69, 70, 73, 74, 76, 78, 79,
    80, 82, 84, 85, 87, 90, 91, 92, 93n13,
    94, 95, 95n32, 95n38, 110, 112, 127,
    130–32, 132n47, 138, 141, 143
Williams, Robert R. 126, 133n55
wonder 130n25, 141, 143, 163n22
Woolf, Virginia 16
World War I, 97
Wrethed, Joakim 132n54
writer 20, 56, 65, 67, 70, 123, 126, 127,
    135, 137, 143, 149–61
writing 13, 14, 16, 18, 20, 24, 26, 40, 45,
    53, 57–59, 65, 69–72, 74, 81, 85, 88,
    123, 124, 127, 129n24, 135–38, 140,
    142, 143, 148–52, 154–59, 161, 162,
    165n49, 166n50, 168, 169